CW01272300

Vice-Chancellor on a tightrope

Stuart Saunders

Vice-Chancellor on a tightrope
A PERSONAL ACCOUNT OF CLIMACTIC YEARS IN SOUTH AFRICA

WITH A FOREWORD BY DR MAMPHELA RAMPHELE

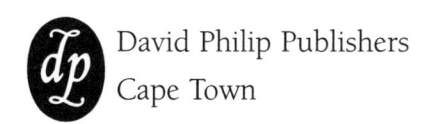

David Philip Publishers
Cape Town

First published 2000 in Southern Africa by David Philip Publishers
(Pty) Ltd, 208 Werdmuller Centre, Claremont, 7708 South Africa

ISBN 0-86486-458-2

© 2000 Stuart Saunders

All rights reserved. No part of this publication may be reproduced, stored in a retrieval system, or transmitted in any form or by any means, electronic, mechanical, photocopying, recording or otherwise, without the prior permission of the publishers.

Printed by
National Book Printers, Drukkery Street, Goodwood, Cape Town

Contents

Foreword by Dr Mamphela Ramphele vii

Preface ix

Acknowledgements xi

Illustrations between pages 20 and 21

1 *Early years (1931–1948)* 1
2 *Student years (1948–1957)* 13
3 *A learning curve (1958–1961)* 24
4 *Politics and the physician (1962–1969)* 39
5 *Head of medicine (1970–1975)* 50
6 *Changing hats very fast (1975–1976)* 63
7 *Personal turning-points (1977–1980)* 71
8 *Not a rose garden (1981)* 92
9 *Scholarship and not ethnicity (1981 continued)* 104
10 *Fund-raising (1982–1984)* 122
11 *Quotas and dreams (1983–1984)* 138
12 *A torrid year (1985)* 156
13 *Freedom of speech & association (1986)* 170
14 *Spies and disruptions (1987)* 185
15 *Some finer points of law (1987 continued–1988)* 198
16 *Still on the tightrope (1987–1989)* 208
17 *The tide turns (1990–1991)* 220
18 *Demise of legalised apartheid (1992–1994)* 237
19 *The road of transformation (1995–1996)* 246

Tables 258

Index 265

Foreword
by Dr Mamphele Ramphele

Historical agents come in many shapes and sizes. They also come from the most unexpected quarters. Gazing onto the uninspiring timber of a toilet roof from one's crib as a baby is hardly a promising start. Nor is the total lack of physical vigour as traditionally measured by participation in sports and athletics. No schoolmaster ever succeeded in getting Stuart Saunders to display the vigour normally associated with schoolboys. What seems to have counted most in Stuart Saunders's rise to prominence as an agent of history was his understanding of, and responsiveness to, the challenges facing his society at a critical moment.

Medical training and practice afforded Saunders excellent preparation for leadership. Dealing with life-and-death situations forces one to make swift decisions. Saunders had the added advantage of engaging passionately in medical research at the cutting edge. It is, however, doubtful that if he had grown up in a 'normal society' he would have considered abandoning the research laboratory desk for a vice-chancellor's office desk. South African higher education is all the richer for his career change.

The Saunders legacy to higher education is not just tied to the dynamic leadership he gave to making the University of Cape Town an innovator in teaching and research over a period of over sixteen years, but to the dogged way in which he pushed the boundaries of an apartheid state to create space for higher education to rise to its responsibilities. The opening of UCT's residences to black students might today look too ordinary to warrant special mention, but taken in the context of the day it was an act of courage. It was not only taking on the State, but also challenging the many ordinary white Capetonians who paid lip-service to non-racialism. So, too, standing between trigger-happy policemen and angry students took courage and passionate commitment to the ideal of creating space for intellectual debates in an intolerant society. Saunders's courage catapulted him to a leadership position in higher education nationally between the mid-1980s and the coming of *uhuru* in 1994. He continues to be a respected active statesman in higher education.

The mark of Stuart Saunders as a great leader was not only in doing the right thing, but also in having the self-confidence to surround himself with a diverse team of strong personalities who held challenging views on a variety of key issues. Saunders had the vision that enabled him to transcend conventional wisdom and prepared UCT for a future with leadership that broke with tradition. He also has the curiosity and intellectual depth to enjoy engaging with controversial issues. There must, however, have been days when he doubted the wisdom of the 'richness in diversity' approach, on the few occasions when debates within his team reached boiling-point. But he is not one to give up.

It is, however, his sense of humour which marks him out as an exceptional person. He is capable not only of seeing the funny side of daily events, but of poking fun at himself. It is not insignificant that the weekly meetings of his team were known as Monty Python sessions. He used humour as an effective tool in leadership as well as in defusing tense situations. Those of us privileged enough to have worked with him are all the richer for it. Readers of these memoirs are in for a treat.

Preface

These memoirs are an account of the personal experiences of the vice-chancellor of an English-speaking university in South Africa during and immediately after the apartheid years. They deal with political events involving the university and the responses to them, as well as the initiatives taken by the University of Cape Town (UCT) against the National Party Government. They are not concerned with the business common to all universities – academic policies, new academic enterprises, new buildings, acquisition of property and a host of other things. These will be included in a full history of the university which some energetic soul will write in due course.

During despotic rule and in the transition from a dictatorial system to a democracy, certain institutions can help to promote civilised norms and to lay the foundations of the emerging democracy. Amongst these, universities can be important. We tried to ensure that UCT played such a role.

I was determined that UCT would be an institution striving to offer an education of quality to its students, to achieve research of the first order and progressively to enrol increasing numbers of black students. Above all, this had to occur in an environment on campus as free from racism as could be achieved. I tried to achieve an island of non-racism in a sea of racism in a country where racial prejudice was enshrined in law.

These memoirs are my personal account of our efforts to achieve those goals. I take full responsibility for the areas in which we failed.

Acknowledgements

Anita gave me unwavering support and encouragement during thirteen years of my vice-chancellorship. I am deeply grateful to her for her love and understanding. I am also grateful for her critique of the manuscript.

My thanks go to Sheilah Lloyd, who did so much research and whose comments and contributions to editing were invaluable, to Maggie Sükel who handled the secretarial work with professionalism and humour, and to Hugh Amoore who cast his eagle eye to check for accuracy.

I am very grateful to John, Jane and Brendan for their support and for their criticisms of the manuscript.

Thanks are also due to the members of the staff of the UCT Archives for their help. Marie and David Philip could not have been more helpful or kinder to me and have been exemplary publishers.

Finally, my sincere thanks are due to the Trustees of the Andrew W Mellon Foundation of New York for their support, without which these memoirs would not have been written.

Early years
1931–1948

My mother Lilian was brought up in Bishop's Stortford in Hertfordshire where Cecil John Rhodes was born, and I was born in Muizenberg, a suburb of Cape Town in South Africa, the place where he died. The University of Cape Town (UCT) was built on a large part of Rhodes's estate. In his biography of Rhodes, *The Founder*, Robert Rotberg* writes, 'Rhodes never wavered in his espousal of a great South African university, based near Cape Town along the warm eastern side of Table Mountain. He dreamed of an Oxford-like teaching institution which would attract pupils from all the white settlements south of the Zambezi, and arouse in those students an enthusiasm which would sustain closer union.' The young white men who attended his university would, he proclaimed, 'make the union of South Africa in the future. Nothing will overcome the associations and the aspirations they will form under the shadow of Table Mountain.' Happily UCT has brought together men and women, black and white, and has broadened Rhodes's limited dream. The association of my mother's home town and of my birth place with Rhodes did not strike either my mother or myself at the time of my birth as being of any significance.

The house where I was born on 28 August 1931 was small and was situated on the mountain side with a view of the sea. A Dr Bosenberg was present at the delivery as well as a midwife, who advised my mother to put my crib in the toilet during the first night of my life because then, she said, my cries would not wake either my mother or herself. And so it was that I spent the first nights of my life in an environment which is somewhat unusual for a newborn child. The effects that it had on the future development of the infant I will leave to the readers who have the stamina to reach the final chapters of this book to determine. It may be that being confined and forced to look at a hanging chain determined my later opposition to the death penalty.

It is established that I was a contented baby and did not mind the absence of congratulatory telegrams or floral tributes. In time I learned that my

---

* *The Founder*, Robert I Rotberg, Oxford University Press 1988 p.357

mother, who corresponded with her sisters in England every week, had neglected to inform her family of the coming event because it had meant the cancellation of a holiday in England. 'I was just angry,' she says now, aged 101, and smiles. After all, the family in Britain knew about my sister, Nanette, who was then two years old and had a mass of naturally curly hair. Showing her to the family had been the main purpose of the proposed trip.

However, I was a boy, which made for a change, and was thought to be quite lovable and so my mother and I soon bonded. When she received news that one of her sisters had been delivered of a girl who was born on the same day as I had been, she was quite reconciled. Thereafter she worried that the angels would fetch me away, as I had become a perfect baby. To this day her only serious criticism of me has been the matter of the cancelled trip. She held that against me until 1981, when I was able to make amends by taking her on holiday to England where we visited relatives and travelled around the Lake District.

Two other notable events occurred during the period when I was a very young infant in Muizenberg. The first was my travelling solo and headlong at a great speed in my perambulator down the steep hill from our house to the main highway. I crossed the main highway, dodging between the traffic, and the perambulator was upended when it hit the kerb on the opposite side. Fortunately I seemed to have been strapped in and suffered no material damage. My mother is not sure what role the angels played on that occasion. The second event was that my mother nearly trod on a puffadder outside the house. I don't recall either incident, but was told about them a number of times.

My parents, who emigrated from England to South Africa in the 1920s, had adapted in different ways to living in South Africa. My father, Albert, spent his first South African Sunday afternoon on Muizenberg beach dressed in a suit and wearing spats and a bowler hat. He did not find the experience a congenial one and I believe that he did not visit a beach again. He told me that picnics, especially those held on beaches, were undesirable. If he wanted to eat sandwiches with sand in them, then he would ask for them to be made in that way! My father was a slightly built, apprehensive man, who had excelled at his school work, had played first violin in a youth orchestra and was also a good pianist. After a stint in the army in World War I, he had been denied the opportunity to study at university because of failing family fortunes. This was a great pity as my father was a natural academic. An omnivorous reader, eager for every scrap of information, he read all the textbooks I brought home as my studies advanced. His good schooling had prepared the ground for life-long intellectual pleasure and, together with his knowledge of French, had helped him as a young man to obtain a position in the foreign exchange department of a bank in London. I believe that if my parents had not emigrated, my father might have made a career in banking and enjoyed more material success and satisfaction, in work which would have appealed to his precise mind. In Cape Town he found employment as the manager of the box-making department of a confectionery company and most of the workers responsible to him were coloured* women. He detested racism and racial discrimination and was a courteous man, who would doff his hat on meeting one of the women working for him. Not surprisingly, he was highly regarded by the employees. After giving loyal and hard-working service for nearly forty years my father was retired without pension. I remember receiving this news with a sense of outrage. Years later, as vice-chancellor of UCT, I was entertained in the luxurious home of one of this confectionery company's heirs. Standing with a drink in that elegant room with a view of sloping lawns and old trees I felt resentment well up in me. My wife, Anita, and I left as soon as it was polite to do so. Fortunately Manfred Bloch, a wholesale merchant in imported fabrics, asked my father to work for him after his retirement from the factory, which he did for a number of years until ill health forced him to stop in his mid-seventies, this time with a modest pension and the important sense of having been valued. Manfred Bloch was gentle and kind, realised my father's worth to the business, and restored his dignity.

My father retained the habits of a Londoner throughout his life. He made good use of public libraries – biographies, textbooks, novels and detective yarns were all grist to his mill – and always had a beer in the pub on the way home from work. He often returned to the local pub in the evening where he joined a coterie of friends. I only saw him under the influence of alcohol once – I was 13 years old and I thought that the world had come to an end. At home he spent most of his time reading. A portrait of my father would probably have depicted him seated in an armchair with his glass of brandy, his cigarettes and an ashtray near him. He often played classical pieces which he loved on the piano and did so quite well, as I remember. He developed severe emphysema but persisted in smoking, even when he was on oxygen. I thought he might blow himself up either in hospital or at home and cause mayhem. He never took exercise, ate bacon and eggs every day for breakfast and died of emphysema in his eightieth year. It seems to me that genes may at times be more important than risk factors in causing dis-

---

* 'Coloured' was the official racial classification in South Africa for people of mixed descent and has retained a colloquial meaning. The other official classifications were Asian for people of Indian or Chinese descent, at first Bantu and later African for black South Africans born in South Africa, and white for people of European descent. The term 'black' came to be used to describe people who were African, Asian or Coloured.

ease. I hope so, because I am not exactly an exercise freak myself. He died of his lung disease not knowing I would be the vice-chancellor of UCT, but very proud that I was professor and head of the department of medicine.

My mother's approach to Cape Town's beautiful beaches was in sharp contrast to that of my father. She loved to go bathing in the long, hot summer and would often spend the day at the seaside. She usually shepherded my sister and me and many of our friends to either the Sea Point pavilion or Dalebrook beach at Kalk Bay, on the False Bay coast. We went there because Jean Cartwright ran a 'teahoose' at Kalk Bay and the Cartwright family were my parents' first friends when they arrived in Cape Town. (Most of the family lived in Wynberg.) To get to Kalk Bay we would commute by bus and by train and the journey took about 90 minutes each way, but that did not deter my mother or the enthusiastic bunch of hyperactive children – often more than 12 in number – whom she took with her. She would also take us to see the sights of Cape Town – parliament, the cathedral, the museum, the botanical gardens – and to the university, particularly to see the hydrangeas there in the summer-time. All these journeys depended on the skilful use of public transport and much foot-slogging. My mother was very energetic, frugal in the sense that she carefully weighed the use of every penny she spent, but was generous in her denial of her own needs while promoting the interests of her children. She had lots of spunk. As a young girl, and one of eight siblings, she had repeated her last primary school year because there were no other educational opportunities open to her and she had to wait until she was 15 and could go to London to work in a large department store. Like my father, she was determined her children would have better opportunities than she did and worked hard to secure them. Nanette and I had happy childhoods and felt secure, although I was always aware of our limited financial resources.

My earliest recollections go back to 1936 when my parents finally went on the delayed holiday to Europe and took my sister Nanette and me with them. We travelled on a Union Castle liner and I can recall the crowds at the dockside at the Canary Islands trying to storm the ship to get food and in a vain effort to get off the island because of the Spanish civil war. The other event of note was that I persisted in my request to be able to feed some penguins which were travelling on the boat and ultimately, in desperation, someone agreed that I could feed them, the only problem being that one of the penguins vomited up the contents of his stomach all over me. Not even repeated bathing could eliminate the overwhelming odour which surrounded me for several days. During that time it seemed to me that I was doing a solo journey on a crowded ship.

My memories of England, where I turned five, include the wonderment of my step-cousin's electric trains and a yacht that could sail in a pond. Then there was the excitement of meeting Audrey, the cousin who was exactly the same age as I was. There was also one very unpleasant experience. I had had a number of attacks of tonsillitis while in Cape Town and so my parents decided that I should have my tonsils out and that this should be done in Great Ormond Street Hospital in London. They decided not to tell me that I was going to hospital for an operation, but instead made the unwise decision to say they were taking me to the Bank of England to see how all the bank notes were made. I can still remember screaming as I was separated from my mother and taken up in the lift by the nursing sister. The nurses were fascinated by my golden tan and my enormous ability to swallow ice cream, even immediately after the tonsillectomy.

My next hospital experience was as a child in Groote Schuur Hospital (GSH) in Cape Town which would later become a second home to me. I had problems with ingrowing toenails for years (the family doctor took off the nail from one of my big toes without anaesthetic, an action used to torture people in oppressive societies) and I lay in a bed with the name 'Saint' ensconced above it. Charles Saint was the first professor of surgery at the medical school and a legend in his own time. I am sure he did not waste his time on my toes, but the romance of the name intrigued me as a small boy. When I was professor of medicine I saw Saint as a patient. He was at an advanced age and had severe gout. While Saint was professor of surgery he once spent a holiday at Gordon's Bay near Cape Town. He phoned Professor Forman (then professor of clinical medicine) to tell him he had acute arthritis in one of his knees. Always taking the thorough approach to differential diagnosis, Forman told him that he had either gout or gonorrhoea and that he had better come in to see him. Saint's reply is unrecorded.

On our return to South Africa from the visit to England my parents rented a house in Sea Point and it was in rented accommodation in this suburb that I lived until after I had qualified in medicine at the age of 22. At that time Sea Point consisted almost entirely of suburban houses large and small. The tall apartment buildings had not yet put in an appearance and the houses, rising up as they did on the hillside, overlooked the sparkling blue of the Atlantic Ocean. Behind us, on the slopes of the mountain, lay adventure. There were trees and shrubs to hide in, rough terrain to stalk the enemy, who could be outlaws, German soldiers (after the outbreak of World War II) or just another tribe of schoolboys, and there were snakes which we caught and took to school in our pockets and satchels. As children, my sister and I had no relatives in South Africa and so the Cartwright family members became our surrogate uncles and aunts as did the Williams family in Green Point. Mrs Williams, Auntie Louie, was a great favourite.

At the age of five I was sent to a pre-primary school in Kings Road and when I turned six on 28 August I was moved to the Sub A class in the Ellerton Junior Co-educational School. Sub A was the entry class of a twelve-year school programme which existed at the time. After three months in the Sub A class I was promoted to Standard One, skipping out Sub B, so I was entering the third year of my schooling having spent a total of three months at a formal school. Shortly after being admitted to Standard One, I was moved to the Special Class where children with learning difficulties were accommodated. This was because the teachers believed that I could not read properly, and I suspect they were right because my reading was largely based upon a very good memory and not a true understanding of how to read. My mother has always denied that I was in a special class, but I have no doubt that I was and that it was because I had been catapulted upwards in the educational system before being properly prepared. That question mark over my ability at school lasted only for that one year, if as long as that, and from the next year onwards I was in the regular class and moved up to the Sea Point Boys' Junior School, where I was for the next two years. My parents, despite very limited means, decided that I should go to a private school. My father spoke to a friend of his, a Mr Burns, who amongst other things at times played the organ at St George's Cathedral. He asked Burns whether I should be sent to St George's Grammar School (an Anglican school) or to Christian Brothers' College in Green Point (a Catholic school). My father was an agnostic. Burns told him that if he wanted his son to become a gentleman, he should send him to St George's Grammar School, but if he wanted him to learn anything, he should send him to Christian Brothers' College. The decision was not difficult for my father, although my manners might have suffered as a result. And so it was that I went to Christian Brothers' College in 1941, staying there until I matriculated in 1947. I was fortunate enough to be placed in the top ten students in the country in the junior certificate examination in 1945, winning a scholarship for my last two years at school, which I completed with distinctions. I was taught almost exclusively by Irish Brothers, a dedicated band of men who were strict disciplinarians and certainly did not spare the rod, so there was no risk of spoiling the boys.

My formative years as a young schoolboy took place during the Second World War, a war which South Africa entered on the side of Britain and the Commonwealth following a small majority in parliament. I had a map up in my bedroom and pinned flags in it to keep track of the movement of the armies. I saw the mighty warships the *Prince of Wales* and the *Repulse* sail out of the bay to the Far East. They were at the bottom of the ocean with great loss of life soon after their arrival off Malaya. Churchill described that as an 'imperial' defeat, a description I once used for a set-back I experienced as a vice-chancellor. My mother busied herself packing eggs in solid blocks of paraffin and parcelling jams, and these were posted to the family in England. My father, who was not a handy man, contrived to dig a bomb shelter in our garden. It proved very useful for storing vegetables. The tragedy of war struck our family when news came that my cousin Audrey had drowned when the *City of Benares* was torpedoed by a U-boat as it approached Canadian waters. She was being evacuated to Canada; my parents had wanted her to come to Cape Town but the voyage to Canada was shorter and thought to be safer on that account.

It was during this period that I learnt to abhor the ambitions and methods of Nazi Germany and those of Stalinist Russia from my father, who also taught me to detest racial discrimination and persecution. He imbued me with the ideal of individual liberty and human dignity. He and I clashed on two issues. Firstly he was dismissive of the South African armed forces in comparison to those of Britain. While it is true in terms of strength, size and fighting capacity there was no comparison between the armies, navies and airforces of the two countries, the South African fighting machine had a proud record and he and I argued vigorously on that score. Secondly, my father was a Freemason and when I left school he asked me whether I wanted to join that movement. I declined on the grounds that (a) being a medical student and subsequently a medical practitioner would claim all my attention and (b) the organisation was segregated in South Africa and blacks were not admitted to white lodges. I told him I could not be associated with such an organisation.

Towards the end of my last year of school my parents asked me what career I wished to follow, and I said that I wanted to be a schoolteacher. My father then asked me whether I didn't want to be a doctor and I admitted that was my first choice, but that I did not believe they could afford to put me through my studies. My mother told me that she would go out to work and that the two incomes would make it possible for me to study medicine, and so I applied to UCT and was accepted into the medical faculty. My mother was concerned as to whether my father had had an undue influence on my choice of career because he himself had always wanted to study medicine and had not been able to afford to do so (he read avidly about the subject, including my textbooks!) and I was not sure whether or not he had had an undue influence on me, nor was I absolutely clear what studying medicine fully entailed, but I instinctively knew that it was the right thing for me to do, and so it proved to be. The financial situation was eased by my winning a Kings entrance scholarship to the university, which I held for three years. My mother did go out to work to make up the shortfall, at first behind the counter in a dress-shop and then subsequently in a pharmacy in Sea Point. She proved to be very popular in her chosen work and became quite an expert, working for many years in pharmacies in Sea Point and always drawing her favourite clientele with her. Naturally gregarious, my mother took a great interest in other people's lives and whereas this was not always a welcome trait amongst our neighbours, regular customers at the pharmacy were warmed by her interest. She stopped working at the age of eighty-one, when she had to look after my ailing father.

Always remarkably energetic, my mother had skilfully given the impression that she was fifteen years younger than her true age, until my sister's sixtieth birthday party shattered her credibility. My sister had worked in the city as a young woman and was a generous source of pocket money while I was a student. At the time of the birthday my mother was living in an apartment block for retired people and she was cornered by a group of blue-rinsed women who faced her with the choice of admitting either to a teenage pregnancy or to a greater age. My mother was then ninety years old but still quick thinking – she calculated and compromised, finally admitting to having shaved five years off her age. In her eighties she finished work late one night and anxious to get home, she hitched a lift on the back of a motorcycle. In her one hundred and second year in 1999, she is still quite a lady!

I had three months' vacation before starting at the university, and plainly I had to work to earn some money. I went to the Sun Building in Greenmarket Square to be interviewed by Mr Alistair McGregor, who was then one of the senior partners in Douglas, McKelvie, Galbraith, and Sons, a firm of chartered accountants. I had on my sports coat, my best shirt and a collar and tie and flannels. The tie was the only tie I owned that wasn't a school tie. It had been given to me by a Mrs Carter, an old friend of my mother. Going up in the lift for my interview, four months into my sixteenth year, a man turned and faced me in that crowded area and asked me when I had been in the Royal Air Force. I said I had never been in the airforce and of course that must have been obvious to everybody. He promptly said, 'That's an RAF tie, take that bloody tie off!' I waited outside Mr McGregor's office, wondering whether he had been in the RAF, because plainly I could not take the tie off. Fortunately, he did not recognise the symbolism of my tie and I got a job as a temporary clerk, going out on audits where I was required to 'cast,' that is add up long lists of figures to check the sum at the bottom of each page. This was before the days of calculators, certainly ages before computers, and this was the way young accountants started their careers. They said it would improve my mind. Somebody told me it was good for my soul. One of the senior articled clerks I worked with assumed that I had a profound medical knowledge because I was about to study medicine, and he was very anxious to know what the most efficient treatment was for a hangover. I said I would find out for him. I can't recall what solution I gave him, but I doubt it was effective. We worked fairly hard most of the time, but there were opportunities for having fun. I remember spending virtually a whole week playing cricket with a ruler and a rubber in the boardroom of quite a prominent company in Cape Town. The only time we weren't playing this sport was when the chairman of the company came and sat at the boardroom table to read some documents. I think he may have had some insight into our other activities, but he never said anything to us or to the partners at head office.

My employers' offices in the Sun Building were near to those of John Stein, who was a very successful stockbroker and the father of one of my closest friends, Edgar. John Stein correctly had the reputation of being absolutely honest and a man of great integrity. He and his wife Bella fled from Germany in the early thirties to escape persecution by the Nazis, who subsequently murdered members of their family. I was enormously fond of them both and had the great privilege of being his physician when we were all much older. Edgar, who eventually joined his father in the business, was a Jew and I was a Protestant in a Catholic school and each of us was therefore part of a minority. (The Brothers never tried to convert us to Catholicism but did impress upon us the importance of developing a strong set of moral values, and the importance of hard work.)

Edgar and I were in the same class at school and we studied together and played rugby badly and tried tennis with slightly more success, though I believe Edgar's game later improved, and together we were ordered off a golf course. Eventually we attended the same university in different courses, but continued meeting regularly. Edgar now lives with his wife Pam in Sydney, Australia, and we are still in touch. His mother, Bella, is with them. It is sad that Bella should once again have experienced the trauma of emigration in the belief that to do so would ensure a better life for the next generation. When we were schoolboys, Edgar and I, like so many other South Africans, anticipated growing old together. The loss of such a talented family was one of the prices that South Africa has had to pay for apartheid. My son John and many other young South African graduates in the 1980s took the painful decision to leave the country of their birth because apartheid was repugnant to them.

I was the first capitalist in my family if owning one's motor car qualifies one as a capitalist. My parents never owned a motor car, but in my fourth year as a medical student I left the vagaries of my holiday job as a junior clerk in a chartered accountants' office, where the pay was quite poor, and worked in the off-sales department of the old Central Hotel (it no longer exists) in Shortmarket Street in Cape Town. There I sold booze of different varieties from opening time in the morning to closing time at night. I was paid well and my package included having lunch in the hotel. The solitary man who ran the off-sales was a bachelor who lived in rooms in the city. He took a great interest in my career as an undergraduate medical student. I of course regaled him with tales, true and not quite so true, and we certainly enjoyed ourselves behind the counter, swopping stories while we went about our work. After the June vacation, in my fifth year, I had accumulated forty pounds and with the help of my future brother-in-law, Stanley Page, who selected the car for me, I was able to buy a 1931 Ford Upright, which had chains on the sides of the door instead of handles and which almost always had to be started with the crank handle in front. The wheels had originally been designed for a motor bike. It was a great car, which took me where I wanted to go (and usually back again) for three years.

I offered to give my father a lift to the factory every morning, the factory being in the Main Road in Salt River, and with some reluctance he agreed because he was quite a nervous man, and was certainly apprehensive about my driving skills and about the car in which he was being asked to ride. Of course it takes some vigour and is not without hazard, starting a car with a crank handle every morning, and so I used to run it down Dover Road where we lived (which was quite a steep hill) and let out the clutch with the car in first gear, igniting the engine. Then I would rev the car by pushing the accelerator up and down, the heel of my right foot on the brake, the sole on the accelerator and my left foot on the clutch.

One morning at the junction between Dover and High Level Roads I had the engine running smoothly, but with very high revs when I let out the clutch. We shot across the road like a rocket and I realised that the accelerator had jammed flat on the floor. I twisted the wheel towards the right and was approaching an electric light pole at some speed, so I flung the wheel to the left and we were then approaching a drop of some twenty feet and as I flung the wheel to the right again my father said, 'You'll turn this bloody car over!', which is what I then did. The car was lying on its side and my father was lying on top of me. I said, 'Open the window.' He opened the window. I turned off the ignition and we stood up with our feet through the window lying on the road and our heads through the open window on my father's side. There was a double-decker bus at a bus stop not far away and as I watched the driver was climbing out and the bus conductor and the passengers were running towards us, presumably to give us first aid. I told my father to pull the chain, which would then open the door to enable us to climb out; this he did, but in climbing out he trod on the gear lever and bent it. I climbed out and there were the ladies from the bus being very solicitous with their handkerchiefs out, ready to apply first aid. Neither my father nor I was hurt, although I did have some grazing on my right hand, and I asked for help to get the car upright. The bus passengers provided this help, and pushed it to the side of the road. They then got back into the bus and I walked with my father up the road to our house, because we had soiled our shirts somewhat and needed to change. It was about a four or five minute walk and my father swore at me throughout that period; I don't think he repeated himself once. My sister insisted that I drive the car immediately because I was naturally somewhat unnerved by the experience. I went down to get in the car to drive to medical school and the only damage that had been done to it was that my father had bent the gear lever. That made it very difficult to get it out of first gear. So I drove along the High Level Road to where Stanley lived; I told him the story and he straightened the gear lever. I went off to medical school, where I gave my first solo anaesthetic.

My father swore he would never travel in the car again, and certainly not when I was driving. My mother, being much more adventurous, frequently travelled with me in the evenings or weekends. Travelling at night was not without its hazards because I had sold the fan belt for two and sixpence to pay for some petrol, so the battery tended to be on the low side and the headlights somewhat dim. Indeed on one occasion when I was driving to the Retreat students' clinic, I found myself groping along roads which were poorly lit and I hit a dog which came up from underneath the car and sat in the passenger's seat barking at me! It wasn't in the least bit hurt – I was somewhat astonished. The dog was able to do that because the car did not have a complete floor and my passengers had to travel with their feet on the steel bars which seemed to join the chassis of the car together.

After about a year, on a Saturday evening in the middle of winter, when the rain was pouring down, my parents were going to Camps Bay to visit friends. They would have had to walk along High Level Road, down to the Main Road, wait for a bus and then walk from the bus stop in Camps Bay for about five minutes to get to the friends' house. It was clear they would have got wet through, so I offered to give them a lift in my car. My father was very reluctant to come but did so and sat in the back left seat. We drove along Victoria Road to Camps Bay and I was astounded by the fact that the car wouldn't pull, but we managed to get there. I opened the door for my mother and she ran inside the house; I looked down at the back left wheel and there was no tyre. The rim was red-hot. I had obviously started the journey with a flat tyre. My father got out of the car, looked at the red-hot rim, gave me one look, said nothing and walked inside and never travelled with me in that car again.

I had enrolled at UCT as an undergraduate, six months into my sixteenth year. South African universities follow the Scottish tradition in medical education and students enrol in a six-year programme, graduating with the bachelor of medicine and bachelor of surgery degree at the end of that time. I had an uncomplicated undergraduate career and achieved some success, graduating at the top of my class and being awarded the Council's scholarship for post-graduate work.

Student years 1948-1957

My first experience of a student revolt occurred when I was in my first year. One of the subjects we took was chemistry and part of the instruction consisted of a whole day's practical each Tuesday, when we worked at a bench doing a variety of experiments. The senior lecturer introduced us to the experiments we were required to perform in that particular practical, and a number of demonstrators would move around the large laboratory to help students solve their problems. One such demonstrator was the wife of the senior lecturer, a Mrs Spong. There were two students at each bench and the student who shared my bench was a man about six foot six inches tall. He came to university wearing an open-neck shirt, short khaki trousers and sandals. This was in 1948, and all the other students wore a collar and tie, a jacket and long trousers and certainly shoes and socks, so his garb was quite unusual. He told me that he had been General Smuts's bodyguard during the war and he certainly was one of the ex-servicemen – those who had served in the South African armed forces during the Second World War – who had been able to enter university because of their war record. There were a number of such veterans in my class in 1948.

During the first practical, Mrs Spong approached him and indicated to him that she didn't think that he knew very much about chemistry. He did not reply. The following Tuesday she approached him again and said that she wasn't sure what he was doing in the class as he seemed to know nothing. He said, 'Don't talk to me like that.' The following week she again approached him and admonished him about his incompetence. At this, he took her, put her across his knee and spanked her bottom! To say that I was astounded is an understatement. I never saw him again, nor did anybody else in the class. Quite how the disciplinary procedures worked, I am not sure, but they certainly were summary in their execution and the bodyguard did not attend the university again. At the end of my term of office as vice-chancellor, if a student did such a thing, the law would require me to give him or her several days' notice to appear before the university court, the student would have a right to legal representation and would have to have full documentation of the charge in a timely fashion. The student would usually be suspended, pending resolution of the matter, but the university would be lucky if the matter was concluded in under a month. The expelled bodyguard's name appeared in the newspapers on three occasions years later: firstly when he was alleged to have tried to blow up an aircraft in which Messrs Goldreich and Wolpe, two political prisoners who had escaped from a South African prison, were to be passengers; again when he was alleged to have shot a diamond dealer; and, finally, when the police were allegedly seeking information about the murder of Dr Smit, a prominent South African.

I first rebelled against university authority in my third year, when we studied pathology, bacteriology (medical microbiology), pharmacology and psychology. I refused to sign the register for the pathology lectures because I believed it was undignified, that we were 'adults', and it was wrong to have a register for a university lecture. That resulted in a confrontation between myself and the redoubtable secretary of the department, Miss Kruger. I can't remember how the issue was resolved, but I think we managed to restore honour on both sides.

We were introduced to clinical bedside medicine in our fourth year and I came deeply to respect Professor Frank Forman, who was the professor of clinical medicine, as a superb clinician and human being. I instinctively felt that clinical medicine was the field in which I wished to work and I tried to model myself on the professor, who had outstanding bedside clinical skills.

Professor Forman had a remarkable memory. On one occasion a patient was admitted with some abdominal problem and after the professor had asked the patient all the details about his current illness, he asked him if his back still troubled him. The patient denied that he had ever had back trouble. The professor asked him if he could recall tripping over a kerbstone in Adderley Street (the main street of Cape Town city centre) and jarring his back in June 1926, 32 years earlier. He reminded him that he had been admitted to the New Somerset Hospital under his (Forman's) care. With an exclamation, the patient acknowledged all the facts to be true. The patient had completely forgotten about that illness, but Professor Forman recalled the details precisely. Professor Forman could also recall with great accuracy articles he had read in the medical literature (and there was not much that he had not read) and was a resource comparable to a modern computer. He was the epitome of a gentleman, renowned for his courtesy and good manners.

In the middle of this year, Dr Marshall (Mark) Horwitz returned to Cape Town from the Massachusetts General Hospital in Boston where he had been working with Dr Fuller Albright, an internationally renowned authority on arthritis. Mark Horwitz was not only an expert in that area, but also a superb clinician, and he became my second role model. That is not to say the department did not have other outstanding clinicians; many of them influenced me at that time and later in my career. Amongst them I would single out Val Schrire, Louis Vogelpoel, Helen Brown, Arthur Landau and Isaac Grayce, but I am deeply indebted to many others.

I don't have the temperament or stamina for surgery, and I realised in my fifth year that obstetrics and gynaecology held no future for me. We did our practical obstetrics in District Six, a suburb adjacent to the city centre, which later became one of the symbols of apartheid. After I had qualified, the Nationalist Government forcibly removed all the coloured people who lived in District Six and made them live on the Cape Flats, many miles away and far from their places of work. But when we were studying obstetrics in District Six, it was a vibrant, exciting suburb, very run down, and we went out in what was called 'The District' to 'deliver' babies. We also worked in the Peninsula Maternity Hospital, which was situated in District Six, and we lived on site. In the early hours of April 1 (which was not a coincidence) one of our number was sent for to come and help with a delivery in the hospital. We were then all sent for and told the first of a set of twins had been delivered, and the second baby was expected and would be a breech delivery, that is feet first. Our colleague was standing there wearing gloves, gown, mask and the first born baby was crying in a nearby crib. The mother was apparently experiencing a lot of pain as she was still in labour. I was asked to go up and palpate her abdomen to confirm that the baby was in fact coming in the breech position. I reported to the obstetrician that I was unable to determine the lie of the child because the contractions were so strong. While I was talking to him the mother sat up in bed and burst out laughing. She turned out to be the cook, who wasn't even pregnant.

I carry with me in my memory a series of clear snapshots, vivid recollections of events which made an indelible impression on me, although one wasn't usually aware at the time that such a 'snapshot' was being taken. One such snapshot relates to the day on which the general election results were announced in 1948, when I was a first-year student. I recall a member of my class running out of the zoology practical room into University Avenue shouting, '*Ons is in, ons is in!*' ('We are in, we are in!') It was the beginning of the apartheid nightmare. I did not anticipate the full horror of the system that was going to be imposed on the country, but I knew enough about Dr Malan's National Party to be dismayed. There had been racial discrimination in South Africa since the seventeenth century but the National Party ensured that Acts of Parliament entrenched and extended it. I also remember walking up the road towards the medical school one day in 1950 and seeing the banner headlines, 'Smuts dies.' That seemed to me to reinforce the position of the ruling Nationalist Party.

When I was a final-year medical student, I was one of the students, as a member of the medical students' council, who hosted the visit to the medical school by Donald Hunter, a distinguished physician with a special interest in occupational medicine, who worked at the London Hospital. We entertained him royally – at least we thought it was grand – and he gave a number of lectures and went on ward rounds, but I remember his visit best for his parting remarks. He described Cape Town and South Africa as the 'gangrenous tip of Africa.' I have been able to point out since 1994 that the blood supply has been restored and that the gangrene has been cured.

After qualifying at the end of 1953 I did my internship at Groote Schuur Hospital (GSH) in general medicine and general surgery during 1954. I started in ward D6 in the old GSH. The extraordinary thing was that at the stroke of midnight students became doctors with powers and responsibilities nobody believed they were able to handle before that magical time. Seriously ill people are in their care. Of course registrars (residents) and consultants would be available, but quite frequently there is quite a long period in which the new doctor has to take that first responsibility, especially in the middle of the night. Young doctors have to come to terms with the enormous responsibility placed upon the medical practitioner in the care of the sick and one has to learn how to deal with the intensely human problems, quite apart from the difficult medical decisions. One has to certify someone as being dead and then write out and sign the death certificate.

During these early weeks I felt very insecure and very isolated. I looked at my fellow interns in the wards, in the corridors and in the doctors' living quarters. They all seemed to be completely confident and free of the intense fears and insecurities which I felt. Of course that was not the case. They, in turn, felt that I was completely confident. Later, when I became a consultant and when I was professor of medicine, I made a practice of taking the new interns aside as soon as they arrived in the ward and telling them what they would feel and of the emotional and other problems which they would have to overcome, but which they would deal with adequately and in doing so they would emerge the stronger for it.

I remember for example having patients in the ward who had diabetes and were on insulin. I felt I couldn't take my eyes off them in case the dose they were getting was too high, so I would make frequent visits to the ward in the middle of the night to wake them up to see if they were all right. The interesting thing is that if a doctor is inefficient and insecure and particularly if he or she makes a wrong decision and then spends a great deal of time with the patient, the reputation of the doctor soars. If on the other hand you are very efficient, make the right diagnosis and give efficient treatment and therefore don't have to spend so much time with the patient, or show so much acute concern, they often feel that the doctor is inadequate. This is illustrated by my experience in a small country shop where the lady behind the till suddenly exclaimed to me, 'Oh, Dr Saunders, I have never forgotten the wonderful treatment you gave me.' I could not recall her at all and said, 'Oh, that is very good of you, what do you remember best?' She said, 'You took my tonsils out and you looked after me superbly.' What she didn't know was that as a house surgeon I had worked for a month in the ear, nose and throat department and the surgeons in that department insisted that I do what is called a tonsil 'slate' that is, be responsible for taking out the tonsils and usually the adenoids as well of patients on a particular day. I think there were six patients who required the operation on that day and the average ear, nose and throat surgeon would have done those operations in about two or three hours. It took me all day, because I was terrified of cutting a major vessel at the back of the throat and killing a patient. I operated successfully in the end, but only after a great deal of terror on my part. The patients being anaesthetised were unable to share my emotions. But one thing they did share was my presence all night at their bedsides because I was afraid that they might bleed to death after the operations. None of them turned a hair and all the operations were successful, but my incompetence and lack of experience were well known to myself. My post operative attention had endeared me to the patient – little did she know this had sprung entirely from my ineptitude. I did not enlighten her in our encounter so many years later – it didn't seem fair to either of us.

It is quite frightening that there is so much luck involved in determining the affairs of men and women. This is especially so when one is at school, at university and in the formative years of one's post-university life. The key to success lies often in the influence of particular individuals and I am very fortunate to have had the great privilege of being taught by outstanding people. I recall in particular the headmaster of my school, Brother McEvoy, and also Dr Mark Horwitz, Professor Frank Forman, Professor Jack Brock, Professor J F P Erasmus, Professor Jannie Louw and Professor D J (Sonny) du Plessis, the latter three all surgeons. I was lucky to have been influenced by them. It is a privilege when one is older to take an interest in and be involved in the careers of young people, but it is also an obligation, one which is often not exercised.

Although I won the prize in surgery when I qualified, it was quite clear what I was going to do because I bought myself a baumanometer to measure blood pressure – something I would use regularly as a physician. I certainly did not buy myself any surgical instruments. My six months as a house surgeon made it clear to everybody that my decision was the right one. Erasmus, who was head of the department of surgery, and Sonny du Plessis, who was the senior consultant of his firm for whom I worked, must have been driven mad by my physicianly approach and by my lack of manual dexterity. On Christmas day I was carving a turkey in the ward when a patient's visitor came to me and commented that he hoped my surgical ability was better than my carving skills!

Surgical interns assist at operations, usually spending their time holding retractors or cutting the catgut once a stitch has been completed. Another task assigned to them is to press a handle on the floor with a foot to complete the electrical circuit for the cautery, which is frequently used to stop blood loss from bleeding-points. On one occasion I was assisting at the removal of most of a thyroid and the surgeon had used many forceps to secure all the bleeding-points. The forceps formed a ring around the front of the patient's neck. I was feeling a bit sleepy and my mind started wandering as did my right foot, which engaged the cautery handle in the floor. Unfortunately the cautery needle was resting against one of the metal forceps. The result was a catherine wheel firework effect with the spark of electricity shooting round and round and a strong smell of smoke filling the air. This was not all that filled the air as the surgeon expressed his opinion of me in unambiguous terms. However, all the bleeding-points had been secured as a result of this and the forceps could be removed forthwith, with the patient experiencing no harm. I reflected to myself that I might have inadvertently introduced a new surgical technique, but I am unaware of its having been widely adopted!

When I completed my internship I was free for a short period before taking up my position for a year as a registrar (resident) in the department of pathology and during that time I acted as a locum tenens for a general practitioner in Salt River in Cape Town, a low-income residential area. Dr Mendel Meyers was the general practitioner and his rooms were in Salt River Road. He told me that his practice was largely amongst the people of the area, most of whom were poor and working class, and that he also was the doctor for a number of factories. It was a busy two weeks.

I was a pathology registrar at GSH and UCT for one year, using that experience to prepare myself to be a physician. I did autopsies, worked in medical microbiology and chemical pathology, and turned my hand to research.

Dr Golda Selzer, Professor Forman's wife, was a senior lecturer in pathology. She was devoted to the work and to the students and was the leading light in the creation of the Students' Health and Welfare Centres Organisation, a student welfare organisation (SHAWCO). She and the professor had married during a lunch break and both were back at work that same afternoon! Golda was doing research on the poliomyelitis viruses before a poliomyelitis vaccine was available. The only way to grow the virus at that time was to passage it (grow it repeatedly) in the brains of living suckling mice, which she did with great skill. I helped her as a lowly assistant, holding my breath in case I inadvertently pricked my finger. It was not the only time that I had held my breath to avoid illness. As a small boy I frequently accompanied my father to the Cape Town docks on a Sunday morning to watch the reclamation of land which was being undertaken to enlarge the harbour. To get to the docks we had to walk down Portswood Road past the Fever Hospital, and I always tried to hold my breath while we were passing the hospital, attempting to avoid contracting a foul infection. As far as I know, my father was oblivious of my fears and the strategy I used.

I became a registrar in general medicine in 1956 and was successful in writing the first ever examination for the Fellowship of the College of Physicians in South Africa in September 1957. This Fellowship was the qualification I needed to register as a specialist physician. Registrars in medicine have to work hard and long hours, but I found that clinical medicine gave me enormous satisfaction, and we had our lighter moments. On a public holiday, then called Boxing Day, the day after Christmas Day, there was a bowls tournament at the King David Country Club. This was a club formed by the Jewish community because anti-semitism denied them membership of another popular club. There was a buffet lunch and, shortly thereafter, when the greens were full of eager bowlers, the majority went down with acute attacks of violent gastro-enteritis. Pandemonium broke out. A number were brought to the casualty department at GSH where I was the senior medical registrar on duty. We had to wash out stomachs and give intravenous infusions. One woman refused to swallow the tube which would allow us to wash out her stomach until her husband yelled at her, 'If you don't swallow that tube I will never let you see the children again!' She swallowed it. Some were quite ill and admitted to the wards, but all recovered completely. Professor Forman referred to it as 'the open bowels tournament'.

Noreen and I were married in 1956, having met in a cinema in Cape Town in the previous year. She and her close friend Unity Walker had done their general training as nurses and were studying midwifery at the Peninsula Maternity Hospital. I have a laugh once described by a reporter as sounding like a donkey's bray and I believe it was this that attracted their attention to Godfrey Radloff (a close schoolfriend and medical colleague) and me, sitting immediately behind them. It was not considered advisable at that time for medical registrars to marry as they were expected to devote themselves to the art and science of medicine, and our marriage raised a number of important eyebrows.

Noreen and I were very happy and she was a great source of support and encouragement to me in my career. We had two children whom we loved dearly. She had an anatomical deformity of the uterus and was prone to miscarriages, of which she had nine before our son was born. She bore all this with great fortitude and was absolutely determined to have children. She worked tirelessly for the African Scholars' Fund, an outstanding organisation started by Margaret Elsworth to help fund the schooling of young Africans, and in later years for READ, an organisation which provided books for African schools.

Noreen came from Pietermaritzburg in Natal where she had done her general nursing training at Grey's Hospital. Her mother was an elderly, petite woman who was the dominant personality in the family. Her father had retired from the railways and in the earlier years of our marriage worked at the market in Pietermaritzburg. I was very fond of them both and particularly liked the feistiness of my mother-in-law. After her death in the late '60s, her husband became very ill. He lived with his son in Port Elizabeth for a short spell and then came to live with us in Driekoppen and it was there that he died. Noreen's sister Daphne and the family were very supportive. Daphne's eldest daughter Leigh (now a respected senior midwife) lived with us at Driekoppen while she trained as a nurse. It was delightful having her with us and she was a great favourite with the children. She and Noreen looked uncannily alike and were often mistaken for sisters.

While a medical registrar I did some research. I worked with Professor Pete Jackson and Dr Raymond (Bill) Hoffenberg, carrying out clinical trials of the first oral agents used in the treatment of diabetes mellitus. I worked closely with Professor Len Eales and Dr Eugene Dowdle and was a member of the renal-metabolic research unit under Eales's leadership. We helped Eales with his research work on the nephrotic syndrome which formed the basis of his doctoral degree, and also worked in porphyria. We did the first haemodialysis for kidney failure in GSH in 1958. The artificial kidney we had bought was the Kolff model, and was like a big washing machine. In our inexperience, and because of Eales's obsessive nature which demanded absolute accuracy, we spent about six hours adjusting the acid concentration of the bath water of the machine before connecting up the patient! The procedure was a success. I was able to publish several papers in the medical literature as a result of my work as a medical registrar, and found that very satisfying.

A natural consequence of my upbringing was for me to find the Nationalist Government's policies, as they developed in the late '40s and the '50s while I was an undergraduate and subsequently throughout almost all of my adult life, totally unacceptable. The draconian laws introduced by the Nationalist Government enabled them to place banning orders on citizens

Lilian Saunders, in front of the pharmacy where she worked for many years.

Albert Saunders.

Prof. JFP Erasmus, head of surgery, teaching the final-year class. SJS on the left.

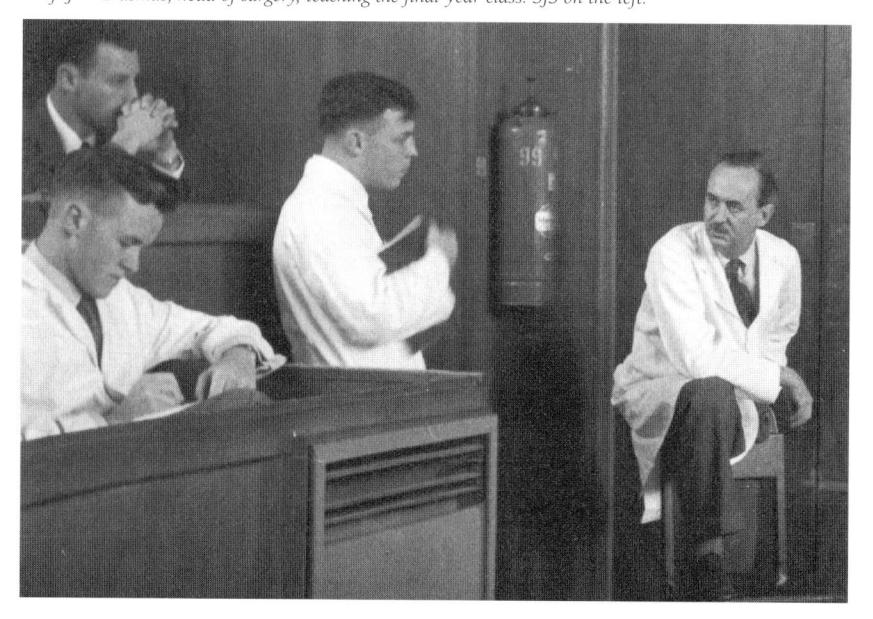

Prof. Frank Forman and Dr Golda Selzer with SJS, 1956.

The 'Gang of Four', clockwise from top left: Prof. Jannie Louw, Prof. Bromilow Bromilow-Downing, Prof. Arthur Kipps, and SJS. (UCT News)

Sir Richard Luyt and Dr Frank Robb.

Dr (now Sir) Aaron Klug and Mr Len Abrahamse. (Bob Steyn, UCT News and Information Bureau)

(Deena Shapiro, UCT)

This page and the opposite page show images from several

(Argus)

occasions of student confrontation with the police, 1985-7.

(Argus)

(Scott Meserve)

Ms Helen Joseph, with Anton Richman, president of the SRC, and SJS, after giving the TB Davie lecture, 1983.

Mr Harry Oppenheimer receiving an honorary degree, 1985. (Argus)

Some members of the delegation visiting the ANC in Lusaka, 1986. Standing from the left, Prof. P Mohanoe, Mr J Samuels, Prof. Charles Villa-Vicencio, Dr Mamphela Ramphele, Prof. James Leatt, SJS, Mr Glenn Goosen. Kneeling in front, Ms Carla Sutherland and Mr Chris Mzamane.

Stuart Saunders welcoming new students. On left, Mr Len Read; on right Prof. Bill Whittaker, Dean of Law.

Prof. John Terblanche and Dr Ralph Kirsch.

Mr Alan Pifer and Mr George Soros in Manhattan.

Mr Hugh Amoore. (UCT News)

Dr Ramphele, Mr Bill Bowen, president of the Mellon Foundation, and SJS, at Princeton. Dr Ramphele and SJS received honorary degrees.

President Mandela receiving his honorary degree from UCT in 1990, with the Chancellor, Mr Harry Oppenheimer. (UCT News)

without charge or trial and people placed under such banning orders could be confined to a particular magisterial district, and could be prevented from entering any particular building or site, including any educational institution. They could be prevented from meeting more than one person at a time and, indeed, could be placed under house arrest, either for twenty-four hours of the day or for a particular part of the day. The Government could also detain people without trial, at first for thirty days, then sixty days, then ninety days and finally, indefinitely. People died in detention – they were murdered there by the police, and citizens were assassinated in their homes or elsewhere by the police or other members of the security forces.

While I was a registrar, apartheid was extended to the universities by law when the Nationalists passed the 'Extension of University Education' Act. Like many authoritarian regimes, they used language to try to hide the truth and to put the best possible gloss on what they were doing to make their actions appear civilised. They were doing anything *but* extending university education. The Act classified universities like UCT and the University of the Witwatersrand as 'white' universities, which they determined were for white students, the University College of the Western Cape was established for 'coloured' people, the University College of Durban-Westville for Asians, the University College of Zululand for Zulu-speaking people, the University College of the North for Sotho-speaking people, and the University College which became the University of Bophuthatswana for Tswana-speaking people.* The Medical University of South Africa was established as a medical school exclusively for blacks. The well-established University of Fort Hare was reserved for Xhosa speakers. To their great credit a number of black academics and other members of staff at Fort Hare resigned in protest. At the same time the Government established the Rand Afrikaans University, which was for white Afrikaans-speaking students, adding that university to the existing white Afrikaans-speaking universities (Stellenbosch, Pretoria, Orange Free State, Potchefstroom) and they also established the bilingual University of Port Elizabeth, which effectively became an Afrikaans-speaking university. If there was extension of university education, it certainly favoured Afrikaans-speaking white South Africans.

Any person of colour who wished to study at UCT had to obtain a permit from a Cabinet Minister! If somebody studied without such a permit it was the student who was prosecuted, not the university. The minister might grant a permit if there wasn't a course offered at a so-called 'black' university suitable for a particular student. This resulted in some courses being specially designed to meet this requirement and using this stratagem there was

---

* The term 'college' was later dropped in each case.

some slight success in overcoming the system. Dr Tom Davie, the vice-chancellor of UCT when I was an undergraduate student, was a staunch opponent of the extension of apartheid to university education in South Africa. He was outspoken in his resistance and together with the University of the Witwatersrand, UCT published a book in 1957 entitled *The Open Universities in South Africa*. Tom Davie defined academic freedom, 'the four essential freedoms of a university,' as 'to determine for itself on academic grounds who may teach, what may be taught, how it shall be taught, and who may be admitted to study.' It is of interest that Judge Frankfurter subsequently used this definition in a United States court.

Tom Davie is one of my heroes. He was uncompromising in his opposition to racism. While vice-chancellor he developed severe rheumatoid arthritis and was put onto cortisone. His face developed the characteristic moon shape and ruddiness. This was the man I faced across a table, as a member of the medical students' council, in my fifth year of study. We had organised a mass meeting to protest against the basement rooms of the medical residence being turned into a cafeteria. I told the vice-chancellor that the students were totally opposed to his proposals and that we wouldn't accept them. He put his gnarled fingers into a fist, slammed his fist on the table and told me that that was exactly what he would be doing, that I would be accepting his proposals, because he was going ahead despite our protests, and that was the end of the matter. Perhaps life was a little easier for vice-chancellors in 1952 than it proved to be in the 1980s! In 1954 Tom Davie had a major complication from a peptic ulcer which had resulted from his use of cortisone, and he had to have an emergency operation, an operation at which I assisted as a young house surgeon.

In June 1957, the members of UCT marched through the streets of Cape Town in academic dress protesting against the passage of the Bill establishing the Extension of University Education Act. The march was led by the chancellor, the ex-Chief Justice the Hon. Albert van de Sandt Centlivres, another man who uncompromisingly and vigorously opposed apartheid, and the acting vice-chancellor, Professor R W James. Many members of the medical faculty took part in that march. As a young medical registrar, I was on duty in the medical outpatients department on that Friday morning and was unable to participate, much to my disappointment. After the march had taken place, the Administrator of the Cape, a Mr P J Olivier, said he was going to ask all members of the medical staff of GSH to inform him whether or not they had taken part in that march, because, except for the full professors who were on university conditions of service, all other staff were on Cape Provincial (Government) conditions of service in terms of the joint agreement between the Provincial Government and UCT. In due course we all got our letters, asking us this critical question. The Administrator and his Government were of course plainly putting pressure on the medical staff and there was a thinly veiled threat to take punitive action against us. The staff held a meeting in the physiology lecture theatre at the medical school and the whole matter was vigorously debated. A proposal for the line of action we should take came from a surgeon, D J (Sonny) du Plessis,* who was later to become a very distinguished vice-chancellor of the University of the Witwatersrand. Sonny du Plessis proposed that we should each tell the Administrator we had received his letter and had noted its contents. I replied in that way, and we all waited for the next development. It turned out Mr Olivier had ischaemic heart disease and while riding in the lift in Leeuwenhof, his official residence, had a fatal heart attack. We heard no more about the letter. The acting Administrator wisely let the matter drop. A few of my colleagues did not emerge from that political confrontation well and I began to develop an insight into the way in which people respond to political threats and pressure.

---

* Sonny du Plessis died in September, 1999.

A learning curve
1958–1961

At the end of 1958 I was awarded a Cecil John Adams travelling fellowship and that enabled me to work for fifteen months at the Hammersmith Hospital and the Royal Post-Graduate Medical School in London under Dr Malcolm Milne. Noreen worked as a factory nurse in Holloway Road. We lived with my aunt in Hornsey, North London, and my commute to the hospital and back was one and a half hours each way.

When I arrived in London, Malcolm Milne was described to me as an irascible man who had a reputation of never speaking to his research Fellows. He was bald with a ruddy, round face and a strong Mancunian accent. He certainly was extraordinary in his forthrightness, but I liked him enormously and we became very good friends and remained so until his death. He had a very keen mind, and was an excellent clinical investigator as well as an accomplished mathematician. He had taught himself advanced mathematics while serving in the Royal Army Medical Corps in the Western Desert in World War II, using his officer's baton to write equations in the sand. Sand must have been a source of inspiration to him because it was during a family holiday at the Scilly Isles that he sat in a deck chair, stared silently at the sand and worked out the principles of the non-ionic diffusion of weak acids and bases across cell membranes – a considerable achievement. He was rewarded for this and other outstanding work when he was made a Fellow of the Royal Society.

The resident medical officer at Hammersmith Hospital was Robin Irvine. His wife Bunty was one of the anaesthetists and the Irvines became lifelong, extremely close friends. Robin played an important role in my decision to become vice-chancellor, but of that later. I successfully wrote the membership examination of the Royal College of Physicians of London during the first six weeks that I was in the United Kingdom and so was able to devote the remaining time entirely to research, which is what I had planned to do. My work with Milne concerned the way in which the interior of muscle cells became more acid when the body was depleted of potassium. This explained why the blood became more alkaline – the hydrogen ions had shifted into the cells. It was only in the 1980s when my second wife Anita and I visited Malcolm and Mary Milne in his retirement that he told me how good he believed that research had been! Up until then I was quite uncertain as to how he had viewed it.

Donald Hunter (of 'gangrenous tip of Africa' fame) was one of my examiners in my 'long case'* for the membership at King's College Hospital. This proved to be fortunate because he used up a fair amount of the time he should have spent asking me questions, regaling his co-examiner with an account of a picnic he enjoyed with the Formans in Cape Town during his 1953 visit. The co-examiner was a man called Borland, who had the reputation of taking his artificial eye out of its socket and putting it on the table in front of the candidate if he disagreed with the proffered answer to his question. Fortunately the eye remained firmly in place during my examination. Of interest is the fact that the written part of the examination included the translation of a passage of Latin or Greek into English. Fortunately my school Latin sufficed. Over 400 candidates took the examination. Some 40 were successful. Some thought this was an illustration of a strong professional club maintaining exclusivity. The truth was that many of the candidates did not have the necessary experience to write the examination. Any doctor could present himself or herself and many did so knowing their chances of success were slim.

The role model in my family for scholarship as a schoolboy was my uncle Tom Macara. A Scot who studied by candlelight in Glasgow, he became a distinguished analytical chemist. He married my mother's sister Dorothy, and their two sons from his first marriage, Rew and John, were both university graduates, and were also held up to me as examples of what could be achieved through study and hard work. Both remain close friends. John and Shirley, his first wife, were very kind to Noreen and me while I was doing post-graduate research in the United Kingdom. Rew was sent to Argentina during World War II as a scientist developing dehydrated and other special food for the troops. Because he settled in Buenos Aires I have seen less of him and his family there. One of the bonuses of my career has been the great pleasure of frequently visiting John and his second wife, Nan, in Buckinghamshire.

I went on several occasions to the Central Middlesex Hospital to watch Dr Avery Jones do gastroscopies because Professor Jannie Louw had suggested that I might acquire that skill, as it was lacking in Cape Town. This was before the days of flexible fibreoptic gastroscopes and the scopes at the time were rigid metal tubes. The patient really had to be an accomplished

---

* The candidate was required to take a history and fully examine the patient in 30 to 45 minutes and was then examined by two examiners. There was also an examination of 'short' cases where only one system was examined in 15 minutes in each instance.

sword swallower to allow the doctor to look into his stomach and, in looking down the tube, all I could see was a flickering light and a very poor view of the gastric mucosa. I was totally disenchanted with the procedure and delighted to hear that Professor Solly Marks was establishing gastroenterology in Cape Town, something he did with great distinction, so I was able to leave the endoscopies in his good hands. Like so many of the special units at UCT and GSH, such as cardiology, pulmonology, endocrinology, neurology, and dermatology, gastroenterology acquired an enviable international reputation for the standard of clinical care, teaching and research.

Professor Jack Brock had become sole head of the department of medicine when Frank Forman retired as joint head in 1953. When I left South Africa in 1959 he explained to me that there were only six specialist posts in the department, that they had all been filled for a long time and he did not anticipate that there would be an opening for me on the full-time academic staff when I returned from the United Kingdom. Mark Horwitz, knowing this, wrote to me while I was in London and told me that he was planning to retire from his practice, which was an extremely busy one in Cape Town, and that he wanted me to take it over. He was effectively giving me his practice, all his furniture, all his equipment and I was quite overwhelmed by his generosity. As a consequence I was in private practice as a physician for some eighteen months on my return from London and enjoyed it very much indeed. Mark used to come with me on occasions to see patients in their homes in the evening so that they got the opinion of two physicians, but of course there was only a single charge. I had got to know Mark well as an undergraduate, had worked with him in the arthritis clinic and he sometimes took me with him as a final-year student, to see patients in their homes in the evenings. I learned an enormous amount from him. He was like a brother to me, and became the godfather of my son John, who was born in 1963. Mark was of average height with a very large forehead and a dome-shaped head which was almost entirely bald. A man of private means who grew up in Kimberley, he was gentle, with a deep understanding of what makes people tick. His approach to medicine was holistic and he gave great attention to the person as well as to the illness. A very kind man, he helped many students in financial need and in many other ways, but all these acts were private ones – he never sought recognition of what he had done, but received quiet satisfaction from the achievement of those he had helped.

While I was in private practice, Brock became very worried because he thought that I was struggling financially, and he gave me seven sessions in the department, eleven sessions being full time. He also employed Noreen to help edit his book on nutrition. At the same time I was running an enormous practice and was working round the clock. I was certainly earning considerably more than a professor of medicine! After some eighteen months Professor Brock approached me and said that a new post had been created in the department for a full-time specialist physician. He wanted me to apply; there would be competition but he thought I would be a strong candidate. I did so, was successful, and began my full-time academic career in medicine. When I discussed it with Mark Horwitz, he said that he had always anticipated this happening. I gave back the practice to him, and it was then closed down. Mark continued as a part-time head of firm in the department of medicine at the New Somerset Hospital. I was his physician and we remained the closest possible friends until his sudden death in 1969.

I had a major political jolt a few weeks after we returned to South Africa from the United Kingdom in 1960, when the police massacred 69 Africans at Sharpeville in the Transvaal and injured 180. The protesters in Sharpeville were part of the Pan Africanist Congress (PAC)-led nation-wide campaign in which large groups of African men deliberately presented themselves to the police without their passes* challenging them to arrest them in large numbers. They had been shot indiscriminately, many of them in the back. There were then widespread protests throughout South Africa and the Government responded by declaring a state of emergency and arresting thousands of people. Two Africans were shot dead in Langa, this tragedy, combined with the pass law protests, leading to a decision by the people of Langa and Nyanga to march on Cape Town. They were led by a young UCT student, Philip Kgosana.

I was having lunch close to the hospital on that day together with some friends also on the staff and we noticed quite a large number of Africans walking past the front of the small restaurant, obviously going to a rallying point. And indeed that afternoon 30 000 Africans marched peacefully into Cape Town and returned peacefully to their homes having been asked to do so by Philip Kgosana. He had been assured by the police colonel in charge that he would arrange a meeting between Kgosana and the Minister of Justice, conditional on the marchers dispersing. Needless to say the Nationalist Government lived up to its reputation, failed to keep its word and arrested Kgosana when he arrived for the meeting.

While the march was taking place, I was giving a lecture in the department of physiology in the medical school where I was a part-time teacher. (It was during my spell in private practice.) The professor of physiology

---

* All African males had to carry a pass or '*dompas*'. If this identity document was not immediately produced for a policeman, they were arrested and flung into gaol. The later introduction of passes for African women resulted in widespread protests.

came into the lecture theatre and announced that all the students had to go home and that they were to avoid public transport and main highways because 'the natives are on the march'. I have never seen a lecture theatre empty so rapidly, but I was bemused by what the students would do if they were in fact to follow the instructions of their professor.

My first exposure as a graduate to general university affairs was when I became assistant warden of Driekoppen Residence (now called Kopano) in 1957 when Professor Walter Schaffer, then a senior lecturer in physics, was the warden. There were over 200 students in the residence and I enjoyed my task of sharing responsibilities with the warden and adding to them the responsibilities of the medical care of these young men. Noreen, who was at that time the nursing head of the ear, nose and throat outpatients at GSH, worked very hard in the residence and was very popular with the students. Schaffer resigned as warden when he became full professor of physics (he later became assistant principal) and he was succeeded by Sammy Skewes, associate professor of mathematics.

Like Schaffer he was dedicated to students, an outstanding scholar and a real character. I learned a great deal from both of those men about how to listen to and to try to understand the views and concerns of students. They both showed great compassion towards students in trouble, including those in trouble with the university authorities. One student, whom Skewes justifiably expelled from the residence, was taken by him to find alternative accommodation. Skewes spent hours doing that, making sure the accommodation was suitable, before leaving the student to his own devices.

My first meeting with Skewes was somewhat unusual. Late on the afternoon of a Christmas day, a student, who was one of the four married students accommodated in the residence, came to tell me that he had met a sailor on the beach during the day and had invited him home for Christmas dinner. The sailor had become progressively more drunk and was creating mayhem in his home. I went with him to his cottage and together we took the sailor to the common room where we decided to play snooker while he sobered up. This was not without hazard to the snooker table because of the drunken state of the sailor and my own well-established lack of snooker skills. While we were playing I heard the night-watchman say, 'And this, Professor, is the common room!' Skewes was inspecting his new responsibilities and entered the room. I introduced myself to him and introduced the student and the drunk sailor, who presented arms with the billiard cue and then stood to attention! Skewes never referred to it – perhaps being treated as an admiral amused him.

In 1961, as I was about to take up my post as a full-time physician in the department of medicine, the then vice-chancellor and principal of the university, Dr J P Duminy, contacted me and asked if I would be the assistant warden of University House, another men's residence, because the warden, Professor Tom Price – a distinguished professor of law – was finding it too onerous to carry out the duties of warden. Duminy indicated to me that I would have to carry out most of the duties and would not be able to rely on Professor Price because of his other commitments. We moved into University House in 1961 and again found it a rewarding experience. The residence occupied prefabricated buildings which had housed returning ex-service women in 1946. It was converted into the Graduate School of Business in 1966 and University House moved to the old Driekoppen site where I had been assistant warden in the late '50s. (The new Driekoppen had been built in the meantime.) When I objected to the move I was told that we would have to move anyway, because the buildings in which we had been housed were temporary buildings and would be pulled down in the near future; the business school would only occupy them for a very short time. Needless to say, the business school occupied them for over 20 years! That was an exposure to university politics which formed part of my learning curve.

When I was the assistant warden of University House, one of the chairmen of the house committee was Cliff Allwood. He already had a degree in science and so was older than the average student.* He asked me if he could invite a youngish African man to have coffee with him. The reason for his asking me was that at that time it was unusual to entertain Africans in one's home. I immediately said he should feel free to invite anybody he wished to have coffee with him, but that as the young black man was a Zulu and my wife was fluent in that language, we would be delighted if Allwood and his guest would come to us for coffee. The man was Gatsha† Buthelezi who was attending the Anglican synod in Cape Town. At that time he had not achieved any prominence as a politician. My wife and I corresponded with him and we became friends through correspondence, a circumstance which is much less common today than it was in earlier times. He often stayed with us as our house guest when he came to Cape Town.

In the early seventies, while he and his wife Princess Irene were our guests, we were all invited to have dinner with Professor Nic Olivier at his flat in Mouille Point. Olivier was at that time a professor at the University of Stellenbosch and a member of the South African Bureau for Racial Affairs, a bureau which formed part of the intellectual justification for apartheid. He subsequently changed his views and became a member of the Progressive

---
* Cliff Allwood is now a senior psychiatrist.
† In later years he preferred to use the name 'Mangosuthu', 'Gatsha' having been a nickname. 'Gatsha' means a branch in Zulu, and he used to joke that he wasn't a special branch.

Party and later was the research officer for the Democratic Party. At the dinner the other guests attacked Buthulezi for being pro-ANC and for not accepting the overtures the Nationalist Party was making to him.

Buthelezi attended the funeral of Robert Sobukwe, the leader of the PAC, in Cradock and was sitting close to Sobukwe's widow. Helen Suzman was also present. A segment of the crowd started chanting slogans against Buthelezi and demanded that he leave. This became so persistent and disruptive that he went to Sobukwe's widow and told her that he could not allow the funeral to be disrupted and that out of respect for Robert Sobukwe, and for her and the family, he would leave. He pushed his way through the crowd accompanied by his secretary and single bodyguard. As they passed through the crowd someone tried to stab him. The assailant was pushed aside and the bodyguard fired a shot into the air. The three men made their way towards an air strip where their chartered plane was waiting. A group of men chased after them. Stones were thrown at the three men, a number of them hitting them. After a short while Buthelezi said to his companions, 'We are Zulus. We do not run away and we will not disrupt the funeral where we are now.' So they turned about and walked towards the crowd which had been following them. The mob ran away. His secretary phoned me (it was a Saturday afternoon) and asked me to meet their plane at Cape Town airport. I drove them from there to my home in Rondebosch where I gave them first aid because they had a number of cuts and bruises. Buthelezi was anxious that there should be no publicity regarding the fact that they had been struck by stones because he feared a violent response by his supporters. The whole matter remained a private one.

On another occasion Buthelezi, his wife Princess Irene and his mother visited us, together with an elderly Zulu man who lived in Langa. They had visited the cell in the Castle in Cape Town where Chief Cetshwayo, his ancestor, had been incarcerated by the British authorities. The elderly Zulu gentleman sat at our piano and accompanied himself while he sang a ballad he had heard sung to Chief Cetshwayo while he was a prisoner. Tears flowed down Buthelezi's mother's face. She was an impressive old lady, who carried herself with great dignity.

On another occasion Buthelezi asked me to fetch him from the Houses of Parliament where he and other black leaders had attended a meeting about the creation of independent homelands for black South Africans. When I arrived there, the others present with him were Sebe of the Ciskei, Matanzima of the Transkei, Mangope of what became Bophuthatswana, and Hudson Ntsantwisi of Gazankulu. They all bundled into my car and I took them to the Mount Nelson Hotel where they were staying. They asked me to join them for coffee and they discussed the meeting they had attended.

They had been offered the opportunity of being presidents of the so-called independent homelands. Buthelezi rejected the idea outright, and he was consistent in that rejection. At that time Sebe and Ntsantwisi also rejected the notion, but the others were quite enthusiastic about it. Buthelezi was the only one who held out against the enticing offers of the Nationalist Government. He was and is a devout Christian and there is no doubt that, at the time when I knew him well, he was a man of peace. As time went on we were busy with our separate careers and our regular correspondence did not continue. We did not discuss politics at any length when he was with us as our attitude was that he should relax completely with us as a house guest, because of the enormous pressures on him in everyday life. When we did so the political realities of the time resulted in our conversation turning on the evils of the National Party then in power. Buthelezi has a strong personality and a good sense of humour, but he is very sensitive to criticism.

Later I was offended by the requirement that students of the University of Zululand should take an oath of loyalty before they could get financial support for their studies and was disheartened by the failure of the Inkatha Freedom Party to take a full and effective part in developing South Africa's new constitution. I believe that the task needed the input of the representatives of all South Africans. The political carnage between the African National Congress and the Inkatha Freedom Party in KwaZulu Natal has been a major South African tragedy. One can only hope that the current moves to eliminate this altogether will succeed. Buthelezi is Minister of Home Affairs in the South African Government and is leader of the Inkatha Freedom Party. By all accounts he is an effective minister.

I subsequently succeeded Skewes as the warden of the new Driekoppen and occupied that position until the mid-seventies, so that I was assistant warden or warden of student residences from 1957 to 1958 and again from 1961 to 1975, a total of seventeen years, and in all that time enormously enjoyed meeting and knowing the students and sharing some of their problems. Noreen was very popular with the students and was very concerned about their welfare. She was a great asset to the residences.

I spent from October 1963 to September 1964 at the Massachusetts General Hospital and the Harvard Medical School in Boston, USA, working under Dr Kurt Isselbacher, chief of gastroenterology. I had been awarded a United States public health service post-doctoral international fellowship and was again extraordinarily lucky to work overseas under an outstanding clinical investigator, certainly one of the leading academic internists in the United States. Our son John had been born in August 1963 while we were living at University House. Taking a 6-week-old baby to Boston by air was one thing; bringing him home 12 months later, another! A paediatrician prescribed a mild sedative for him but this seemed to make him hyperactive, to the consternation of the passengers on the Boeing 707.

In Boston I established that certain sugars would interfere with the transport of amino acids across cell membranes. This related to some of Milne's work on genetically determined linked transport defects of amino acids in the gut and the kidney. The work in Boston formed the basis of my thesis for my Doctor of Medicine degree at UCT. I dedicated my thesis to John F Kennedy, who was assassinated while I was living in the United States. Everyone remembers what they were doing when they heard that Kennedy had been shot. I was working at the bench in the laboratory at the Massachusetts General Hospital, and a technician ran in screaming the dreadful news. I admired Kennedy for his leadership of the free world and for his commitment to liberal values. I know there has been much criticism of him down the years, but he had that rare quality – the ability to inspire those who were members of generations younger than his own.

When I became a full-time physician I established the liver clinic at GSH and the liver research group in the medical school. John Terblanche, who later became professor of surgery, was doing post-graduate work in Bristol and when he returned I asked him to join me in the clinic and in the research group as co-director. A long, close partnership came about, physician and surgeon working harmoniously together, both in the clinical area and in research. When I resigned to become vice-chancellor of the university, Ralph Kirsch became the co-director, and the partnership between physician and surgeon has continued and has resulted in the establishment of the liver research centre in the hospital and medical school, a centre which continues to do outstanding work under their joint direction. When I resigned as co-director of the liver research group I had authored or co-authored 190 research publications.

In the laboratory, our research took us into areas such as amino acid metabolism, protein synthesis and liver cell regeneration. I continued my interest in porphyria for a while. In the clinical area I remained a general physician, but with a special interest in liver disease. Arising out of work which had predominantly been done by Derek Burns and Charlie Trey in the department when they were registrars, we became interested in the treatment of acute liver failure. Trey and Burns had explored the use of exchange transfusion in this syndrome and the three of us had written up a series of patients treated in this way who, it seemed, had a better survival rate than other groups of patients. As is proper, we published this work in the scientific medical literature and were astonished to see it reported in *Time* magazine as well! After treating a larger number of patients we came to the conclusion that the treatment was not conveying a significant benefit to these patients. Charlie Trey* and I had sat next to each other on our first day at university in 1948. Larger than life in more ways than one, Charlie established a reputation for himself as a liver expert in Boston.

Like others elsewhere in the world, we used the isolated animal liver perfusion technique to try to help these patients, again with no real detectable success, and on one occasion cross-circulated a patient with a living (heavily sedated) baboon to try to use the animal's liver to restore the patient to sufficient health while her liver regenerated. That was a successful procedure, but the patient subsequently died of other complications. Together with Chris Barnard's group we had developed a technique to remove all the blood from the animal, to replace it with low temperature physiological saline, and then to replace that, in turn, with human blood compatible with that of the patient. We knew that these animals could live for several days in that state and during that time would be suitable for cross-circulation with a patient. We did not follow up that work any further because of the dangers of the transmission of simian viruses, a number of which are known, and some of which are very difficult to detect. I remember the evening when we had to take the decision to try this extraordinary procedure on the patient who we were convinced was about to die. When I agreed to do it I felt like somebody standing on a cliff and throwing a stone into the darkness below, not knowing exactly where it would land. Of interest is the 1996 decision in the United Kingdom to place a moratorium on the use of pig organs in man because of the potential danger of infection with viruses.

We did a large number of experiments on animals, especially in the field of liver transplantation (the liver clinic now has a very successful human liver transplantation programme) and in the course of that work the group detected a strain of pig which developed a very high temperature (malignant hyperpyrexia) on exposure to halothane. This syndrome also occurs in human beings and has a very high mortality. Further work in the medical school was able to identify the metabolic basis for the disease and a cure for and the prevention of it in patients. One of the publications arising from this work became a 'classic citation' in the science citation index. Professor Gaisford Harrison, the anaesthetist, played a key role in this work.

While I was a senior lecturer in Brock's firm in the 1960s, Dr Burger, the medical superintendent, phoned to tell me that Dr Nico Malan, the Administrator, had been ill for some time. He asked me if I would see him professionally. Dr Burger said that if I could help him it would be good for the hospital! It turned out that Dr Malan had had his prostate removed at the Karl Bremer Hospital, at that time the teaching hospital for Stellenbosch

---

* He died in January 1999.

University's medical school, and that he had had three episodes of pneumonia in the post-operative period over six or nine months. The pneumonia had always been in the same segment of the lung. One did not have to have great insight as a physician to realise that he had a localised area of bronchiectasis or dilatation of the bronchi in a particular part of the lung. I advised him and his wife Hester to be sure that he did postural drainage every morning and every evening – he should bend over the bed and she should pummel his back. I demonstrated it to them and to their astonishment, very large quantities of sputum were produced. The amount gradually diminished each time until there was very little sputum. He did that every day for the rest of his life and never had another attack of pneumonia. And so with that simple manoeuvre after listening carefully to the history of his illness, I convinced the Administrator that I was a medical diagnostician of note! As a consequence he asked me to see several members of the Cabinet and folk in other prominent positions in public life, all of whom I saw *pro deo* in my little office at GSH.

One Sunday evening I went to see Nico Malan, who was ill in bed in his official residence, Leeuwenhof. He told me that Dr L A P A Munnik (then member of the executive council responsible for hospital services in the Cape Province) and Professor Fransie van Zyl, the dean and professor of surgery at the Stellenbosch medical school, had just left him. They had asked him to close down radiotherapy at GSH and UCT and to confine it to the University of Stellenbosch teaching hospital. He informed me he had told them 'to go to hell'.

The Provincial Administration built a grand Opera House on the Cape Town foreshore and named it after the Administrator. One day when Nico Malan was consulting me as a patient, he said he assumed that I would not attend the opening of the Opera House (he knew my views on racial discrimination). I said that I would not because it was accessible only to white South Africans – as patrons, that is. Blacks could and would of course undertake menial tasks. But I said I would go to the Opera House one day. 'Oh,' he said, surprised. 'Yes', I said, 'when it is open to all races and it will be.' Years later it was opened to all races and Noreen and I went to see a ballet. By some weird coincidence we were sitting next to Nico Malan and his wife! 'You see, Nico,' I said, 'I have come as I said I would.' He just smiled.

On another occasion Professor Andries Brink, the professor of medicine at the Tygerberg Hospital and the Stellenbosch University Medical School, asked me to see Dirk Opperman, a leading Afrikaans poet. He was in liver failure and in a coma. His wife, who had heard of our liver clinic, wanted a second opinion. I saw the patient with Professor Brink and could not improve on the excellent care he was giving the patient, and I told Mrs

Opperman so. However, she had him transferred to the Stellenbosch hospital and then agitated for him to be placed in my care at Groote Schuur Hospital. I phoned Brink and told him what was going on, and he agreed that Opperman should be transferred to Groote Schuur Hospital. We treated him in precisely the same way that Professor Brink had treated him and he made a full recovery! The reason he recovered was the unstinting and devoted care his wife gave him. She never left his bedside, made sure his intravenous line remained patent, checked all his medication, drove the nurses and medical staff to be meticulous in their care of him and saved his life. I mention this story because in a comprehensive biography of Opperman and in other writings about him no one acknowledged Mrs Opperman's vital role, but then again no one asked me! Opperman went on to write his masterpiece *Kommas uit 'n Bamboestok* with one verse entitled: *Spesialis teen spesialis* ('Specialist against specialist'). Brink and myself!

In 1963, Len Eales, Eugene Dowdle and I organised an international conference on diseases of porphyrin metabolism and Rudi Schmid was one of the distinguished foreign speakers. Rudi was then working in Boston but later became chairman of medicine and subsequently dean at the medical school, University of California, San Francisco. That started a long association between Rudi Schmid and the department of medicine at UCT. He has visited the department on many occasions, has given invaluable advice on research and many other matters. He is a true friend to the department of medicine, especially to the liver research group and subsequently to the Liver Centre. Rudi, Kurt Isselbacher and Win Arias were three of the most outstanding research physicians in the United States of the '60s, '70s, '80s and '90s. After I became professor of medicine and when the time was ripe for Ralph Kirsch to work overseas, I went to see Win Arias at the Albert Einstein Medical School and arranged for Ralph to work with him, which he did, gaining enormously from the experience of working with such an outstanding scientist and physician. I had a policy of identifying centres of excellence for bright young physicians to work in overseas, and I made sure as many as possible returned to the department, which most did.

In 1973, John Terblanche and I organised an international conference on liver diseases on the UCT campus, which was well attended by distinguished research workers from many countries and from elsewhere in South Africa. Caroll Leevy, who was then President of the International Association for Study of the Liver, made a big impression as a distinguished African-American delegate. Others came from the rest of Africa, including Nigeria, and there were other delegates from North America, Europe and the Far East. Accommodation was provided on the university campus and the entire conference took place there. Of course no delegate to the conference or the accompanying persons experienced any form of discrimination at all on the campus. But apartheid was well established in South African society in general and we were grateful to the delegates for coming and supporting our work in the knowledge that the medical school and university rejected racial discrimination. I shall return to the issue of the academic boycott.

Life as a warden in a UCT residence was congenial. Noreen and I enjoyed the contact with the students from all the faculties and we got to know many of them well. At the new Driekoppen we lived in a house apart from the main buildings, overlooking the sports field used for soccer in the winter and baseball in the summer. My son John became the mascot of the baseball team. Years later he played for the UCT baseball club. Both Jane, my daughter, born in 1966, and John were great favourites of the students, many of whom came to entertain them and taught them the intricacies of other sports as well, including rugby and cricket.

John played cricket well for his school and opened the batting. There was a tradition at the school that the first cricket XI of the preparatory (junior) school played a cricket match against their fathers in the year before they advanced to the college (senior school). The fathers were required to play in the same 'positions' as their sons. The match took place at the college and was watched by large numbers of parents and staff and of course by all the boys. For the match which concerned John and myself I did not have clothes suitable for cricket and I borrowed a shirt and long white trousers from the operating theatre at the hospital. The trousers had a long slit up one side and were kept up by a cloth belt, which one tied in a bow on one side. When I went in to open the batting, John came to me and insisted I wear a 'box' or protector in the front of my trousers as a cricket ball is quite hard and comes at some speed, even when delivered by a schoolboy. Perhaps he was concerned about my future and feared that a blow in an unprotected vital area might compromise it. To my astonishment I hit the ball on several occasions and had to run down the pitch to score a run. Every time I did so, the 'box' migrated down my leg and fell out onto the pitch in full view of everyone and each time I had to run back to retrieve and reinsert it. The laughter from the spectators could be heard some miles away. I thoroughly enjoyed myself but I don't think that John appreciated my antics.

Jannie Louw, professor of surgery, and his wife Cathy had a holiday house at Yzerfontein, on the west coast north of Cape Town. When Noreen and I were looking for a seaside holiday house in the early sixties they encouraged us to build there, which we did. For years the roads were not tarred and there was no electricity and very few houses. John and Ann Terblanche also bought a seaside house there, as did Ronnie and Pam Kottler – he was the professor of radiology. John Terblanche and I, ably helped by our children and sometimes by our wives, caught crayfish in ring nets launched from my very small dinghy.

In the mid-sixties, during the first holiday we spent at Yzerfontein, I was invited to attend a meeting of the local ratepayers' association. It was held in the lounge of the house of one of the members and there were about a dozen people present. The meeting rapidly went through the agenda and reached 'any other business'. A Dutch Reformed Church *dominee* (parson) said he wanted to raise the issue of the *'klonkies op die strand'* (the young coloured boys on the beach). Everyone else in the room was a staunch supporter of segregation. I was the only English-speaker present and clearly regarded as a dangerous liberal. The chairman went on to say that people at Yzerfontein had got into the habit of letting coloured youths oversee their small children on the beach together with the coloured *meide* (young girls) while their 'masters and mistresses' had their afternoon snooze. These coloured youths were watching young white girls playing at the water's edge and swimming and this was intolerable. The chairman and other speakers vigorously supported the proposal that male coloured youths should be prohibited from the beach. It was depressing. Here I was on holiday trying to relax and have a good time, but it was clear that I was about to enter into conflict with everyone else in the room. I decided on a particular strategy. I told them that my clear understanding of the laws of apartheid as they applied to beaches was that *no* people of colour were allowed on those reserved for whites and that if they pursued their proposal I would insist that the *meide* (coloured girls) not be allowed on the beach either. The effect of this would be an end to all afternoon snoozes for at least half of the parents. There was silence in the room. The *dominee* got slowly to his feet and said, 'Mense, ons moenie te haastig wees nie.' (Folks, we must not be too hasty.) The whole matter was dropped and the *klonkies* continued to roam the beach.

On a later occasion a coloured schoolboy in his early teens, whose father was a labourer on a neighbouring farm, was buying sweets in the small beach-front shop. A white youth of about the same age started taunting him. In the end the coloured youth punched the white boy, who ran home crying. The white father soon arrived, picked up the coloured teenager and threw him through the window of the shop and told him never to come back. When I learned of these events I made enquiries and found out where the coloured youth was living and I went to see his mother. I offered to pay their legal expenses so that the white father could be tried for assault. It soon became clear that such action was not possible because the white father was the owner of the farm on which the coloured boy's father worked and the whole family lived on the farm. If they took any action at all, let alone legal action, the father would be dismissed and the whole family evicted from the farm. The mother did not lay any charges. The farm labourers in the area were often living like serfs and they had no rights. Fortunately in the new South Africa this is all changing, though in my view the pace of change is too slow.

Politics and the physician
1962-1969

During the 1960s I had worked as one of the two full-time senior lecturers and consultant physicians in Professor Brock's firm. The department of medicine was divided into five firms, each headed by a senior physician. The other senior lecturer in the firm was Raymond (Bill) Hoffenberg. He was senior to me and taught me pathology in 1950. He was a man I greatly admired and still do. We worked closely together and he taught me a great deal. Bill Hoffenberg and his wife Margaret (who was the first social worker at SHAWCO) were actively opposed to apartheid and he was acting chairman of the Defence and Aid Fund when it was banned in 1966 under the Suppression of Communism Act. Its main work had been to provide legal defence for persons alleged to have committed offences because of their political beliefs. Its work was financed by donations from South Africans and from overseas sources, which included the International Defence and Aid Fund established in London under a body called Christian Action. Bill had also been a prominent member of the Liberal Party, which was the only truly non-racial party in South Africa until it was prohibited in terms of the law.

On the afternoon of 28 July 1967 I was at a home in Constantia where I was seeing the father of a close colleague and great friend, Ralph Kirsch. In the middle of the consultation I was called to the telephone and Bill Hoffenberg asked me if I could come to the medical school immediately. I said that I was in the middle of seeing a patient but that if it was urgent I would come, because the patient wasn't seriously ill and I could always return to see him later in the day. He asked me to come immediately and I did. When I entered his laboratory at the medical school, he was looking ashen. He turned to me and said, 'The police have been here. I thought they were coming to me regarding an unpaid fine for a parking ticket, but I have been banned.' He was, plainly, absolutely astounded that they had done this to him. Bill had wanted to see me as Professor Brock, who was head of the department, was at that time my patient in the hospital because he had suffered a heart attack, and Bill wanted my permission to tell him.

The notice in the Government Gazette indicated that Hoffenberg was prohibited from attending gatherings from 28.7.67 to 31.7.72. In terms of the banning order, Bill Hoffenberg was forbidden to enter any educational institution. The five-year banning order confined him to the magisterial districts of Cape Town and Wynberg, prevented him from being a member or office-bearer of any organisation which in any way criticised the Government, and from playing any part in student activities. He was forbidden to attend any gatherings and was prevented from entering any 'non-white' areas, factory or premises on which publications were produced. He had to report to the police weekly and was told that he could continue his academic and research duties only until the end of the 1967 academic year. He was forbidden to write or to make any statement for publication. He wrote to the Minister seeking an explanation for the actions taken against him. He was told he furthered some of the aims of statutory communism, had served on the Defence and Aid Fund Committee and that it was 'not in the public interest' to say any more than that. I wondered whether B J Vorster, then Minister of Justice and later Prime Minister, was just being vindictive because of Bill's action in the court against him regarding restrictions on the Defence and Aid Fund. Subsequent revelations about the Nationalist Government have made it clear how evil it was. I also believe they were alarmed at the influence Bill was having on medical students at the Afrikaans-speaking University of Stellenbosch. Bill is such a remarkable person that the students could not help being impressed by his sense of fairness and the need for justice for all in South Africa. This was not to the liking of our political lords and masters.

Professor Brock led the opposition to the banning of Bill Hoffenberg but he did not receive the support that he deserved from a number of his senior colleagues in the medical school, nor did he receive adequate support from the then vice-chancellor, Dr J P Duminy. In his articulate opposition, he was quite isolated in the hierarchy of the medical school in a sense, although the vast majority of the faculty and students were behind him, as was the vast majority of members of the staff of the university. There was a wide public outcry about the banning. The chancellor of UCT, Mr Harry Oppenheimer, spoke out strongly and the vice-chancellors of the Universities of the Witwatersrand and Rhodes supported him. The council of UCT expressed its 'grave disquiet' and agreed unanimously to ask for an interview with the Minister of Justice to seek reasons for the banning order and to ask for its removal in the interests of medical education and research. The deputation consisted of Mr Oppenheimer, the chairman of council Mr Clive Corder, the vice-chancellor Dr J P Duminy, and Professor Brock. The meeting took place in October and their submissions were rejected out of hand. The International Atomic Energy Agency, the University Teachers' Association of

South Africa, Sir de Villiers Graaff, leader of the United Party, the Progressive and Liberal Parties, the Civil Rights League, the National Union of South African Students (NUSAS) and other bodies all protested, to no avail. There were protest meetings and poster demonstrations on the campuses of English-medium universities and a petition was signed by university staff (including 16 members of the University of Stellenbosch) by medical and other students and by leading citizens. The silence of the overwhelming majority of staff at the Afrikaans-medium universities was deafening. Sixteen British medical professors and twenty-four South African doctors doing post-graduate work in the United Kingdom signed a letter of protest.

The department of medicine held a meeting and elected an action committee consisting of Professor Brock, Dr E B Dowdle, Dr H Gordon, Dr S Shapiro and myself to organise the protests against Bill's banning. One of the most valuable and staunchest supporters of that committee was Professor Frances Ames, a neurologist and psychiatrist. We all felt vulnerable as the protests mounted and as the controversy raged. There was a proposal that all the staff of the hospital and medical school should resign, giving three months' notice to that effect. Brock dissuaded the staff from acting in that manner because in his view it would run counter to the Hippocratic Oath and medical ethics. The patients would be put at risk and we knew that the supporters of the Government in the medical profession would try to nullify the effects of the resignations; but it was the ethical issue that concerned Brock. A mass meeting in the Jameson Hall (the main hall of the university) was called by Professor H M Robertson, chairman of the academic freedom committee, and was addressed by Brock. I sat close to him, ready at any time to help him medically because I was his physician and I knew he was having severe angina pectoris throughout all this period.

Some colleagues who should have known better were telling me, 'There is no smoke without fire.' Again I saw how people ran for cover if there was even an indirect threat to their security. One afternoon Brock and I were walking into the medical school and he turned to me and said, 'It's very difficult to accept the fact that the Government of your country is evil.' His comment has always remained with me. It raises the crucial issue of what the appropriate form of protest should be against a thoroughly evil regime. We said a lot but did very little. Should we have done more on this and other occasions when we protested against apartheid? We probably should have done so, and I regret what could have been shortcomings. We could have put ourselves at greater risk, but I could not have resorted to violence.

The Cape Western branch of the Medical Association of South Africa called a meeting in the physiology lecture theatre at the medical school. The lecture theatre was packed. Professor Fransie van Zyl, professor of surgery at the University of Stellenbosch medical school, was there, and had arranged for large numbers of Government supporters on the staff of the University of Stellenbosch medical school and many doctors of like mind from surrounding areas to be present. As would happen so often under the apartheid regime, the Medical Association failed to protest.

Bill Hoffenberg was forced to go into exile. His departure at the Cape Town airport was a remarkable one, with large numbers of students and staff and many citizens from all races there to give him a rousing send-off. The security police took photographs of us at the airport. I saw Captain van Dyk of the security police watching the proceedings. Bill covered himself with distinction in his subsequent career, becoming professor of medicine at the University of Birmingham in the United Kingdom, President of the Royal College of Physicians of London and Master of Wolfson College, Oxford. He was knighted by the Queen in 1984. I have absolutely no doubt that Bill Hoffenberg had not done anything which could have justified any action being taken against him and that he was innocent of any of the secret charges made against him except that he was legitimately opposed to the ideology of the State. The whole system of banning was repugnant and totally unacceptable in itself.

While writing these memoirs I consulted the university archives and had access to documents which were confidential at the time. They confirmed my view that Dr Duminy had not given the leadership required at the time.

At Driekoppen the house committee members were elected by the students, but I appointed the sub-wardens after consultation with students whose views I valued. The sub-wardens received a small stipend and acted as tutors and 'senior citizens'. Hugh Amoore, who was later to work very closely with me when I was deputy principal (planning) and later when I was vice-chancellor, entered Driekoppen in 1970 as a first-year student. He was a very good student academically, a fine athlete, and became secretary of the students' representative council. I recognised that he was a very talented and outstanding young man. He became a sub-warden. As I write, my mind fills with the faces and names of so many fine young men from University House and Driekoppen – it is impossible to name and describe them all. When we meet I feel a sense of warmth and good fellowship, a strange mixture of nostalgia and paternalism.

My philosophy as the warden of undergraduate and postgraduate residences was that the students' behaviour determined the rules. I indicated to them that students could play music in their rooms, but if they abused that privilege and played it too loudly and interfered with other people, the privilege would be withdrawn. The students could drink alcohol but anyone who abused that would be called to account, especially if it resulted in anti-social behaviour. I indicated to them that if they abused the privileges they had, I would require them to leave. I told them I expected them to behave like gentlemen. This may sound quaint, even naive and prissy in the contemporary world, but it certainly worked well in the late 1950s, '60s, and early '70s. I doubt it would be as effective in the '90s.

I remember at University House a group of students making a great deal of noise, some of whom had certainly drunk far too much. As I went out to talk to them I saw them all going into the gents' toilet next to the common room. I followed them into the toilet and stood in front of one of the basins in the customary way. Silence had fallen on the group and while I faced the tiles I said, 'You are not behaving as you should. If you continue to behave in this way I am afraid you will have to find accommodation in another residence.' I walked out. I never had any trouble with that group of students again.

In those years, my relationship with the local constabulary was quite different from what it became when I was the vice-chancellor during the states of emergency in the 1980s. In the '60s and '70s, the police were perhaps overly tolerant of student pranks and misdemeanours and I fetched a number of inebriated students from the charge offices of Mowbray and Rondebosch before they were charged, and had them released provided that they were appropriately punished within the university.

Students get up to all sorts of pranks. On one occasion, the cannon balls which were carefully piled on the stoep of Groote Schuur, the house of the then Prime Minister Mr John Vorster, were discovered one morning to be painted light blue, dark blue and white, which are UCT colours. This caused great consternation amongst the security personnel responsible for the safety of the Prime Minister. They wanted to know how it had been done but realised that they would never be able to find out who had done it. What had happened was that a group of students had sat in a black Mercedes car on De Waal Drive, the highway leading from parliament to the Prime Minister's residence. They waited until three black Mercedes cars with police travelling in front and behind the Prime Minister, who was in the middle car, had swept by and then slipped in so as to become the fourth black Mercedes in the cavalcade. They followed, without hindrance, into the Prime Minister's residence and when the other cars swung to go to the entrance at the back, the students drove round the front, picked up the cannon balls, put them in the back of the car and drove off. They painted the cannon balls and returned them in the same way the next day.

On another occasion, three Mercurius jet trainers, flying in formation, tragically crashed into the side of Devil's Peak. Within hours the whole area was cordoned off to prevent the public getting access to the scene. A few days later I was contacted by the police who said that they would like to be able to recover any parts of the planes which the students at Driekoppen might have, because they were important in establishing the cause of the crash and if the parts were returned, no enquiries would be made as to how they had got into the hands of students. I put a notice up on the notice board asking any student who had a piece of the aircraft to put it in my garage and when I went to get my car the next morning, an entire cockpit of one of the aircraft was there. Just how the students got it down the mountainside and through the cordon and who exactly they were, I never established.

There was an incident when one of the students defied one of the rules that had been agreed by the house and which were enforced by the house committee, which was that residents were required to wear a tie to the evening meal. When he first defied the house committee its members fined him a modest amount. He defied them again, they fined him again and he defied them a third time. The house committee came to me in despair. I asked the student to come and see me and he was a member of a group of students whose dress and overall appearance were somewhat unconventional amongst the general public at the time. His hair had not been cut for eighteen months and he was sloppily dressed, but what impressed me about him was the fact that he was clearly very intelligent and his academic results were good. I explained to him that if you have over 250 young men living in a residence you have to have rules, and that the rules he was being asked to abide by were rules which had been drawn up by the entire house and were, according to the constitution of the house, rules which had to be enforced by the house committee. I explained to him that the rule could have been that everybody was required to come into dinner naked, or wearing pyjamas, or wearing a dinner jacket and that the rules were not an infringement on his personal dignity or his freedom, but were purely establishing a convention for the residence and that because of that he should wear the tie. He told me that he understood the situation and would now wear a tie to dinner. I informed the house committee and they decided not to press with the fines because they believed he had not 'fully' understood the position. I waited with interest to see what would happen at the next evening meal, which I attended. There was a sense of expectancy in the dining room. Eventually the student arrived. He did indeed have a tie around his neck, but he had no shirt on. After that he wore a shirt and tie, but he had made his point.

In 1975 Noreen and I decided it was time to leave residence life and we bought and moved into a small house in Rondebosch. We were presented with a golden labrador puppy by the Driekoppen students as a farewell gift.

He was the second of three golden labradors we had as a family. We also had a small white mongrel called Vadoek (Dishcloth) alias Moppet.

The College of Physicians and Surgeons of South Africa was founded in 1956 and offered its first specialist examinations in 1957, at which I was one of the first candidates, as I have mentioned. In 1962, Professor Brock asked me to come and see him together with Professor Guy Elliott, who at that time was the president of the college. They asked me if I would become the honorary registrar of the college, that is the chief administrative officer, acting in an honorary capacity. The first honorary registrar was Mr T B McMurray, an orthopaedic surgeon. After being initially co-opted for three years I was an elected member of the college council for fifteen years until I resigned as senior vice-president of the college in 1981 when I became the vice-chancellor of UCT. Mrs Ella Skea, the granddaughter of President Steyn, President of the Orange Free State, was the college secretary, a very able woman who was fluent in English and Afrikaans and was dedicated to the college's well-being. We had a small set of rooms in the medical centre at the bottom of Adderley Street in Cape Town and she was the only member of staff.

The college had been founded by far-sighted doctors in South Africa who wanted to establish a college similar to the Royal Colleges of Great Britain, Australasia and Canada, so that young South African doctors could specialise in South Africa without having to travel overseas to do so and could hold an internationally recognised qualification. The establishment of the college was vigorously opposed by the Afrikaans-speaking medical establishment, led by Professor Fransie van Zyl, who was professor of surgery and subsequently dean of the medical school of the University of Stellenbosch. They regarded the college as a British institution and Fransie van Zyl said quite clearly that he intended to destroy it. We determined that the college would be a national institution, that it would be a home for all specialists, irrespective of language, race or creed, and that is how it has always been. We also determined to overcome the prejudice of the Afrikaans medical establishment by ensuring that the college would carry out all its functions in both English and Afrikaans and, to try to ensure that I was completely fluent in Afrikaans for college purposes, I conducted all business within the college office in that language. This policy of inclusiveness and becoming a truly national South African college was successful and we overcame the prejudices of the older generation of Afrikaans doctors, to the extent that for many years it has no longer been an issue in South Africa. The college has grown to nearly 9 000 members, and is a home for doctors coming from all sectors of society. It is now called The Colleges of Medicine of South Africa and offers examinations in all the specialties as well as in family medicine. From its inception the college was non-racial.

My insistence on using Afrikaans in the college office had its amusing side. The college council had decided to give the State President, Mr C R Swart, an honorary fellowship. Mrs Skea and I called on the chief of protocol to discuss the proceedings. The conversation was in Afrikaans. The chief of protocol said, '*Nou kom ons by die saak van die ampstafdraer*' ('Now we come to the matter of the mace-bearer'). I asked in English what '*ampstafdraer*' meant and he enlightened me. We went straight from his office to the State President's secretary, a Mr Pretorius. During our conversation he said to me, 'Dr Saunders, this is a bilingual country. Please feel free to speak in English.' I promptly replied, '*Ek is Afrikaans-sprekend*' ('I am Afrikaans-speaking'). I will never know what possessed me to say that, and Mrs Skea nearly fell off her chair. Mr Pretorius took it in his stride and the conversation continued. I later said, '*Nou kom ons by die saak van die ampstafdraer*', and Mr Pretorius asked in English, 'What is that?!' Blandly I replied, 'The mace-bearer!' Whenever we met subsequently he asked me how my English was getting on!

As honorary registrar of the college responsible for overall management for over ten years, I gained a great deal of administrative experience and insight into the medical politics of the country. I was particularly pleased to propose, and to see become a reality, the establishment of medical missions to states in sub-Saharan Africa to try to help them with the delivery of health care. Such an arrangement has persisted all these years with Malawi, with teams of specialists regularly visiting that country under the auspices of the college. I was also part of a team consisting of Jannie Louw, then professor of surgery at UCT and president of the college, a member of the Department of Health of South Africa, and Dr Marais Viljoen, secretary-general of the Medical Association of South Africa – who was later to accuse me in secret correspondence (made public in 1997) of wanting a political platform to attack the Government and others after Steve Biko's murder by the police. We went to Lesotho, Swaziland and Malawi to assess the health care delivery systems in those countries.

Towards the end of the '60s I had an experience which changed my attitude to the way in which I would respond to public affairs. Up until that point, I had always allowed my response to be influenced to some extent by what my colleagues in the medical profession would think of my behaviour. I recognised that the profession was a conservative one and knew that there were conservative elements in the medical school which had some influence in the affairs of the faculty. I tended to go with the herd and to avoid rocking the boat. But towards the end of the '60s Noreen was arrested for selling soup in the black townships. She was working with a charitable organisation which provided soup for the destitute and, as a policy, they required those who could to pay the smallest amount possible, for example one cent, for a bowl of soup. They were trying to avoid a culture of dependency. Plainly, many of the people receiving soup were not able, and were not required, to pay the one cent, but many did. A black police sergeant in civilian clothes deliberately paid my wife one cent for a bowl of soup and promptly arrested her for trading without a licence. She and the woman working with her in the mobile soup kitchen were required to appear in the magistrate's court in Wynberg on a formal charge. The woman who was charged with Noreen was an outspoken eccentric person and repeatedly interjected during the procedures and made it quite clear that she thought the whole thing was a nonsense. The case turned on the definition of the word 'charity' because Noreen and her co-accused were claiming that they were a charity and therefore did not require a trading permit. The magistrate called for a dictionary and he was given the smallest possible pocket Oxford English dictionary, from which he read out that charity was the giving of something and as they weren't giving the soup away, they couldn't be a charity. He found them guilty and they were cautioned and discharged. During the proceedings I was anxious about the impact this would have on my conservative colleagues, an anxiety which I kept to myself, but at the end of the proceedings I was so outraged by what had happened to my wife that I urged that she appeal because it was quite clear that all the State was trying to do was to intimidate those doing charitable work and to stop white people from going into the black townships. After a great deal of debate, Noreen and her co-worker decided not to appeal as they had only been cautioned. I made a firm resolve then and there never to allow any consideration of my reputation, or the way in which people might see me, to interfere with the response that I would give publicly to matters of public concern. Principle and values should rule, not expediency. I have tried to keep to that resolve ever since.

Chris Barnard became famous when he performed the first human heart transplant on Louis Washkansky on 2 December 1967. I had been in the lift at GSH at about 10 o'clock on the night before the first heart transplant was done. Chris Barnard got into the lift and told me he was going to do a heart transplant. It didn't impress me at all. The significance of it completely passed me by and it was only when I opened my newspaper the next morning and read the banner headline that I realised something of moment had occurred!

He asked me to see Dr Philip Blaiberg, the second heart transplant recipient, in regard to one of the complications that he developed post-operatively and when I arrived in the ward Barnard was doing a ward round accompanied by some thirty-odd people. I declined to examine the patient at that time and said I would examine him by myself and give him my opinion privately, which I did, but while standing there trying to catch his attention, I spoke to the man next to me and asked him who he was. He told me he was a writer and that he was going to write Barnard's biography in co-operation with him. I asked him where he came from and he said he came from Rome, Italy, and that his wife was a sculptress who did mega sculptures, that his house was three storeys high, built around a courtyard, and that she did her sculptures in the middle of the courtyard and they had to get a crane to lift them out. I came to the conclusion that he was pulling my leg and was about as unconventional as the number of people on the ward round. Much to my surprise, six months later *Life* magazine carried a story which confirmed everything he had told me.

Mark Horwitz described Chris Barnard as a '*Naturkind*' – a child of nature. He has been criticised for his more flamboyant behaviour. One must remember that not many of us have had the experience of arriving at an airport like Rome and finding that the whole airport had come to a standstill simply because we had arrived! Such adulation is hard to deal with unless one has been prepared for it over a long period of time. It did occur to me at the time that it was a pity that the heart transplant had not taken place a little earlier, before Bill Hoffenberg was banned, because it might have stayed the hand of the Nationalist regime in banning him, the hospital having achieved such international prominence, and Bill Hoffenberg being one of its leading physicians. There is no doubt in my mind Barnard would have consulted him in regard to some of the problems which occurred post-operatively in the transplant patients.

After Hoffenberg left, Brock involved me more and more in the administration of the department. Brock retired after a very distinguished career, at the end of 1970. He was the father of medical research in South Africa, an outstanding human being, an excellent administrator, who never went back on his word; a man who made enormous contributions to the medical faculty of UCT and to medicine in South Africa in general. He was a superb administrator and it was from him that I also learnt a great deal about administration and, above all, never to make a promise that you do not keep. Brock was a deeply religious man who, as a young Rhodes scholar at Oxford, became a member of the Oxford Movement. He had a strong moral sense and advanced the cause of social medicine. In that, as in so many things, he was far ahead of his time. He had the habit of dropping off to sleep at unfortunate moments. He would frequently introduce a guest speaker, sit down, and to the consternation of the speaker almost immediately fall asleep. What upset the speaker more profoundly was the fact that at the end of the lecture, Brock would open his eyes and ask the speaker a question relevant to his address, which he or she usually could not answer! Brock had a quiet courage and the force of his intellect and personality made him one of the most important guiding forces in the medical school and hospital.

Head of medicine 1970–1975

Early in 1970 the university set about finding Brock's successor. I was one of the applicants, was appointed without being interviewed, and took up the position on 1 January 1971. When I was appointed I wrote to Bill Hoffenberg and I told him that, in my view, *he* should have been occupying the chair and headship of the department of medicine and not myself. I realised that as head of the department of medicine I would have to subordinate personal ambition to ensure that the department maintained its position and grew stronger. I would not have as much time to pursue personal interests and would have to put the needs of the department first. The same applied to my position later as vice-chancellor of UCT, but on a larger scale.

In the latter half of 1970 I visited medical schools and in particular departments of medicine, in Australia, New Zealand, the United States, Canada and the United Kingdom. Throughout the ten years that I was professor of medicine I maintained close international links, particularly with research workers in the field of liver disease, which was my interest, but also with heads of departments of medicine around the world. I was able to go to many conferences, large and small, and soon discovered that one had to be selective otherwise one could easily find oneself on the 'conference circuit' and doing that and little else. I don't think that is a productive use of anyone's time. I am a firm believer that one has to 'stay in the kitchen': to do the work which is one's first responsibility and that other matters should receive secondary consideration.

Overseas medical congresses do have their value, especially because they give research workers the opportunities of meeting their colleagues and discussing current problems with them, but they have their lighter side as well. On one occasion I attended an International Association of the Liver meeting in Versailles and as part of the recreational agenda of the congress, we went on a bus tour of the Loire valley. We visited a number of châteaux and were able to sample the French wine both at lunch and at a number of wine tastings during the afternoon, ending in the late afternoon drinking champagne. We then set off to a *son et lumière* performance at a château and when we got there, the heavens opened. Professor John Terblanche (professor of surgery) and I decided to stay in the bus and remain dry. We then saw some garden umbrellas in a tea room close by and decided to borrow one of them. Accompanied by a number of hepatologists, all sheltering under one umbrella, we set off to the *son et lumière* event. We had walked about 100 metres through the mud in the pouring rain when we found ourselves surrounded by gendarmes who wanted to arrest us for stealing the umbrella. We did an abrupt about turn. All our companions fled except for one short German hepatologist who loyally joined us as we were marched back towards the bus and restaurant, accompanied by the gendarmes. Fortunately, our example had been followed by three other groups of enterprising liver experts from around the world and, to the gendarmes' consternation, three umbrellas were approaching them, protecting the heads of our international fraternity. In the confusion we took the opportunity to return the umbrella to the restaurant and to re-enter the bus, so that we were able to avoid being arrested. I thought that the South African newspapers would certainly make something of the fact that the UCT professors of medicine and surgery were arrested in France for stealing a beach umbrella in the pouring rain. Incredibly the story was already known to the medical students when we returned to Cape Town. Quite how that information reached them, I never established.

During this conference there was the grand dinner in the Hall of Mirrors in Versailles. A world-renowned harpsichordist entertained the dinner guests. The table closest to the harpsichordist was occupied by a number of our colleagues from Japan, one of whom had clearly had too much to drink and, during the harpsichordist's recital, he gradually started slipping off his chair and under the table. At first he was visible from the chest upwards, then from the shoulders, then only his neck and head could be seen, then his forehead, until finally he disappeared completely from view. Needless to say, everybody's attention was focused on the disappearing liver expert and I don't think anybody heard what the harpsichordist was playing. At the end of the recital his colleagues carried him out and he was not seen at an international conference for many years.

In the mid-seventies I was invited by the Ciba Foundation of London to conduct a workshop at its headquarters in Great Portland Place. I spoke on medical care in Southern Africa. Well before I left for London, the Director of the Foundation wrote to tell me that there was great interest in the workshop and that I could expect a considerable amount of criticism from South Africans in exile, including members of the African National Congress (ANC) and of the anti-apartheid movement. I prepared myself well and had slides dealing with every aspect of health in sub-Saharan Africa that I could think of. The workshop consisted of a very congenial buffet supper followed by my speaking in a room which allowed the audience to sit in a semi-circle in front of me and very close to me on the same level. It was a case of Daniel in the lion's den! I made no apologies for the shortcomings in health care in South Africa and highlighted the adverse effects apartheid was having on adequate health provision. I was very critical of many aspects of the South African Government's policy, including the iniquitous differentiated salary scales and the restrictions placed on black doctors and nurses regarding where they could work. I faced many critical questions and at the height of the criticism a tall African stood up, introduced himself as a member of the health ministry of Zambia, and said that the critics should remember that when Zambia received its independence from Britain, there was one medical practitioner left in the country. By the end of the evening I think it was clear to all that we were agreed on the evils of apartheid and what we had to do was to look beyond it and plan for a new health programme. None of us underestimated the problems facing the whole of sub-Saharan Africa in health care provision.

Professors are members of the university senate and I sat next to Professor Troskie, professor of statistics, at my first senate meeting. He tells me that as we walked out at the end of the meeting I swore and told him that that would be the last senate meeting I ever attended because it had gone on interminably and most of the discussion was quite pointless. Little did I realise how wrong I was and that I would chair senate as vice-chancellor for some years. Professor Leon Kritzinger, professor of accounting when I was professor of medicine, and later dean of the faculty of commerce when I was vice-chancellor, and I, both had the reputation, as members of senate and as heads of department, of being intolerant of bureaucracy. As a consequence each of us, in our own way, at times acted outside of the rules and established our own procedures; and so in the central administration of the university, the word was that there were university rules, Kritzinger rules and Saunders rules. Nobody can say they weren't warned!

While I was a senate member on the University of Cape Town council, a number of members of staff were banned. I made it plain at the council meeting that if the university did not continue to pay the salaries and give appropriate increments which the banned members of staff would have received had they not been banned, I would find it difficult to have anything to do with the university. My strong words were not necessary as council resolved to pay the salaries of all banned or in other ways restricted members of staff who had not been found guilty of any crime. Others banned in South Africa were not always treated in that way.

I was elected to the university council in 1975 as one of three senate representatives on that body. The other senate representatives during the years that I was a senate representative on council, which extended up until my appointment as deputy principal (planning) in 1981, were Professor Jack de Wet, dean of science, and Professor Anton Paap, dean of arts. The three of us would lunch together at Peter's Pancake Place in the Main Road, Rondebosch, on the first Wednesday of every month immediately before the council meeting, which began at 2.15 in the afternoon. Over lunch we would go through the main issues on the agenda and discuss their implications for the senate and for the university as a whole. Many other issues involving university affairs were brought up as well. We were able to achieve a remarkable consensus between the three of us, representing senate on the most senior body in the university. Jack de Wet was a fine mathematician completely devoted to the faculty of science and to UCT. He had the remarkable ability of identifying talent both locally and overseas, and of moving mountains to attract outstanding people to his faculty. Often unorthodox, always outspoken, he certainly made enemies amongst some of his colleagues, but I had an enormous respect for his intelligence, his energy and for his loyalty to the university. Anton Paap was a quiet, distinguished classical scholar, reserved and thoughtful, the perfect foil for Jack de Wet.

The council was made up of the following members:

Vice chancellor and principal, deputy principal and assistant principal, 3 members appointed by the State President, 6 members elected by convocation (graduates of UCT), 3 members elected by senate, 2 members chosen by city council (local government), 3 members elected by past students and life governors (nowadays this means by donors), 1 member chosen by Diocesan College constituency (a matriculant from the D.C. who had obtained a degree from the university), 2 members chosen from their members by the board of governors of the UCT Foundation.

There were no student representatives. Members of council served three-year terms and were eligible for re-election. There were no blacks on council and only one woman. The State President's (National Government) nominees on the university council saw themselves as being appointed in their own right and as not having the obligation to report back to those who had appointed them to the council. There was one exception, a young man who was appointed to the council to compensate for the fact that he had failed in a parliamentary election for the National Party. He was partisan and biased to a degree that astounded us all and even those Government nominees who were active supporters of the National Party despaired. Stephanus du Toit, one of that number, criticised him very severely when he said he would report back to the Government to tell them of his concern about what was going on in the university council. On a number of occasions Du Toit and some of the members nominated by the Government, as well as a few others, severely criticised NUSAS, the National Union of South African Students, an organisation which was representative of the students on English-speaking campuses and was actively opposed to the Government. It was in fact the only 'named' organisation in South Africa, that is to say it was unable to obtain financial support from overseas, and many of its leaders had been banned or detained and a number had gone into exile. Students automatically belonged to NUSAS through the SRC affiliation to it and NUSAS was guaranteed an income from its constituent universities. This was a system I would not ordinarily have supported but NUSAS was under constant attack by the Government and we would not weaken its financial base.

NUSAS was a national student body at that time, representing students on the English-speaking campuses. The Afrikaans Studentebond (ASB) had broken away from NUSAS because of NUSAS's non-racialism and represented students on the Afrikaans-speaking campuses. The South African Students Organisation (SASO) had broken with NUSAS as part of the black consciousness movement and represented black students. NUSAS, SASO and other black student organisations had consistently campaigned against apartheid and 1972 was no exception. It resulted in my first personal experience of police action against demonstrators. On 22 May NUSAS launched its 'free education' campaign. Mass student meetings, public meetings, and the distribution of information took place on all NUSAS-affiliated campuses. Attention was focused on recent events at the University College of the North, Turfloop, where there had been police intervention and over 1 000 students had been expelled.

In Cape Town UCT students held a protest meeting on the steps of St George's Cathedral. The meeting was broken up by police, who launched a baton charge and pursued students into the cathedral. Tear gas was used. This incident gave rise to a snap debate in parliament, and fierce public debate over 'police brutality.' Wide international publicity followed. I was told of the events at the cathedral by students returning to Driekoppen and I immediately advised them to ensure that any injured person was taken to the casualty department at GSH where I arranged for senior surgeons (Professor Ed Immelman was one of them, I recall) to take care of them, and to record injuries in detail in case the victims wished to take legal action. I went to the hospital to do what I could.

My other link with the steps of St George's Cathedral occurred during those events when a group of people, mainly from UCT, crowded on to the steps to demand the right to peaceful public protest. Any meeting on the street had been banned. I was standing between two elderly women, one of whom was Madge, wife of Jack de Wet, the dean of science, when the police officer in charge announced through a loud hailer that we had five minutes to disperse. A large number of police were drawn up on the opposite pavement. I suggested to the women that we should go into the cathedral as others were starting to do, but they would have none of it. That caused me some anxiety. I did not feel I could leave them there but it did occur to me that I would be a more likely target for the police than they would be! Fortunately they agreed at the last moment and we moved rapidly into the cathedral.

In acquitting students charged for protesting illegally, some judges affirmed the right of persons to protest – and senior members of the Government subsequently made threatening statements on the subject. In October, Marais Viljoen, Minister of Labour, referred to UCT and Wits students as terrorists – and, in a statement to the *Cape Times*, said that all student demonstrations should be stopped, whether peaceful or not. Senator Owen Horwood, Minister of Indian Affairs (he was a former vice-chancellor of the University of Natal!), and Mr Jimmy Kruger, Deputy Minister of Police, warned that police would not hesitate to act against demonstrating students, despite recent acquittals by the courts. Horwood claimed in the Senate earlier in the year that an edition of *Wits Student*, lampooning the Prime Minister, 'was part of a communist conspiracy to subvert law and order on university campuses. This is a matter of the security and the very way of life of the country, and when it comes to that, the issue of whether university autonomy is being infringed or not becomes irrelevant.' Rightwing terrorism against students continued during the year. Death threats were received by various student leaders, and also by Mr Justice Watermeyer, who had granted an interdict restraining the police from intervening in meetings at UCT. The house of Geoff Budlender,* SRC president, was burnt out by a bomb attack.

The student newspaper *Varsity* was repeatedly banned and the council was concerned about this, so it set up a sub-committee, on which I served, to look into the matter. Professor Murray, a retired professor of philosophy at the university and a Government nominee on council, was a member of the censor board and said that he would find out why the latest issue had been banned. At the only meeting the sub-committee held, Professor Murray informed us that there were two reasons for banning the last issue of *Varsity*. One, it contained a four-letter word (which was indeed so but I had not spotted it when I first scrutinised the publication) and secondly, that at the top of the editorial column there was a quill held in a left hand and

---

* Geoff Budlender is currently the director general of land affairs.

this was a known symbol of communism! Our sub-committee decided not to take the matter further because we were totally opposed to any form of banning.

I belonged to the Book of the Month Club in New York and regularly acquired books in that way. On one occasion I had ordered the novel *Couples* by John Updike. To my astonishment, I received a letter from the Department of Customs and Excise informing me that I had imported a banned book and had therefore broken the law, but that if I cared to come and see them the matter could be discussed. Accordingly, I went to their offices near the harbour in Cape Town and was shown into an office which was occupied by two men, one very fat and one very thin. It was a hot day and they were sitting in their shirt sleeves in a room piled with books. While we waited for an official to bring the forbidden book we got into a conversation and I told them that I was totally opposed to censorship in any form. 'Doctor,' the fat man said to me, 'you don't know what you are saying. We look through all these books and films and we make most of the decisions here; they are just rubber-stamped by people in another building. We see all the material and last week I saw an illustrated book from Sweden which was pornographic. It was just like a crude bioscope.' I was singularly unimpressed by these two men and very alarmed by the powers which they had. In due course, the official arrived with my book and the usual invoice. The fat man told me that if I posted the book back to the United States that would be the end of the matter and I would not have broken the law. I said to him that if I returned the book without explaining to the club what was happening, it would be returned to me. Accordingly I received one of their official letterheads on which I wrote to the Book of the Month Club: 'Dear Sirs, for reasons best known to themselves, the above will not let me read this book. Please credit my account.' That was folded up, put with the book which was wrapped up in paper, tied with string, and the customs officer accompanied me to the nearest post office where he watched me post the book to ensure that it safely left South Africa and didn't contaminate the national air. Quite what the people in New York made of that letter I don't know. I always imagined that it might be framed and hanging on a wall somewhere.

The whole issue of censorship is a difficult matter and anyone who has lived in a society where it has been abused is wary of it. There are dangers in exposing those vulnerable in a society to techniques of crime, pornography, sadism and the like, but there are also dangers in placing such powers in the hands of Government and their bureaucrats, powers which allow them to decide what the population may read and see and hear. I believe that on balance it is better to take the risks involved in living in a society free from censorship.

I will give two examples from the '70s and '80s in South Africa to demonstrate how power can be abused. When Judge Mostert, who had been a commissioner looking into the information scandal which later brought down Prime Minister John Vorster and Minister of Information Connie Mulder, had held a press conference despite having been 'told' not to do so, the news bulletin was cancelled because the South African Broadcasting Corporation had not had time to decide just how they would inform the South African public of this. On another occasion in 1987 a television newscaster reported on events in Mossel Bay where the Reverend Allan Hendrickse, who was a member of the Cabinet in the Tricameral Parliament and the leader of the House of Representatives (for coloured people), had committed a cardinal sin by deliberately swimming in the sea at the same time as some white folks. There had been words between him and President P W Botha as a consequence and the newscaster was reporting on this. He suddenly stopped with a stunned look and there was a temporary break in transmission. The newscaster reappeared, saying that he would read the first item again, upon which he gave a completely different version of the events. It transpired that the President had phoned the television station and had successfully insisted that the news be changed to suit his version.

My ten years as professor of medicine and head of the department were enormously satisfying. The department grew rapidly, both in consultant and training staff and in the number of special services which it offered. I received outstanding support from the members of the department, many of whom had taught me as a student. People of the calibre of Val Schrire, Pete Jackson and others gave me unstinting support. John Terblanche and I were able to continue developing the liver research group and the liver clinic and Ralph Kirsch played a crucial role in that work. He had been a research fellow with Bill Hoffenberg and was working with him at the time when he was banned, doing his PhD on certain aspects of albumin synthesis. Bill Hoffenberg's laboratory was next to mine and Ralph latterly worked more and more with me. As a young senior lecturer, my laboratory also doubled as my office. It was a small room with my desk on castors so that when we did experiments the desk at which I did my administrative work could be pushed under the work bench and out of the way. I had learned from Malcolm Milne that one doesn't need a great deal of space to do good work. One only needs enough, and a certain amount of pressure for space is not a bad thing.

1977 had seen the demolition of squatter camps at Modderdam and Werkgenot – and warnings were issued to the Unibel squatters of the pending demolition of their camp. These squatter camps of improvised shelters made of wood and corrugated iron sprang up to house mainly Africans coming to the cities in search of work. Appeals to the Government from many sources – medical and social workers, the churches and welfare organisations – had no success. Professor Folb, the professor of pharmacology, asked on 13 January 1978 that the UCT medical faculty send a delegation to the minister, asking for demolition plans to be dropped, and suggested that other medical schools do the same. But on 16 January 1978 demolition commenced, and over a period of five days the bulldozers wreaked havoc. The SHAWCO mobile clinic encountered difficulties in entering the area, but was welcomed by the principal of the University of the Western Cape, and allowed to park in the UWC grounds. Noreen and I accompanied Professor Folb to Unibel on the second day of the demolition. Professor Folb, who had served as a medical officer in the Israeli forces, reported to the medical faculty meeting, 'The last time I saw anything like this was during a war.' I agreed, saying, 'You're right – it is war.'

A report was drawn up on the medical aspects of the demolition of Unibel by Folb and Kirsch and Dr Elaine Clarke, who had worked in the camp for the past year. The report was sent to the dean of medicine at UCT and was published in the *Cape Times*, *Argus* and *Die Burger*, the local daily newspapers in Cape Town. It set out the views of the three doctors who, among many other concerned people, spent time in Unibel during its demolition. They were shocked by what was happening. The reaction to the publication of the report was swift. A press release by Dr Schalk van der Merwe, Minister of Health, refuted the report and questioned the motives of its authors.

The dean requested a meeting with the Minister of Health. Folb and Kirsch and Clarke provided a memorandum which was sent to the Minister. The UCT delegation, which saw the Minister, consisted of the dean, Prof. J C de Villiers, professor of neurosurgery (also chair of council of the University of the Western Cape), and myself. This meeting took place in February 1978 by which time Crossroads, another squatter camp, was under threat of demolition. I reported to Folb and Kirsch that the Minister had taken a fairly conciliatory attitude in private.

Professor Spencer, the professor of community medicine, was critical of our actions and had been urged by the Director-General of Health to try to stop us. He writes in his autobiography,* 'The staff and students spoke out loudly against segregation, and the iniquities of apartheid; voices of some, it seemed to me, all the more strident because of unspoken guilt arising from their white status and position.' As one of those who spoke out loudly and as the colleague closest to Spencer professionally, I was aware of this criti-

---

* *Hope Beyond the Shadows* by Ian Spencer, Forest Publishing, 1992

cism and of the fact that some colleagues thought we were seeking publicity for ourselves. I gave careful thought to those accusations at the time, rejected them and, on reflection, do so again now, but, in doing so, am aware that unconscious influences can play a role in shaping our actions.

Unibel was destroyed, as I have said, and now Crossroads was threatened with demolition. At the start of 1978, surveys carried out seemed to indicate that it was a reasonably settled community, with most of the people in employment in the Peninsula and only a small percentage unemployed. SHAWCO had started a clinic at Crossroads in 1977 and Professor Kirsch of the department of medicine, and active in SHAWCO, knew that the health statistics compared favourably with those in the Peninsula and were better than those in the so-called homelands. The head of criminology at UCT stated that the crime statistics were lower than in established townships. However, Brigadier van der Westhuizen, chairman of the Peninsula Administration Board, pointed to the extreme overcrowding in the township, and claimed the area was a health hazard and that crime was a problem. Harassment by various authorities continued: demands of rent arrears payment, under threat of shack demolition, pass raids leading to arrests and fines and, during September, clashes with the police and some shootings – which caused widespread reactions, protest meetings and condemnations. Throughout the year, the fight against the proposed demolition of Crossroads continued. It became clear that Crossroads was destined for a fate similar to Unibel.

The police set about fomenting the trouble which had broken out between two rival groups of squatters, and fighting and torching of houses were rife. Many shacks were destroyed in the fighting, the police siding with the 'vigilantes' against the younger residents, who bitterly opposed the proposed moving of the squatters to the new township of Khayelitsha. Ralph Kirsch was phoned very early one morning by a young nun (Celeste) who was a social worker in Crossroads. She appealed desperately for help – and Kirsch, Folb and I rushed out to Crossroads at about 5 a.m. with white coats and stethoscopes and did what we could to help while the police mounted a raid on 'illegals' in Crossroads, beating people indiscriminately. We documented the beatings, to the fury of the police, recording about thirty cases.

The three of us were frequently there, at the SHAWCO clinic, moving among those who had been badly beaten up. It was clear that among the genuine 'vigilantes' there were many members of the police, their faces blackened with boot polish. A resident who had been badly beaten up took the matter to court – and won his case. He had been charged with resisting arrest. The magistrate commented that it was not necessary to break bones in order to arrest someone. I was sure that the police were at the root of the violence. During the 1970s Noreen and I received a number of anonymous, abusive phone calls, some threatening our children. We also had reason to believe that our telephone was tapped.

For administrative purposes the teaching hospital was divided into a number of divisions: medicine, surgery, obstetrics and gynaecology, etc. For the ten years that I was professor of medicine, I was also head of the division of medicine, carrying responsibility for general medicine, psychiatry, dermatology, neurology and, initially, paediatrics.

Jannie Louw was the head of the department and of the division of surgery all the time that I was professor of medicine. He taught me as an undergraduate, was a brilliant surgeon and teacher, but ruled the department and the division of surgery with a rod of iron. A short man, he was a bundle of nervous energy. His staff and students quaked in their shoes when he turned his very direct gaze upon them and questioned them on their shortcomings. He had a devastating turn of phrase when the occasion demanded it. On one occasion the professor of medical education from a sister medical school gave a Saturday morning seminar for the teachers in the medical faculty at UCT. I found it very boring. Towards the end of the morning the visitor was unwise enough to ask who had got what they had expected to get out of the morning's session. Jannie Louw put up his hand. The visitor was delighted – here was the famous professor of surgery about to describe the value of the session. 'What did you get out of it, Professor Louw?' he asked. 'Absolutely nothing,' was the reply.

On another occasion the first professor of community medicine gave a lecture to the joint meeting of the physicians and surgeons at my request, because his was a new discipline and I felt everyone in the faculty should know how important it was. His slides were very simplistic, often consisting of a single word such as 'primary', 'secondary' or 'tertiary'. As we left the lecture I jokingly asked Jannie Louw if he had followed the lecture. His reply: 'I did not understand the slides!' Jannie Louw and I did not often disagree in our work at the hospital and medical school, but when we did the feathers flew.

In passing I would observe that my medical colleagues all over the world have a penchant for using slides to an excess. In my experience there can be a tendency to read from the slides and often little else until question time. The last lecture I gave to the medical faculty as professor of medicine was given without any slides. I told them that I wanted to demonstrate that it was possible to do so.

The dean of medicine was Professor Bromilow Bromilow-Downing. (When he was an undergraduate his fellow students said that he didn't have a name, he had a war-cry.) Bromilow-Downing was a conscientious administrator. He was not well informed on modern medicine and its advances, but he was absolutely honest, loyal to the university and played a pivotal role in maintaining good relationships between the university and the Provincial Administration (local government), where he had worked before becoming the dean of the medical faculty. The four of us, the dean, Jannie Louw, Arthur Kipps (head of microbiology and a distinguished virologist) and myself, were labelled the 'gang of four' after Madame Mao's group in the cultural revolution in communist China. We certainly wielded great influence in the medical school and the dean leaned heavily on the three of us in making decisions which were vital for the school. There was criticism of us because we allegedly did not consult widely and took decisions without doing so. While there may well be some justification in those criticisms, it is also true that I held a monthly meeting with all the full-time teaching staff in the department of medicine and the heads of firms, part-time and full-time (the department was divided into five firms each with its own wards and head), and discussed with them all the issues of the day. I made available to all staff the Principal's Circular from the university and all the other university circulars. I kept the heads of departments in the division informed of all major decisions and of all the issues that were coming up and obtained their advice on the major decisions which had to be made. So from the point of view of the department of medicine in particular and the division in general, they had some influence on the views that I was expressing in the 'gang of four,' although I would be the first to admit that it was hardly democratic.

If I was too forceful as a young professor, it was because I knew that a medical school is as strong as its department of medicine and that I was succeeding a man (Brock) who had dominated the scene for many years; that I was young (38 years old), had been taught by all the senior professors at the medical school and that I had to establish my position early in my time as head of the department of medicine. I was determined to ensure the department maintained its strength, and became stronger.

I was much younger than the other professors in the faculty and cocky enough to go against the stream. At a trivial level, there was a rule that no air conditioners which protruded beyond the window could be installed because this would make the buildings unsightly. I find it easier to work in a low temperature environment during the hot Cape Town summers and so I bought an air conditioner using funds from a donor, who was happy that they should be used in that way. It was like starting an epidemic of measles, because within a few weeks there were at least a dozen air conditioners in the medical school. Once installed, there was very little the dean and others could do about it.

On another occasion my secretary asked me whether she and the other secretaries in the department could wear trouser suits. Wondering why on earth she asked me, I said that I didn't care what they wore, as long as they were smart. Trouser suits were fashionable at the time and soon all the secretaries were wearing them. About two weeks later I was called to a meeting in the dean's office where Kipps and Louw waited. We were plainly assembling as the 'gang of four.' After some desultory introductory remarks the dean announced that it was against the rules for any woman to wear trousers while on duty in the medical school. 'Well,' I said, 'if that's all this meeting is about, I have more important things to do than to talk about what the women should wear. As long as they are smart, I am satisfied.' With that I got up and walked out. It was the last I heard about the matter.

During this time I started a refresher course for physicians which lasts several days and still occurs biennially. The late Bernard Pimstone, an outstanding endocrinologist and close friend, and I reorganised the department's annual research review into a formal research day which has continued to the present time.

Changing hats very fast
1975-1976

In the mid-1970s I was invited to be the visiting professor at the medical school in Salisbury, now Harare, in what was then Rhodesia, now Zimbabwe. Professor Michael Gelfand was the head of the department of medicine there. While I was there I asked whether I could see a mission hospital. A young English physician and I drove out to the Eastern Highlands and we were met at a crossroads by a middle-aged Italian woman doctor driving a four-wheel-drive vehicle. We followed her to the mission, which was in a remote area of the Rhodesian veld. We did a ward round and saw many extremely ill patients with a variety of diseases, many of them characteristic of the tropics. The Rhodesian war was in full swing and there was fighting all around the mission and I asked her whether she wasn't frightened. She said yes, she was very frightened. I asked her what frightened her most and she said that she feared making the wrong diagnosis! At lunch we were joined by the matron, also an Italian woman, and by the local Catholic priest, an African who arrived with a bottle of Cinzano. The lunch consisted of freshly made ravioli and spaghetti bolognaise and was served with apologies from our hostess who said her cook was only able to produce Italian meals. During lunch I learnt that both the church and the hospital had been built by Italian prisoners during the Second World War.

Later that afternoon she took us to visit a leprosarium at Mutemwa, where the patients were 'burnt out' cases, most of them blind with severely mutilated hands and feet. They crawled on their elbows and knees which were protected to some extent by a piece of cloth. An African nurse took care of them. The Italian doctor then took us to meet with John Bradburne, who was living in an aluminium wigwam, set in the blazing Central African sun. There was only one chair inside the wigwam and I was obliged to sit on it, as being a professor apparently meant that I took precedence when it came to seating arrangements. John Bradburne, the English doctor and the Italian mission doctor sat on the floor, or rather on the earth. The young man's hammock and mosquito net was in one part of the wigwam. In another there was an altar with a cross and also the star of David, the crest of Islam and a Buddha. But he was clearly a devout Catholic. We discussed the problems at the leprosarium and I was deeply impressed by his devotion to those suffering there. For the following details of John Bradburne's life I am indebted to Charles Moore, who wrote an article about him in the South African *Sunday Times* on November 13 1994. The article originally appeared in the *Daily Telegraph* in London.

John Bradburne was born in 1921. His parents were High Anglicans and his father was a country parson. Amongst his cousins were Terence Rattigan, the playwright, and Christopher Soames, the last governor of Rhodesia. An officer in the Gurkhas in World War II, he survived in the Malayan jungle for about a month after the fall of Singapore until he escaped to fight with Orde Wingate's Chindits. (My predecessor as vice-chancellor, Sir Richard Luyt, had also served under Wingate.) A fellow officer and now a Jesuit priest, John Dove, became a life-long friend. In 1947 Bradburne converted to Roman Catholicism and three times unsuccessfully tried to become a monk. He made a pilgrimage to Jerusalem, was caretaker of the Archbishop of Westminster's house in Hertfordshire and, while living subsequently in Italy, made a private vow to the Virgin Mary to remain celibate.

When he was nearly 40 he joined Dove in Rhodesia, having asked him if he knew of 'a cave in Africa which I can pray in.' He was deeply shocked when he saw the condition of the leprosarium, became its warden and improved the living conditions of the lepers immeasurably. He bathed their sores and took care of them in a most compassionate way. He knew them all well and wrote a poem about each of the 80 or so of them.

After about three years, the body responsible for the leprosarium, the Rhodesia Leprosy Association, denied him access. He had overstepped the mark by giving a loaf of bread to every leper once a week and by refusing to put a number around every leper's neck for purposes of identification. He had good reason to believe that the person who had been made responsible for the lepers was denying them dapsone and was selling the tablets. He took the matter up, at first privately, but getting no response, publicly, and this was the last straw for the Association, which obtained a court order preventing him from entering the settlement. He went to live in a tent and later in the tin hut where I met him, just beyond the fence of the settlement. There was no electricity or water. He built a chapel beyond the settlement's grounds and the lepers crawled on their elbows and knees to take part in the services he conducted. He played music for the mass on a harmonica. He also played Bach for them and taught them Gregorian chants.

Moore describes how he met with Coletta, a leper, who had seen John Bradburne daily during the fortnight before he disappeared. She was worried about Bradburne's safety and he had told her he had seen a 'big angel' and that he was safe. One midnight, ten youths came to his hut – not guerrillas but 'messengers' for Mugabe's army. Moore thinks they were probably acting on a tip-off from the man Bradburne had denounced at the leprosarium. Moore relates how Bradburne was taken to a meeting of hundreds of mainly teenagers in the bush, where he was taunted in a degrading manner. The next day he was tried by the local guerrilla leaders. Moore writes, 'The guerrillas were in an uncomfortable position. They had been inundated with local reports that their prisoner was a good man, and they were angry with the mujibhas ("messengers") for kidnapping him. But they were nervous of taking him back to Mutemwa now that he had seen so much. They interrogated him (according to Denford Nyandimu, who at the time had been a new recruit to the guerrillas, but had known Bradburne and respected him) and, after about ten minutes he knelt and prayed, which infuriated the guerrilla commander. When he was offered food, he passed most of it on to others. 'Why don't you come with us,' the guerrillas asked him, 'and we'll let you live in a foreign country? You could go to China' (Mugabe's chief foreign ally). At this, Bradburne burst out laughing. They tried to persuade him to come with them to Mozambique and help their people there, but he refused, and said he must go back to the lepers at Mutemwa.

For the rest of that day, Bradburne was guarded. He slept and prayed. In the evening, there was a pungwe in the bush, a Marxist consciousness-raising session for about 500 local people. Bradburne sat quietly on the edge of the crowd. A mother of twins gave him her babies to look after while she joined in, and they slept in his lap. After the crowd had dispersed, about 50 guerrillas, including Denford, set off with John Bradburne and made for the main road. Just before they reached it, in the early hours of Wednesday morning, the security commander ordered Bradburne to walk a few paces ahead and then stop and face him. He did so, and fell on his knees and prayed for about three minutes, again showing no sign of fear. Then he rose to his feet, and as he did so, the commander shot him. His killer is now a businessman in Zimbabwe. Horrified by what had happened, Denford deserted the guerrillas.

Father Gibbs was told a couple of hours later that a white man's body had been found. As he drove to Mutemwa, he saw the corpse on the side of the road. It was still warm.

The Italian woman mission doctor was subsequently faced with a freedom fighter who had been shot in the arm, fracturing his humerus. She set the fracture, gave him antibiotics and told him there was nothing else she could do and that he should go to the next hospital down the road, a hospital which, of course, did not exist, but it was her way of sending him on his way. The regulations at the time required her to turn him over to the police or the Rhodesian armed forces, but she did not do that. As a consequence, she was arrested and put on trial in Salisbury. There was an outcry, and she was not required to serve any prison sentence. Unfortunately some time later when driving towards the mission, she turned off into a side road some three or four hundred yards away from a Rhodesian military road block. They thought that whoever was driving the vehicle was deliberately trying to avoid them and they opened fire and killed her.

Pilgrims now visit Mutemwa and Moore writes of the possibility of the sanctification of Bradburne. My meetings with the Italian doctor and with John Bradburne are as clear in my mind as I write this, as they were when I saw them over twenty years ago. They were two extraordinary people who made a deep impression on me.

In all the years that I had worked at GSH, up until the time that I became professor of medicine, the hospital had been segregated. Half of the hospital was for white patients, nursed by white nurses and the other half was for Indian, coloured and African patients (black patients) nursed by coloured nurses. African nurses were not allowed to work in the hospital and coloured theatre sisters were not allowed to assist at operations on white patients. Despite this, all patients got the same quality of care in the hospital. Indeed, the more experienced full-time consultants usually worked in the black wards because the patients there were frequently more ill than the patients in the white wards, had a greater variety of illnesses and presented at a more advanced stage of disease. A number of people in the hospital had been agitating for change, but in the '60s that wasn't easy to achieve.

In 1971 it was still the practice for those coloured and Indian doctors who wished to specialise to undertake their specialty training at the New Somerset Hospital, which was one of the teaching hospitals in the GSH group, but no black doctor had ever done specialty training in GSH itself. Plainly that was fundamentally wrong and was increasingly becoming a disability, given the special services which were developing in GSH. I decided that this should end. Thinking it best not to consult anyone, I approached Bryan Kies, who was starting his training as a medical registrar, and told him I wanted him to be the registrar in my ward, Ward D6 at GSH, but since this was against hospital regulations he would have to eat in the ward and sleep in my office because the bureaucracy would not allow him to use the doctors' bungalow. He agreed. Jerry van Aswegen and others followed him. Bryan Kies is now a senior full-time consultant in neurology at GSH and Jerry van Aswegen is in practice as a specialist physician in Cape Town. The neurology department was also active early on in eliminating discrimination.

Gradually more and more people of colour did their training at GSH and naturally they started taking their meals in the doctors' bungalow. One day the medical superintendent, Dr J G Burger, called me to say that the housekeeper at the doctors' bungalow had lodged an objection with him because coloured doctors and their wives were eating in the bungalow. He had told her that if she didn't like it she could resign, which she did. That was a turning point. Quite soon after that the coloured and Indian doctors and their wives were living in the doctors' bungalow and black doctors were seeing patients in both the white wards and the black wards in GSH. At this time African doctors had great difficulty in getting permits from the Minister to register at UCT as postgraduate medical students, a necessary provision for their appointment as registrars. The Cape Provincial Administration would not have appointed them in any case. We were able to begin integrating the hospital without crises and confrontations, and a great deal of credit for this must be given to Dr J G Burger, the chief medical superintendent, who understood what we were trying to achieve and gave us his support. Dr Burger had been appointed medical superintendent while he was still in the Transvaal and his appointment had been opposed by UCT because the university thought he was a dyed-in-the-wool Nationalist. It was the one senior administrative provincial appointment that the university had the power to oppose. However, it didn't have the power to do any more than delay the appointment, which it did. The Administrator overruled the university and appointed Dr Burger, who paradoxically became a great supporter of the university and closely identified himself with its ideals. He was an outstanding man.

We also succeeded in getting rid of apartheid in the intensive-care wards, claiming that we could not afford to have separate services because the personnel were not available to duplicate the staff. Since we knew that the Administration would willingly fund the duplication of equipment in order to ensure apartheid, we could not argue that there was a shortage of equipment or of accommodation. Indeed, they would make money available to enforce apartheid. When the University of Stellenbosch's new teaching hospital was opened, expensive equipment was duplicated on the white side and the black sides of the hospital. This illustrates the waste that occurred with apartheid, not only in human terms, but in material terms as well.

At GSH Dr Reeve Sanders became the chief superintendent at a later stage and continued helping with the integration of patients in the hospital as she had as deputy to Dr Burger. After I had resigned as professor of medicine and had become the vice-chancellor, the progressive integration of the hospital continued under the able leadership of Professor Solly Benatar, who succeeded me as professor of medicine and head of the department. The heads of other divisions were also actively involved. GSH became the first and for a long time the only public hospital in South Africa that was not segregated on the basis of race and this applied to professional staff, patients, students and everyone else. There were quite frequent complaints by constituents and friends and relatives of members of parliament, including Cabinet members, which the medical superintendents had to field. To the credit of Dr Burger and Dr Reeve Sanders they did so, but it required a lot of fancy footwork.

The medical and nursing staff at the New Somerset Hospital were deeply resentful of the effects of apartheid on the hospitals where doctors and nurses of colour received lower salaries than their white colleagues. This iniquitous situation continued despite repeated protests by, amongst others, members of the UCT faculty.

In 1976 the schoolchildren of Soweto took to the streets to protest against being forced to be educated in Afrikaans and there were bloody riots in Soweto and in the rest of the country. Many schoolchildren in the Cape were involved as the schools were disrupted in sympathy with the Soweto scholars. This drew fierce reprisals from the police. Victims sought treatment and refuge at the New Somerset Hospital and at GSH and the police demanded that nursing and medical staff report all cases treated for birdshot and bullet wounds, and those who had been sprayed blue (the police used water cannons to mark protesters). When staff refused to comply, the police stationed their own people in the wards and this was deeply resented.

At a meeting for all staff at the New Somerset Hospital addressed by Dr Louis van der Poel, a registrar in obstetrics and gynaecology, it was decided to march in protest and to hand over a memorandum expressing their anger, and the reasons for it, to the medical superintendent. This went according to plan and the marchers dispersed peacefully. At 4 a.m. the next morning Van der Poel was arrested at home. He was a young husband and the father of two small children. I was in my office at the medical school early the next morning when Dr Roy Keeton, who was head of the medical firm for which I was responsible at the New Somerset Hospital, phoned to warn me that the doctors and nurses at the hospital were going on strike because of the arrest and detention without trial of Dr van der Poel, and that Livingstone Hospital in Port Elizabeth and King Edward VIII Hospital in Durban were going to strike in sympathy. I asked him if he could delay the onset of the strike for a few hours, during which time I would try to find ways of easing the situation. Obviously a strike would have caused great problems and I was concerned about patient care. I rushed to Professor Bromilow-Downing, the dean, and told him that we had to see the Administrator, Dr Lapa Munnik, and effect the release of Dr van der Poel immediately. Bromilow-Downing was very agitated and not at all sure that what I was suggesting was appropriate, but did not have much option but to agree. Arthur Kipps and Jannie Louw undertook to come with us. We saw Munnik in his office in Wale

Street where I told him that the matter was very serious and that unless they released Van der Poel he (Munnik) would as a consequence face strikes in three major hospitals, two of which were within his jurisdiction. Munnik said that he would contact the commissioner of police and do what he could, but he was very critical of the protests which were going on in the country. He then made a chilling prediction saying that dire things would happen to people. His comments alarmed me.

I reported back to Dr Keeton and the strike action at the hospitals was postponed pending the outcome of Munnik's discussions with the police commissioner. Dr van der Poel was held in detention for about twelve days. The strike was postponed while negotiations continued. While he was imprisoned the Cape Provincial Administration terminated his hospital appointment and I have no doubt that the threat of strike action was responsible for both his release and reinstatement. The actions of the police and of the hospitals' department of the Cape Provincial Administration were reprehensible. Dr van der Poel is now a specialist obstetrician and gynaecologist practising in Cape Town.

Shortly after the events surrounding Van der Poel, the nurses at the New Somerset Hospital marched in the streets outside the hospital to protest against apartheid, especially as it applied to the hospitals. They were particularly incensed about restrictions placed on where they could work and what they could do, and on income discrimination based on colour. They held a peaceful protest but as a result they were threatened with dismissal. The heads of firms at the hospital came out in their support and I addressed a meeting of a very large number of all the staff at the hospital, expressing my total support for the nurses and condemning the hospital authorities. No nurses were dismissed.

The 1976 riot in Soweto and the consequent events in the country caused a great deal of turmoil in the department and I called a general meeting of members of the department and pointed out to them that our primary obligation was to the care of the sick and to the teaching of undergraduate and postgraduate students, nurses and other health professionals, and emphasised the importance of medical research for all the people living in South Africa. One or two members of staff were revealed as lacking any substance at that meeting; a number of staff emigrated during the next six to nine months. As Bernard Levin once wrote, 'There is no steel in a pork sausage.' For some, emigration was the final rejection of apartheid, but many emigrated simply because they felt very insecure and their decision to leave was not based on an abhorrence of apartheid, although many of them would subsequently make more of the moral issue than did those who had truly left for that reason.

In June 1977 a group of us from the medical faculty formally called on the vice-chancellor and principal to discuss salary and other forms of discrimination in the faculty. White doctors earned more than coloured doctors, who in turn earned more than Indian doctors, who earned more than African doctors. Sir Richard Luyt reported to council, which resolved that the discrimination should be brought to an end as soon as possible. It was agreed that when Sir Richard approached the Administrator he should be informed that the University of Cape Town felt so strongly about this matter that it was prepared to consider bearing the financial cost of ending the discrimination.

The meeting with the Administrator took place in September 1977. UCT was represented by Professor Maurice Kaplan (acting vice-chancellor and principal), Professors Uys and McKenzie from the medical faculty, and myself as professor of medicine. The discussions concerned salary and other forms of discrimination and a memorandum dated 17 February 1977 which had been prepared by the staff of the New Somerset Hospital in this regard.

The Administrator said the Government was committed to the ultimate goal of parity in salaries for all for equivalent work done by persons of equivalent qualifications, but that the current financial climate was preventing rapid attainment of the goal. He agreed to raise the matter with Government but did not believe it to be administratively and legally possible for the university to make up any difference in funds. We could achieve nothing more at the time, but he was essentially fobbing us off and it was not until mid-1979 that these discriminatory practices began to be eliminated. These were years of shame and injustice.

I was receiving anonymous phone calls threatening my family, about whose movements the caller seemed to be very well informed. This really did worry me.

Personal turning-points 1977–1980

Towards the end of 1976 Sir Richard Luyt, the vice-chancellor and principal, asked me to see him. I thought he wanted to discuss a problem concerning his health as I was his physician, but learned instead that Professor Maurice Kaplan, the deputy principal, was to take long leave and that Sir Richard would also take leave after Kaplan's return. He then asked me if I would act as an assistant principal during this time. I was taken aback, not having considered fulfilling such a role. My reaction was to say that I would do it part-time while continuing with my responsibilities in the medical school and hospital. At its meeting in February 1977 the university council appointed me part-time acting assistant principal from 1 April to 30 November of that year.

While Kaplan was away I occupied his office in the Bremner (administration) Building. Miss Mouat was Kaplan's very efficient secretary and a friend of Dormee Hirschberg, Sir Richard's secretary. They were a formidable pair. Before I took up the new appointment Miss Hirschberg would phone me and say, 'I don't like the look of the principal. He won't listen to me. Please phone him and ask how he is. He is working too hard.' I always followed her instructions.

As my secretary at the time, Miss Mouat was very helpful but she had a fine-tuned sense of the niceties within hierarchy and was set in her ways. On my first morning as acting assistant principal she asked me what time I would like my tray of tea. I replied that the timing did not worry me and that all I needed was just a cup of tea. Miss Mouat replied that I would have a tray of tea. I restated my position – I wanted a cup of tea. 'But Professor always had a tray,' she said firmly – and a tray of tea was what I got!

My duties as acting assistant principal were not particularly onerous. I was appointed chair of the residences and of the student affairs committees; I had been a member of both for some time. I had other committee responsibilities and found myself responsible for approving applications for sabbatical leave. One of the first of these applications to reach me was from an anatomist who proposed to do research on the brain at an overseas institution for a year. As he had no record of research of any consequence over the previous several years I turned his application down. Sabbatical leave had come to be regarded as a right and there was quite a reaction. I stood my ground but was overruled by Professor Axelson, who was acting as deputy principal. As I suspected, the anatomist used his sabbatical trying to get a more senior position elsewhere and did not add to the little he knew about the brain before he went on his leave. In later years as vice-chancellor I ensured that sabbatical (study and research leave) had to be earned and that the programme which was proposed was built upon a proven track record at UCT. Academic staff at the university are entitled to apply for twelve months' sabbatical leave every six years, or six months after three years. This is as generous a provision as obtains in any university anywhere, but is necessary when a university is situated at the southern tip of Africa. Most academics put their sabbatical leave to very good use, but it is essential that the privilege be earned.

Early in 1976 Mr Len Abrahamse, a member of the university council, had proposed that the London firm of management consultants, Peat, Marwick, Mitchell and Company, be asked to undertake a comprehensive review of the university's administration at an approximate cost of R100 000. He said that he was not happy about the council having to concern itself with trivia and that many of the administrative procedures were cumbersome and needed to be streamlined. While I agreed with his concerns, I was opposed to spending so much money on such an enterprise and said so. Abrahamse had a strong personality and was not deterred by my opposition. The council approved his proposal with my voting against it and the ensuing report changed my life, but I was not to know it at the time.

When I joined the university council as one of the elected representatives of the senate, Mr Frank Robb was the chairman. He was also chairman of the University Foundation, the university's independent fund-raising structure in South Africa. He was an outstanding man, who chaired the council with great ability. A liberal, he was an implacable foe of apartheid, and his wife Noël was a leading member of the civil rights organisation, the Black Sash, who worked tirelessly amongst the poor and dispossessed. The women of the Black Sash wore the sashes to symbolise their opposition to injustice and courageously defied the Government on many occasions. I greatly enjoyed Robb's quiet sense of humour. He continued to take an active interest in university affairs after his retirement as chairman of council and as chairman of the University Foundation at the end of March 1976, being president of convocation until 1981. Robb had been one of the original trustees of the foundation. Len Abrahamse succeeded Frank Robb as chairman of council in April 1976 and occupied that position until the end of February 1991. When Abrahamse retired he had been a member of the university council for close on sixteen years, fifteen of them as chairman. In 1976 he also succeeded Robb as chairman of the University Foundation in the formation of which he had played a key role. He had been a governor of the Foundation for thirty years and a trustee for fifteen, and he served as chairman for thirteen years.

Abrahamse made it clear at his first meeting as the council's chairman that he believed the council should not concern itself with minutiae and that it should concentrate on broad areas of policy; that it should leave academic affairs to the senate and not interfere in them; that the council should leave it to the vice-chancellor and the rest of the executive to undertake their leadership and managerial roles and that the council should not meddle in those areas, but should be supportive of them. As will become apparent, I worked closely with him when I was vice-chancellor and was indeed fortunate to have him as the chairman of council during many difficult years. He was one of the finest men I have ever known.

Len was orphaned at the age of three years and was brought up by an uncle and aunt. They were folk of limited means and Len went to school at Observatory Boys' High School. He saw service in North Africa during World War II and it was there he met his future wife Nel, his life-long companion, a quiet and self-effacing person. Nel has an inner strength, and their deep mutual love and affection was a source of strength to them both. While he was in the desert he learnt to love Shakespeare's plays, carrying a copy of the Bard's complete works in his kit. On his return from active service Len obtained a bachelor of commerce degree from the University of South Africa by correspondence. He joined the Shell Oil Company and rapidly rose through the ranks of that organisation, occupying very senior positions in South America, the Philippines, Sri Lanka and in Holland. While in Holland he played a key role in overcoming the oil problems experienced by Europe following the OPEC crisis. He was chairman of Shell South Africa and on his retirement was, or subsequently became, a member of a number of boards of leading South African companies. He also played key roles in the Urban Foundation and the Independent Development Trust and worked tirelessly to try to secure a just and prosperous South Africa. He was passionate about UCT and saw it as a vital force for the education of young South Africans from all walks of life and from all sectors of society. It was my privilege to count him as one of my closest friends. Sadly he died in April 1994.

In 1976 the council received the Stage I report from Peat, Marwick, Mitchell and Co. Mr John Fielden and Dr Anthony Waters had spent some time at the university before drawing up the report and Hugh Amoore had played a significant role in their investigations. It turned out that no South African university at that time was engaged in structured, systematic, academic planning, and they pointed out that, 'As a university is an institution with academic objectives, the basics of planning should be the academic plan.' They went on to recommend the formation of a small academic planning committee to undertake the detailed work for planning, with all major academic policy matters passing through senate for approval. Faculty boards could also appoint faculty planning groups. They recommended the creation of a post for a second deputy principal to co-ordinate all aspects of planning in the university. The council accepted Stage I of the report.

I was a senate representative on the selection committee for the deputy principal which was chaired by Len Abrahamse. The post was widely advertised and candidates were short-listed and interviewed, but the selection committee failed to identify a suitable candidate. At a meeting of the committee to take the matter further Len Abrahamse asked me if I would leave the room. I protested, saying I was a member of the committee elected by senate. He insisted that I do so, and I withdrew. When I was called back to the meeting he informed me that the selection committee had unanimously decided that I should be offered the post. I had not anticipated this development at all and I needed to think it through. Subsequently I informed Len that I would accept the position of deputy principal (planning) but in a part-time capacity, as I wished to continue with my responsibilities as professor and head of the department of medicine. At the council meeting in November 1977 the members unanimously recommended my appointment on that basis. I had made one other stipulation and that was that Hugh Amoore should be appointed to the post of planning officer. Sir Richard was reluctant to agree to this proposal as he had his own plans for Hugh, but I was adamant and Hugh was appointed to that position. I knew what an able and hard-working person Hugh was and considered him ideal for this role.

The lecturers' association's newspaper *Forum* was edited by a social anthropologist, Mike Whisson. Its next issue carried a front-page cartoon with Abrahamse, symbolising the Shell Company, offering a fish with D.P.(P.) [for deputy principal (planning)] on it, to a dolphin which rather resembled me. Another fish marked 'P' (principal) lay waiting in a bucket. The inference was clear.

Hugh Amoore and I started academic and overall planning in three small offices, one for each of us and one for a secretary. The files were completely empty and the table tops were bare! Monday meetings were initiated to identify new directions for the university. These lasted one hour before the day's work began and were open to all members of senate after their first three years. (Later they were open to all interested staff and students.) No-one would be held to anything they said at the meeting and nobody could be quoted. It was a forum for new ideas and the source of a number of new developments, and those meetings have continued beyond my retirement.

From the 3rd to the 10th of April 1978 I attended a British Council course on 'Academic planning and university development: the vision and the reality' which was held at the universities of Lancaster, Warwick and London. The course was organised by Sir Charles Carter, vice-chancellor of the University of Lancaster, and Professor Alec Ross, professor of educational research at the same university. I got to know them both well and they subsequently visited UCT. The delegates lived in the university residences, and on the first evening we were entertained at a cocktail party. I thought that Sir Charles and Alec were a little apprehensive at the cocktail party, but I didn't realise that I was the cause of their anxiety! The registrar of a Nigerian university, together with some other university administrators, had objected to my presence there as a South African, and Carter and Ross were not sure how things would develop. We sat down to a meal after the cocktail party, and as chance would have it, I sat next to the Nigerian registrar, who was on my right. On my left was an Australian colleague. The Nigerian lost no time in attacking me on the general subject of apartheid, and I was not slow in indicating to him my total rejection of apartheid and the fact that this had been my view for many years. The Australian came out in my support and I was grateful to him for it. The evening passed off uneventfully. The next morning, as I left my room to go to the communal bathroom, the door opposite mine opened at the same time and the Nigerian registrar emerged. He looked at me and said, 'Good morning, sir,' and I realised that at least part of the battle had been won and that he was no longer aggressive towards me. On the final evening there was a dinner for all the delegates and I had to make a speech on behalf of all those who had attended the course. The evening ended with my putting the Nigerian registrar to bed, because he was somewhat under the weather. I did think of the ambivalent attitude which some had had towards me as a white South African when I first arrived on the course. Thirty people from nineteen countries attended, but once we got to know each other and recognised each other's values, the initial suspicions fell away.

I was chairman of the residences committee in the late 1970s and had become aware of the serious accommodation problems black students had, even though Africans in particular were few in number. In November 1977 council accepted a recommendation, which was supported by the students, that a house belonging to the St Francis Xavier Seminary be used for this purpose and that UCT make a financial contribution to the seminary in return for this. The students were eligible for boarding bursaries. At that time the student residences (dormitories) were open to white students only. This was because the Group Areas Act, an apartheid law, forced people of different 'racial groups' to live in defined and separate areas. UCT was in a 'white' area and blacks could not live there. Blacks who were employees such as domestic servants could do so, but had to have special permits.

When UCT reached its 150th birthday in 1979, the chancellor, Mr Harry Oppenheimer, made a personal donation of R150 000 and Sir Richard asked me how UCT could use these funds most effectively. My reply was that the university would have to introduce an academic support programme (ASP) because, increasingly, the students would be coming from school systems (black) which left a great deal to be desired and that they would need special help to 'bridge the gap' between their schooling and the university. In 1980 I looked at academic support programmes in the United States.

As deputy principal and later throughout my tenure as vice-chancellor I gave strong support to the ASP. I sought financial support both inside and outside South Africa, with some success, but it was time-consuming and often difficult. My actions were criticised by most of the leadership of the Afrikaans-speaking universities (which were not admitting these students!), who echoed the Government line that students who were not fully prepared at high school should not go to university and that ASPs were therefore unnecessary and were not the business of a university. This argument could only lead to the exclusion of the vast majority of African students. I was a member of the advisory council for universities and technikons and consistently failed to obtain funding for these programmes. Most of the committee members and the Department of National Education were simply not interested. The white paper issued by the present Department of Education states that academic development programmes (the successor of ASP) will be funded by Government, but that has not happened yet. All the time I was vice-chancellor I had to allocate precious internal resources and raise funds to ensure a successful ASP (later called the academic development programme (ADP)).

The general framework was to have a small central unit with staff in a number of departments. By 1995 there was a total of forty-four staff working in this area, plus tutors. Associate Professor Ian Scott, the director, and Ms Nan Yeld, the deputy director, are dedicated to this task and, in my view, are the best exponents of academic development in South Africa and are equal to their peers internationally. Not only are numerous courses in place to help disadvantaged students, but also an alternative admissions procedure with special tests in English and mathematics has been developed over the years, and this has proved to be a good indicator of success at university. These procedures are now used by several universities and some corporations to detect potential. The academic development programme is closely linked to the writing centre and the computer literacy project. Initial resistance from students who understandably did not want to be viewed as 'second rate' was overcome by the attitudes and conscientiousness of the staff, who made it clear that students were at UCT because they were bright and had the potential to succeed, but if their formal schooling had gaps, the ADP could help them to succeed. The failure of the Nationalist Government to fund these activities and the lack of support we received from Afrikaans-speaking universities reflected the apartheid ideology of the time.

Meeting the duties and obligations of being deputy principal (planning) and head of both the department and the division of medicine at the medical school at Groote Schuur Hospital was a considerable challenge. I would do my ward round at the hospital from 07.45 to 08.45, requiring the students to be there to be taught at the bedside. When students from medical residence told me that it was impossible for them to come on a ward round at such a time because they would miss their breakfast, I told them they could encourage the residence to give them breakfast earlier, or have their breakfast at the usual time and miss the ward round, or they could come to the ward round and not have any breakfast. The decision was up to them. The medical residence adjusted its hours for breakfast. Before going on the ward round I would leave a tape from my tape recorder on the desk of my secretary in the department of medicine at the medical school, which reflected the work I had done the previous evening, relevant to the department's needs. I then spent the morning in my office at the university, busying myself with academic planning and other matters, and during the lunch hour and early afternoon I would be in my office at the medical school. Then I would attend meetings either at the university or the medical school, or I would be supervising the liver research group of which I was still co-director, or I would be seeing patients in the hospital. In the evening I would work, either on university or medical school matters. My ward admitted emergencies on Mondays and every Monday night at 22.00 I was in the ward to see acutely ill patients. Final-year students assigned to the ward were required to be present. I worked in this way for three years, which certainly put me under a great deal of pressure and in its turn must have reflected on the time and commitment that I could give to my family. I spent as much time with the children as I could, especially at the weekends, and while I was unaware of not paying enough attention to Noreen's needs, and to the quality of our relationship, it must have been very difficult for her.

Joan Smith was my excellent senior secretary in the department of medicine, but after a while my new lifestyle proved too much for her. She told me she was resigning to take up another post in the medical school because she couldn't relate to a voice on a tape recorder – she needed to see the professor more often than she did! I understood that and I was very sorry when she left. She was succeeded by Mrs Gladys Stubbs, an equally delightful person who was a tower of strength and remained with me until I resigned to become vice-chancellor. Looking back I am not sure why I was arrogant enough to take on so many responsibilities simultaneously. Was I overly ambitious? I had no desire to follow a career in university administration. One explanation might be that I have a congenital inability to turn down a challenge. Such a quality can be weakness.

Sheilah Lloyd was Sir Richard Luyt's personal aide – a woman with a very well-rounded personality, well educated in the broad sense, with a deep understanding of the university and capable of forming very good judgements of the people working in it. She was (and is) a very highly regarded member of the university community. One afternoon she called me to the vice-chancellor's office while I was chairing a meeting in the senate room on the floor above. Sir Richard Luyt, the vice-chancellor, was clearly having a myocardial infarction. At the time he had severe compressing, central, chest pain which was radiating up into his jaw and down the inner surface of his left arm. The pain had been present for twenty to twenty-five minutes when I saw him. I immediately telephoned the coronary intensive care ward at Groote Schuur Hospital and informed them I was bringing him directly to them. I asked him to walk with me very slowly to my car, which we then did. I then drove at great speed to the hospital and as I approached my parking bay I called out to the parking attendant and asked him to fetch a wheelchair as quickly as possible. Sir Richard Luyt was in bed, in the intensive care ward, within ten minutes of my seeing him. The most critical period of the myocardial infarction is in the first hour or two after the onset of the attack. Sir Richard made a complete recovery and embarked enthusiastically on the rehabilitation programme which was very popular at the time. This consisted of the patients undertaking graded exercise, until they were really exerting themselves quite a lot. I went to see Sir Richard during one of his rehabilitation periods and came to the conclusion that I would probably survive a myocardial infarction if I had it, but that I would never survive the rehabilitation. Sir Richard, who had been a very distinguished rugby player and cricketer, was ideally suited to the physical jerks which the cardiologists were imposing on him. My own lack of involvement in physical jerks reminds me of a cartoon which shows a man dressed in shorts, looking out of a window at a large number of people doing exercises. The speech bubble had him saying, 'Physical jerks? Oh yeah. I can see hundreds of them.'

Sir Richard had been appointed vice-chancellor of the University of Cape Town in 1967 and was an outstanding incumbent of that post. As Professor John Reid, the university orator, said when Sir Richard received an honorary

Doctorate of Literature from UCT in 1982, he had come full circle because he was born in the house that stood next to the old College House in Breda Street, then the university's only residence. Three years after obtaining his BA degree in economics at UCT he was awarded a Rhodes scholarship to Trinity College, Oxford, where he received his MA degree. He qualified to enter the colonial service. He had excelled at rugby and cricket, receiving a double blue at UCT and a rugby blue at Oxford. After a short period in the colonial service, he enlisted in the East African forces as a sergeant under Brigadier Orde Wingate and after five years' service he was demobilised with the rank of lieutenant colonel.

I remember seeing the movie 'Breaker Morant' in the university's Baxter theatre and Noreen and I sat next to Richard and Betty Luyt. During the movie I thought that Dick Luyt would be very critical of the way in which it portrayed the court martial procedures of the British army. After the movie was finished I asked him what he thought of it and he said, 'I thought it was a very good movie but I don't think the scenes portraying the court martial procedures of the British army were accurate,' and I felt very full of myself for making such an accurate prediction of his reaction. Sir Richard then went on to say, ' ... Wingate ordered me to shoot a prisoner.' I looked at him in astonishment and asked, 'What did you do?' and he replied, 'Fortunately Wingate forgot.' I then realised Richard Luyt had personal experience of the challenges which the film had raised and felt ashamed of my presumption of anticipating his reaction to the court martial. Professor Heese, the professor of paediatrics, had been to the same film show, and in the foyer I asked him what he thought of the movie. Boetie Heese told me that the preacher shot by the Australians had been a great-uncle of his. I was really quite dumbstruck, especially as Boetie's charming wife is indeed Australian. I thought to myself what a fool I had been to think I could make judgements when I lacked real insight.

Richard Luyt led Haile Selassie into Addis Ababa after it was liberated from the Italians and described to me a hair-raising flight in a reconnaissance aircraft over the highlands of Ethiopia, where he worked behind the lines. After the war he joined the colonial service, becoming a district officer in Northern Rhodesia and subsequently senior labour officer in the Copperbelt. In 1953 he was transferred to Kenya as their labour commissioner, and thereafter was appointed Permanent Secretary in the Ministry of Education, Labour and Lands and Secretary to the Cabinet. In 1962 he returned to Northern Rhodesia as Chief Secretary, and was for a while Acting Governor. He became a close personal friend of Kenneth Kaunda.

In 1964 Richard Luyt was appointed Governor of British Guiana during the stormy years when that country moved towards its independence. When civil war broke out he was forced to declare a state of emergency. He handled the situation with tact, firmness and fairness. In February 1966, shortly before the country became independent, Queen Elizabeth and Prince Philip paid a royal visit to British Guiana at the start of their Caribbean tour. An investiture ceremony was held in the ballroom of Government House, at which the Queen awarded Sir Richard the K.C.V.O. (Knight Commander of the Victorian Order). The following day she received him privately in her sitting-room on board the royal yacht *Britannia*, and awarded him the G.C.M.G. (Grand Cross of St Michael and St George).

When independence was declared in May 1966, Sir Richard became Governor General of Guyana. It was from there that he took up the position of vice-chancellor and principal of the University of Cape Town.

Lady Luyt (Betty) was Sir Richard's second wife, his first wife having died shortly after the birth of their daughter Frances. Betty had trained as a nurse and was a devoted wife and mother. She was much admired by all at UCT and continued to be an enthusiastic supporter of the university until her death in September 1999. She was a woman of sterling quality, with that rare ability of taking a real interest in what you told her and making you feel you were doing something worthwhile.

At the time of his appointment the relationship between the vice-chancellor and the students had reached a very low level, but Sir Richard soon gained the respect and confidence of the members of the students' representative council and of the entire student body. He was forthright in his condemnation of the policies of the South African Government, firmly opposed to apartheid, a strong supporter of the National Union of South African Students (NUSAS) of which he was an honorary vice-president, and a staunch opponent of conscription, an area in which the Government found it difficult to criticise him, given his distinguished voluntary war record and their total lack of it during the World War II. Indeed, most of them had opposed South Africa's entry into the World War II to fight against Nazi Germany. He was a man of great physical courage, who had integrity and was patently honest. He believed strongly in civil liberties and was active in the End Conscription Campaign and the Civil Rights League. He enjoyed talking and was too polite to cut short others who also wished to wax eloquent, especially at the meetings of senate and other committees. As a consequence, the senate meetings were intolerably long and not much to my liking. To sum up his career at the University of Cape Town, one cannot do better than to quote from the *Cape Times* editorial on the announcement of his retirement: 'Sir Richard Luyt carried out the duties of his office with dignity and tolerance, often in difficult and provocative circumstances. On taking leave of the university, he may look back on thirteen years of outstanding service which had its roots in a total commitment to the cause of basic human rights and the preservation of academic freedom. It is greatly to Sir Richard's credit that in a period when the university was often under attack by Government spokesmen – a situation which often smacked of harassment – he stood his ground with timely expositions of the university's right, in any society that laid claim to Western standards, to teach students of its choice in the long tradition of academic freedom. His term of office saw a confrontation between police and students which came to a head with a clash on the steps of St George's Cathedral. He gave invaluable support to the student body and the institution as a whole when the Government seemed determined to subdue a university that had long roused its suspicions of harbouring liberal leftists and the like. Through it all, the principal retained his dignity and his commitment to what he believed was just and fair.'

I considered it a great privilege to have known Sir Richard, who died in February 1994, and to have followed him as vice-chancellor of the university. He was a close personal friend. I will always remember a photograph of him in his retirement, standing in the pouring rain and blustering wind on a street pavement with a placard protesting against conscription and supporting the End Conscription Campaign, the campaign which was vilified and the members of which were actively persecuted by the Nationalist Government.

There is a palm tree in the middle of the quadrangle in Smuts Hall (a men's residence) and another similarly placed in Fuller Hall (a women's residence). The former is higher than the latter allegedly because of the tradition at Smuts Hall of urinating at the base of the tree after major social events in the residence. After one of these annual formal dinners the men of Smuts Hall went to Fuller Hall and carried out the ceremony there. In my capacity as chairman of the residences committee I was phoned by a very annoyed medical colleague from Natal, whose distraught daughter had witnessed the event together with many other young women. A few days later I assembled the whole of Smuts Hall in the senate room. It was very crowded and they had to sit on the floor. They were each given two charges in writing. Charge 1: entering Fuller Hall and urinating at the base of the palm tree; charge 2: entering Fuller Hall and watching others urinating at the base of the palm tree. As I asked each student in turn, they nearly all pleaded guilty to charge 1 – after all, their honour was at stake! Near the end a young man said he did not know how to plead. 'Why not?' I asked. 'Because I tried but could not,' was the reply. I managed to remain serious and found him guilty of charge 2. There was some smothered student laughter. Their total fine was

R1500. They did not do that again.

The post of vice-chancellor was advertised in May 1979. In the months before this happened there had been a great deal of speculation inside and outside of the university as to who would succeed Sir Richard Luyt, but this intensified after the post was advertised. Jack de Wet, the ebullient and influential dean of science, had spoken to me on a number of occasions about my putting my name forward and became more insistent in his request. Sir Richard had encouraged me to do so. Others approached me. My great friend Robin Irvine,* then vice-chancellor of the University of Otago in New Zealand, and his wife Bunty, broke their journey to Europe and came to Cape Town to talk to me about it. We had an on-going correspondence and I had mentioned the pressure being put on me. I was very reluctant to leave my chosen profession of medicine and my teaching and research. I drove Robin and Bunty to Hermanus (about one and a half hour's drive from Cape Town) to see an old friend of theirs and on the way there and back they spoke at length about their experiences while Robin was vice-chancellor and urged me to put my hat in the ring. Robin had had a long session with Sir Richard the day before. Noreen believed I would miss medicine and my work in the medical school too much, but said she would accept any decision I made. I remained reluctant until I heard some of the names being bandied about (none were amongst the final candidates) and I was arrogant enough to feel that the university meant too much to me and that I identified too much with its liberal ethos and its opposition to racism to allow any of these candidates to be selected without my name being considered. This view was strengthened when Frederik van Zyl Slabbert, whose name had been mentioned in the press and who was active in politics, was clearly not going to be a candidate. He had been my choice. So in the end I put in an application.

A notice was sent to all members of senate on 31 August 1979, indicating that the full list of names before the selection/search committee had been available in the vice-chancellor's office for scrutiny by members of senate for two weeks and that the committee intended submitting a short list of candidates to senate on 11 September. The short list of four candidates was included in the notice and senate members were told that ten members of senate could together request the addition of names to the list. Accordingly ten senior members of the medical faculty requested that a fifth name be added. Senate voted by secret ballot to indicate its support for each candidate and four names (including my own and that of the 'added' person) were

---

* Robin died in 1996.

short-listed to be interviewed by the selection committee, which was chaired by Len Abrahamse and consisted of seven members of council and seven of senate. I did not know why my medical colleagues did this and to this day remain uncertain. Either they thought I was unsuitable to be the vice-chancellor or they did not want me to leave the medical school! I like to feel it was the latter and I feel it was possibly so because Professor Jannie Louw, the first signatory of the ten making the request, had protested to Len Abrahamse that I should remain professor of medicine as I was needed in the medical school, but who can be sure? I have never asked.

The short-listed candidates were interviewed. It was the first and last interview for a post I have had and only one of the questions posed remains with me. Professor Francis Wilson, the economist, asked me if anything the students did was likely to surprise me. My reply was that as a teacher and as a warden of residences for many years I thought that I had experienced just about everything students could do! Little did I know how wrong I was.

In the event I was appointed in November 1979 by a unanimous decision of the university council on the recommendation of the selection committee. I had always identified with UCT and the values for which it stood. It was the most important reason for my staying in South Africa despite my rejection of the South African way of life at the time, and I was determined to try to live up to the examples set by Davie and Luyt in their rejection of apartheid. I believed that education held the key to South Africa's success – I still hold that view – and that it was vital to ensure that black South Africans were able to get an education of quality. That was not only just but also important for the future of the country, particularly when apartheid went. I did not think I would live to see that happen but realised the importance of UCT's role in preparing for that day. I firmly believed that the shared experiences of young people from different backgrounds and cultural experiences would increase understanding and tolerance and help to ensure a peaceful future for South Africa. I was determined to eliminate racism from UCT and, to the extent that I could do so, to work towards the removal of apartheid from South Africa. I would try to challenge Government policy wherever I could do so.

I felt it was important for the university council to have the opportunity to review my appointment long before the usual retirement age of 65 years because I was only 48 years old. Accordingly, at my request, I was appointed for a five-year period from 1 January 1981 at the end of which time both the council and I would review the position. This occurred twice and I remained in office until 1996 when I reached the age of 65. My letter of appointment included, inter alia, the following 'further conditions':

(a) You will be required to exercise general supervision over the university, subject to such guidelines and regulations as may be framed by the university council.
(b) You will be ex officio vice-chancellor of the university and, in the absence of the chancellor, you will exercise the powers and perform the duties appertaining to the chancellor's office as prescribed in the university statutes.
(c) You will remain a member of the university council, be chairman and chief executive officer of the university senate and an ex officio member of all standing committees and boards of faculties of the senate.
(d) You will become a member of the committee of university principals which, as you know, is a statutory body comprised of the principals of the South African universities subsidised through the department of national education.
(e) As principal, you will be the recognised representative of the university at all public and social functions and will be required to act on behalf of the university in dispensing hospitality when it is necessary to do so on such occasions.
(f) As principal, you will have a special responsibility for maintaining a standard of conduct and discipline, questions of academic policy and the smooth administration of the university and its residences, and its management.

Quite an overwhelming set of conditions!

I had been professor of medicine for ten years and the question arose as to what title I should use. Professor Falconer, the first professor of medicine who had also become vice-chancellor, relinquished the title of professor and Tom Davie had used the title of doctor as had Beattie before he was knighted, and Sir Richard by virtue of his knighthood had no decision to make. I elected to use the title of Doctor. The registrar confirmed that in the past the university appeared to have favoured this practice and the council agreed. This decision caused great consternation amongst some of my colleagues who occupied similar positions at other South African universities. With one exception, they used the title of professor and some had acquired that title only on appointment to the post. They could not understand why I did not want the 'honour' of being a professor. When they asked me I said that I professed nothing! Titles had never been important to me, nor had the other trappings of office. It seemed to me that what one did was important, not what one was called. A vice-chancellor has a great deal of power, but only as much power as he or she can achieve through actions which result in him/her getting the confidence of the various sections of the university. I made it clear that if at any time I felt I had lost the confidence of council or senate, I would resign. I asked and was granted the right to return to the department of medicine as a full professor of medicine without any administrative duties should I stand down before my sixty-fifth birthday.

In the period between my appointment and my taking office on 1 January

1981, I continued to act as deputy principal (planning) and played an active role in academic and physical planning in the university. Sir Richard Luyt discussed any issue with me which required a decision and which would impact on the university in 1981 and beyond. The South African military had approached him asking for the reinstatement of the University of Cape Town regiment as part of the compulsory service which young white males in South Africa had to undertake when they left school. As a result, two senior military officers came to see me in my office. It was pointed out to them that the University of Cape Town regiment had been a volunteer organisation during World War II and had acted with distinction. The university community as a whole was opposed to conscription as was the present vice-chancellor Sir Richard Luyt, and I, the incoming vice-chancellor. It would be abhorrent if students conscripted into the University of Cape Town regiment were asked to defend apartheid in any way, and in particular if they were asked to act against fellow citizens within South Africa. The senior military officers said that it was inconceivable that the South African army would act against fellow citizens within South Africa. (The events of the 1980s were to prove me correct in my fears.) I said to them that the university could consider re-establishing the University of Cape Town regiment if it was a voluntary organisation which would have nothing to do with conscription, but that the issue of a voluntary regiment would have to be put to the university as a whole. The senior officers were enthusiastic about the possibility of a voluntary organisation, but subsequently wrote to say that that would be impossible. The matter simply fell away.

I visited universities in the United Kingdom in May 1980 and in the United States in October. The visit to the United States was arranged by Mr Alan Pifer, then president of the Carnegie Corporation. As in the UK, discussions were held with colleagues about the problems facing universities in the '80s, but particular attention was paid to academic support programmes for poorly prepared students. It was just before I was leaving to visit the United States that the issue concerning the death of Steve Biko in detention came to a head for me personally.

I had met Steve Biko at the conference held at UCT under the auspices of the Abe Bailey Institute for Interracial Studies (now the Centre for Conflict Resolution) in 1970 and I had been impressed by his eloquence and his obvious qualities of leadership. Steve Biko died after sustaining severe head injuries while being detained at police headquarters in Port Elizabeth in September 1977. He had been examined repeatedly by district surgeons but the medical certificate, written at the request of the security police, was falsified, as was the medical record. The clinical examination and laboratory tests showed that he had suffered severe brain injury, but the doctors accepted the police refusal to transfer him to a hospital. In the end Biko was transferred in the back of a landrover to Pretoria, 750 kilometres by road, and it was shortly after he arrived in Pretoria that he died.

At the inquest the magistrate found that there was a prima facie case of professional misconduct and/or negligence against the district surgeons treating Biko, but the sub-committee of the South African Medical and Dental Council took no action, a decision which was ratified by the full council. I had been appalled by that decision. The Medical Association of South Africa declared that the South African Medical and Dental Council had been correct in its findings, and the executive committee of the federal council of the Medical Association of South Africa published its conclusions in an article in the *South African Medical Journal* on 13 September 1980. I read the record of the inquest several times and was equally appalled by the decision of the Medical Association of South Africa. I was deeply ashamed of its attitude towards what I saw as a gross violation of human rights and what amounted to murder on the part of the police, an action which was being covered up by the medical profession. Having read the article in the *Medical Journal* very carefully, I came to the conclusion that there were serious inconsistencies in their statement, which underlined the fact that the record was not a true reflection of the events.

On the Saturday morning I went to see Richard Luyt at his official residence, Glenara, and gave him the article by the executive committee of the federal council of the Medical Association of South Africa, asking him to read it. I said that I would not comment until he had read it. He also came to the conclusion that what was written contained serious inconsistencies. He then told me of his experience when he was the Governor of British Guiana. The country was in a state of revolution and a state of emergency had been declared. There were Royal Naval warships in the harbour and a senior superintendent had been sent out from Scotland Yard to be in charge of the police and of all security. The situation was very tense. A certain individual was taken to the jail and beaten up after explosives had been found under his bed. They threw him into a cell and fired tear gas at him. When they came back, he was dead. The superintendent of police was sent for, and he in turn called for the doctor who was in charge of the military hospital. The two of them arranged for the corpse to be taken to the military hospital and they alleged that he had died in the hospital. Luyt insisted on a full inquiry, and the facts emerged. He fired the superintendent of police and the doctor, and all those concerned with the matter were disciplined. The superintendent of police was a very efficient and able man, and was indispensable to Luyt at the time of the state of emergency, but despite this, he fired him. Sir Richard went on to say that if one did not deal properly with illegal acts performed by the police or other security forces, then all is lost. It was plain to us both that this was exactly what was happening in South Africa.

I went home and wrote a letter to the editor of the *South African Medical Journal* indicating in it that I was resigning from the Medical Association of South Africa as a protest against its failure to condemn the South African Medical and Dental Council's attitude towards the district surgeons who were in attendance on Steve Biko at the time of his death, and shortly before it. I was particularly annoyed that the executive committee of the Medical Association had endorsed the decision of the ethical committee of the local association branch in Port Elizabeth, that 'Having scrutinised the court records carefully, the committee has come to the unanimous conclusion that a charge of unethical conduct against the doctors responsible for Steve Biko's care during his detention prior to his death, should not be sustained, and in the circumstances advise that the matter now be closed.' A month earlier, on 16 August 1980, Professor J N de Klerk, who was chairman of the federal council of the Medical Association, wrote an editorial for the *South African Medical Journal* (which did not carry his name) in which the South African Medical and Dental Council's decision not to discipline the doctors concerned was fully endorsed, and the editorial concluded by stating that, 'Much harm can be done to the profession ... in this country if we do not temper our concern (regarding the Steve Biko case) with a modicum of unemotional savvy.'

My letter to the *Medical Journal* was not published nor were many others which were critical of the association's actions. I recently learned the following. The secretary general of the Medical Association of South Africa wrote to the assistant editor of the journal on 22 September saying, 'Thank you very much for your letter of 10 September 1980 with attachments of letters you have received in respect of the Biko case. With regard to the Biko letters it has been agreed, as far as I am aware, that all correspondence concerning this matter, following the publication of the executive committee's declaration as well as the chairman of the federal council's letter, closes the matter.'

The Biko letters kept coming and Dr Turner, the assistant editor, was put in an impossible position, particularly with regard to a Dr J J Isenberg who wrote repeatedly. Turner wrote to Professor de Klerk, the chairman of the federal council, saying, 'I received the enclosed letter from Dr J J Isenberg. I have already returned two of his letters and have told him that they are no longer relevant. Now he writes again. Must I publish it?' On another occasion, Dr Turner wrote, 'Here is another Biko letter. I don't like the insinuations in it, what do you think?' In his answer, the secretary general gave the true reasons for their attitude. 'We cannot allow the *South African Medical*

Journal to become a political platform for attacks on the Government, the Medical Council, and least of all the Medical Association – this is what Professor Saunders and Dr Isenberg are determined to do.'*

The Truth and Reconciliation Commission meeting in mid-1997 reviewed the events leading to Steve Biko's death and the present editor of the *Journal*, Professor Daniel Ncayiyana, published part of my previously unpublished letter on the front page of the journal together with Dr Marais Viljoen's unpublished reactions. I reproduce my letter here:

The Editor, South African Medical Journal.

Dear Sir, I refer to the statement by the executive committee of the Federal Council, MASA, regarding the conduct of the doctors responsible for the treatment of the late Mr S B Biko which appeared in the journal on 13 September 1980. Having read the official record of the evidence given at the inquest of the late Mr Biko with great care, I am forced to the conclusion that I can no longer belong to an association which has a regional and federal ethical committee and an executive committee which have come to the conclusions recorded in the above-mentioned statement. A full public enquiry is necessary before such conclusions can be reached. I have accordingly resigned from the Medical Association of South Africa. I invite all members of MASA to study the official record of the inquest and to decide for themselves whether they, too, wish to resign from MASA. I would like to ask the executive committee two questions:

1. *Does the committee believe that a medical practitioner should be influenced by factors other than the care of the patient and his or her well-being in deciding on where he or she should be treated? For example, does the committee believe that a police officer can make that decision and that the doctor should acquiesce?*
2. *Does the executive committee believe that it is proper for a severely ill patient to be transported without any medical (or nursing) supervision over hundreds of kilometres in the back of a land rover under any circumstances? Would its view on this question be influenced by the fact that a neurosurgeon advised that a particular patient should be carefully observed, and yet such transportation occurred?*

With regard to the decisions of MASA I note that the 'court records' were scrutinised – this is the same information to which I have previously referred. Clearly the decisions were not influenced by additional information.

May I also comment on Professor J N de Klerk's letter in the journal of the same date. Could the chairman of federal council explain what he means by 'taking into consideration the particular circumstances surrounding this whole matter' in the sixth paragraph of his letter? Are there considerations other than the patient's wel-

---

* This correspondence was first published in the *SA Medical Journal* in mid-1997.

fare which Professor de Klerk is asking us to take into consideration? Some clarity is needed here. Finally, does he really believe (exclamation mark and all) that medical ethics belong with the medical profession 'and nowhere else'?/ Does society as a whole have no interest in and concern for our ethical standards? Patients have every right to judge our ethics and to be fully informed.

The ethical issues raised by Mr Biko's death go much further than the immediate tragedy – the whole question of society's trust in and regard for our profession is at stake.
Yours sincerely
(signed) Stuart J Saunders
Vice-chancellor and Principal elect, UCT Professor and Head of the Department of Medicine

The Medical Association issued a long statement in 1997, part of which is also published in the May 1997 issue of the journal, apologising for the actions of the Association in the 1970s. The journal also contained a number of other letters from South African doctors which the editor had refused to publish at the time.

I was deeply ashamed by the attitudes of the medical profession in South Africa as expressed by the decisions of the South African Medical and Dental Council and the Medical Association of South Africa. I knew that my action would receive a lot of prominence and indeed it made newspaper headlines. Reporters had been in touch with me and I told them of my decision to resign. I was not in the country when that happened, having left shortly after writing the letter to visit universities in the United States. During the flight I asked myself whether my actions had been motivated purely by my repulsion with regard to what had happened to Steve Biko, or whether my actions, knowing that they would receive publicity, were in any way motivated by personal political or other less admirable motives. I came to the conclusion that I was acting entirely because I was so ashamed of my profession and of my country.

I felt very isolated. I was leaving the medical school to become the vice-chancellor of the University of Cape Town. I had first entered the medical school as an undergraduate in 1948, had been a lecturer, professor of medicine and head of the department of medicine, and head of the division of medicine for ten years. I had spent my entire adult life, up until that moment, working in the medical profession. I knew many members of the profession throughout the country. I had played a prominent role in the College of Medicine of South Africa. I was now not only leaving the profession to become the vice-chancellor, but I had resigned from the association which joined the profession together and I had expressed my contempt for the actions of senior members of the profession. Despite this feeling of isolation, I was convinced I was doing what I had to do.

On my return from overseas considerable pressure was put upon me to reverse my position and to be more 'understanding' of the complexities of these issues. I remember one morning going into the staff toilet in the medical school where I was joined, somewhat to my surprise, by three senior professors. To have four senior professors passing urine at the same time was not a common event in the medical school, but it became clear that they had taken the opportunity, on seeing me enter the toilet, to tackle me on the issue of Steve Biko. They were polite, friendly and collegial, but made it clear they thought I was rocking the boat unnecessarily. I made it clear that I was unimpressed by what they were saying to me.

After I became vice-chancellor, the chairman of the federal council, Professor de Klerk, and Dr Norman Levy, an office bearer in the Medical Association, tried to persuade me to rejoin the Medical Association. They told me that a prominent member of the department of medicine at the University of Cape Town had examined the record of the inquest very carefully, and had come to the conclusion that no blame could be attributed to Dr Tucker and Dr Lang, the two doctors concerned. I was not convinced by their arguments and unimpressed by my colleague's analysis and I refused to re-join the Medical Association.*

Professor Frances Ames, head of UCT's department of neurology, also resigned from MASA. She continued to press for disciplinary action against the doctors involved and decided to challenge the South African Medical and Dental Council in the courts. There was considerable doubt as to whether the courts had jurisdiction in the matter in terms of the law and some lawyers believed the action would be rejected out of hand. The costs would be daunting. I indicated to Frances that I did not have the financial resources to take the South African Medical and Dental Council to court. She told me she was prepared to mortgage her house to do so. She is a widow and has four sons, who were quite young at the time. I decided I could not take that step and so she and three others proceeded without me. They won the case without incurring financial penalty. The Medical Council was forced to hold a disciplinary hearing six and a half years after Biko's death and pay the costs of the applicants. I greatly admired the financial risk Frances Ames was prepared to take on as a matter of principle. Very few people show that commitment. I am not as brave as Frances. The Medical Council found Dr Lang guilty of improper conduct and he was cautioned and reprimanded. Dr Tucker was found guilty of disgraceful and improper

---

* I joined the new SA Medical Association in 1998.

conduct. The evidence given to the Truth and Reconciliation Commission has confirmed the brutal torturing of Biko. Professor Peter Folb played a leading role in the protests around Steve Biko's death.

Dr Mamphela Ramphele, who was closely associated with Steve Biko, had been arrested and banished to a remote area of the Transvaal shortly before he was killed. In her autobiography *A Life* she gives a very moving account of these events. She was to succeed me as vice-chancellor of the University of Cape Town.

Not a rose garden
1981

On 5 January 1981 I sat behind the vice-chancellor and principal's desk for the first time. On the desk was an envelope with my name on it. Inside was a letter dated 4 January 1981. It was from Sir Richard to me and read:

> Dear Stuart
> Welcome to this seat and may you and the university prosper throughout your occupancy of it!
> Best wishes,
> Yours sincerely,
> Dick

It is only when one sits behind the desk of the vice-chancellor and principal of a university, and especially one in the political environment of South Africa in 1981, that the full impact of the responsibilities involved is driven home. There is a world of difference between being a deputy vice-chancellor and deputy principal and being in the hot seat. I was aware that the buck stopped with me and that I would have to take the critical decisions affecting the university and take responsibility for them. Frankly I was not at all confident that I had the qualities which would make me equal to the task.

The first month in office was quiet enough. The undergraduate and many of the postgraduate students were on vacation as were many of the staff, January being the middle of summer in South Africa. It is the only month of the year when the university council does not meet. The council is the highest decision-making body in the university and sets policy except for academic matters, which are the concern of the university senate.

I introduced a weekly meeting with the acting deputy principal, Professor Donald Carr, and the registrar. We met from 0815 to 1300 one morning a week and I continued that practice until I retired. All deputies and the registrar (chief administrative officer) attended these meetings and later, when a post of academic secretary (and effectively senior deputy registrar) was created, the incumbent also attended, as did my personal aides. All matters of import were fully discussed and we usually reached consensus. If there was disagreement I had to make the final decision, and all my colleagues always supported me. My standing instructions were that if any of them thought that I was about to make a fool of myself they should say so, and they often did! Many a time I was saved from taking the wrong decision. I could not have done my job without the loyal and whole-hearted support of my colleagues. I referred to these meetings as 'Monty Python' after the British comedy series, which I had heard about but strangely had never seen! After seeing a Monty Python programme I did not change the name. Everyone else insisted on calling it 'top executives' or, later, 'executive management meeting', but I consistently referred to it as Monty Python. One of my colleagues told me I was being flippant by calling it Monty Python, but I let that ride and admit to enjoying the continued use of that title for our Friday morning meetings.

When Richard Luyt had asked Donald to be an acting assistant principal Donald had declined because he wanted to continue as professor of chemical engineering. I suggested to Sir Richard that I approach him and Donald then agreed on condition that he could continue his research. Sir Richard agreed, and it was settled. I told Len Abrahamse that I wanted to abolish the posts of assistant principal and wanted the executive officers to be titled deputy vice-chancellors and deputy principals. I wanted Donald to be one of the two deputies. He was an energetic, intelligent and committed academic with considerable administrative skills. John Reid, the professor of physiology at the University of Natal, was my choice for the second deputy position. With Len's agreement I phoned John, who said before he could consider the offer he had to be sure that we shared the same ideals for the university and for South Africa. He flew to Cape Town, we talked and found ourselves to be kindred spirits, and he agreed to his name going forward. Early in the year a selection committee met and endorsed my recommendations, and council agreed to both appointments. John, a deeply religious man, had been a Rhodes scholar and was the first to describe the 'floppy valve syndrome' which affects the mitral valve of the heart. A lateral thinker of great integrity, he and Donald were superb deputies and complemented each other well; they have remained firm friends to this day. I do not believe that it is wise for a university to appoint deputy principals against the wishes of the vice-chancellor and principal, and that the latter should have the major say in identifying the candidates. When other systems are used, harmony and good management are less likely to result. Len Abrahamse shared this view. But the actual appointments came about a little later.

I met with Sarah Cullinan, the president of the students representative council. She was a slight young woman who impressed me greatly with her grip on university matters and on national politics. She proved to be an outstanding student leader, showing courage and good judgment. Student leaders were harassed by the security police and they did not spare her, or her successors, despite my protestations. Tragically she died young in a motor car accident.

I arranged to meet with the registrar (chief administrative officer) Mr Len Read and with other university officials. At each meeting I stressed my determination that UCT would be a first-rate teaching and research institution, that we had responsibilities to the community around us and to the nation, and that we would be implacably opposed to racial and any other form of discrimination. They all supported me fully. In time I realised how lucky I was to have Len Read as my first registrar. He had wide experience of university affairs and a deep knowledge of all aspects of the administration. He was a tireless worker and lived and breathed the university. No one was more loyal or more committed. Len Read was the head of the administration and was responsible to me. I did not interfere in his or his successors' affairs but in matters where I was concerned he always carried out my decisions to the full, even if he disagreed.

Danie Fourie, who was a long-time member of staff and held the title of Principal's Liaison Officer, brought a police colonel and lieutenant to meet me. They were anxious to improve relations with the university. I told them that they would have no trouble with me if they stuck to conventional policing, if they acted as 'peace officers' and not as secret agents. If they or the security police interfered in the affairs of the university or with our staff or students, I would have no truck with them and I would make their actions and my reaction to them public. They assured me that the police would only act if the need arose, but I did not believe that they would change their ways, and I was right. Danie was a Mr Fixit and worked hard to help students in trouble. I was concerned about his membership of the police reserve, where he held commissioned rank, because of the unacceptable actions of sections of the police at the time, but I did not ever have reason to believe that he acted against any member of the university. He retired in 1984.

I met with the committee of the workers' association to discuss their problems. This was before the time of unionisation in South Africa and their relationship with the university management was a consultative one. I believe in strong unions and am of the view that they result in better labour relations, so I welcomed the unionisation of the workers when it occurred in later years. I am not happy about the unionisation of academic staff as that changes the relationship between them and the executive and, of course, many of them play an active role in management. Fortunately the academic staff have retained their collegial relationship with management and have not unionised.

I opened conferences and went to cocktail parties – the latter being a less desirable part of a vice-chancellor's duties. One thing soon became very clear to me. When I was professor of medicine no one, not even members of my own profession, would attack my professional competence or claim to know more about my area of expertise than I did (although it may well have been the case on some occasions) but as vice-chancellor I was fair game. Many claimed to know what was best for the university much better than I did and claimed to be experts in higher education. Criticism became the name of the game!

Noreen, John, Jane and I moved into Glenara, the official home on the campus of the vice-chancellor. In terms of my contract I was required to live there as had my predecessors. Glenara, a tall Victorian house, set in large grounds, was built in 1882 and is a national monument.* The university bought Glenara for £8 500 in 1924 and Sir Carruthers Beattie, the first vice-chancellor, moved there in January 1925. His antique desk remains in the study and working at it underlines one's responsibilities yet again! Dr Falconer, who succeeded Beattie, and had also been professor of medicine at UCT, had a lily pond built in the garden, which leaked from the outset. As a consequence it was called Falconer's Folly, or so Richard Luyt told me. I thought that if that was the only folly committed by him as vice-chancellor, he had been luckier than I was likely to be. The bulk of the furnishing in the house was the responsibility of the incoming vice-chancellor. We bought quite a lot of furniture from the Luyts, and there was some university-owned furniture, but it was no mean matter to furnish a house with large reception and dining rooms, a study, a second large downstairs sitting room and five substantial bedrooms. The wall space posed a particular challenge. Fortunately I was able to get some fine paintings on loan from the university's Irma Stern museum – Irma Stern is known as one of South Africa's greatest artists and a powerful expressionist. We had no horses or cows (Beattie had had a milk cow) but we did have two golden labradors much beloved by the whole family, especially by my daughter Jane.

Jane was in high school and John at Abbots College, trying to improve his school-leaving marks to get into medical school, which he had failed to do. Some have expressed surprise that my son could not get into our medical

---

* The house stands on land which was once part of the earliest formal farms at the Cape – de Hollandsche Tuin, granted in 1657 by Jan van Riebeeck, the first Dutch governor of the Cape. Over the years there were subdivisions and in 1881 part of the resulting Zorgvliet estate was sold to a Cape Town merchant, one L A Vincent. The house was designed by the architect A.W. Ackerman, who had been responsible for the old Cape Town railway station. The contract price was £6000. In 1898, after Vincent's death, the property was sold to Stephen Trill with its vineyards and orchards and paddocks for horses and cows, stretching down to the Main Road.

school, but I have never believed that one should 'pull strings' for one's children and John certainly did not want me to do so. It underlined the fact that our admission procedures were fair and it turned out to be a trump card down the years for the deans of medicine and for me in dealing with irate parents whose children had failed to gain admission. On one occasion I was asked to go to a leading business in Johannesburg to receive a cheque on behalf of the university. I had drinks with the directors while we waited for the chief executive to join us. He was one Wim de Villiers, known to be a tough and unpleasant customer who later became a Nationalist Cabinet Minister. I knew he would be unhappy about his colleagues' decision to support UCT, because of its open opposition to apartheid, but I was rather surprised when he entered the room and said to me in a very aggressive manner, 'If I had my way I would not give you a penny!' 'Why?' I asked. 'Because you did not admit my daughter to your medical school.' (She had gained admission to an Afrikaans medical school.) I replied, 'Join the club. My son did not gain admission either.' He was completely deflated.

John then did achieve the marks needed to gain admission to the medical school but decided he wanted to do a business degree instead! It was the right decision as he is a real entrepreneur. When John left school, while waiting to enter university he helped at a fast food outlet at the popular Muizenberg beach and employed his friends to help him. As a school choirboy he went on a tour of Botswana. He saw an assegai he wanted in a shop and told the shopkeeper he did not have enough money but that he would sing for him if he would give him the assegai. The bemused shopkeeper consented and I still have the assegai in safe-keeping for him. After emigrating to the United States, to avoid being conscripted into the South African army to fight to defend apartheid, he worked for an accounting firm, then for Unilever and now has his own successful business in California.

Jane gained admission to the medical school, and qualified well. After a stint with her classmate husband Brendan O'Malley at the Cecilia Makiwane hospital in the Ciskei, both worked in Canada in a remote part of the prairies. She is now a psychiatrist in the UCT department of psychiatry. Brendan has obtained the FCP, the qualification needed to be a physician (internist). Both are very accomplished young doctors, she winning the gold medal for the first part and second part of her psychiatry examination, the first person to do so. I get great pleasure from knowing all three of them and having them as my friends.

At the end of January I went to Port Elizabeth, to my first Committee of University Principals (CUP) meeting as vice-chancellor. I had attended some meetings with Sir Richard when I was deputy principal (planning). The Afrikaans vice-chancellors (who had the title of rector as well) were in the majority and I believed most, if not all of them, were members of the Broederbond. The Broederbond was founded as an Afrikaner self-help organisation, but became a sinister force in South Africa when secrecy was combined with power. It aimed at ensuring Afrikaner dominance in all walks of South African life and did so successfully. Members had clearly caucused before the CUP meetings and the liberal English-speaking vice-chancellors were unable to make much headway in removing any of the restrictions of racism in higher education. The Afrikaans vice-chancellors blocked any discussion of the higher education of blacks, because they said it did not fall within our jurisdiction in terms of the law.

In the plane travelling back to Cape Town I sat next to the registrar, Len Read. I told him I would open our residences to all students irrespective of race, in defiance of the Group Areas Act, and that I wanted it to happen in the same year, 1981. A few days later he came to me and said that the university official in charge of the student residences was afraid to carry out my instruction because he feared that he would be prosecuted in the courts. I wrote out an instruction ordering the official to integrate the residences, taking clear responsibility for the decision. It was the only time as vice-chancellor that I was forced to give a written instruction to an official. Consequently, a handful of black and Asian students were admitted to the residences that year. There were no problems amongst the students and it all went off very quietly. Len Read said that if I was prosecuted he would seek to be prosecuted with me. That was a measure of his commitment and support.

Just before I took office, a friend who had recently retired from Syfrets (a finance house in Cape Town where Len Abrahamse was chairman) told me that Len had a very strong personality and would try to dominate me. (He was quite wrong about that. Len was an enormous support to me and never acted improperly.) Perhaps because of this advice I decided not to tell him (or anybody else on the university council) what I was doing in regard to the residences. I wanted them all to know what I thought my role as executive officer was. A few weeks later I informed Len of what I had done. He looked at me quizzically and said, 'Good.' In due course the council was told and gave its support. Ten months later I had the Minister of National Education, Dr Gerrit Viljoen, to lunch at Glenara, Len Abrahamse being the only other guest. Viljoen had previously been vice-chancellor and rector of the Rand Afrikaans University. A classical scholar, he was usually among the few more enlightened (*verligte*) members of the Government. I spoke of the difficulty black students had in getting adequate accommodation. If they had to live in the poor African townships they studied under overcrowded, intolerable conditions and commuted long distances. Viljoen said that children of diplomats could be admitted to residences irrespective of race, as a result of new regulations.* I replied that I knew that and, quite deadpan, added that of course we also admitted the children of blacks who were not diplomats. He glanced at me, got the message, and said nothing. The Government obviously had their informers and knew what we were doing but over the years as we steadily increased the numbers of black students in the residences in defiance of the law, they took no action against us. I think they were aware what an almighty row it would cause and no one was complaining in the residences. From our point of view it had been a great success as we knew it would be. The benefits for the black students were enormous and, as the years went by, making sure we acquired more and more accommodation for them became a top priority.

Dr James Moulder joined me at the beginning of February as my special assistant. His major assignment was to deal with the particular problems experienced by black students, including financial, housing and academic difficulties. He showed real initiative in finding accommodation for these students and in trying to find solutions to their problems with transport, particularly if they were living a long way from the campus. James is a philosopher and had taught in both South African and Australian universities. He was wise and thoughtful and capable of working very hard. He had been persecuted by the Government in an earlier career when he was a minister of religion. He played an important role in raising funds for black students, both for their academic fees and their residence costs (this became a recurring major problem), in finding them accommodation off campus if we did not have space for them, and helping in many other ways. He joined the Monty Python show. In all my dealings with the deputies, the registrar and with my personal assistants, I put everything on the table. Only information entrusted to me as strictly confidential by someone else was not revealed, but there were no other secrets. James responded well to this environment and we had a good working relationship.

As time went by I was being repeatedly questioned by reporters on various contentious issues. I had resolved never to say anything which was not true, but of course there were some questions I preferred not to answer. James told me to read *A Man for all Seasons*, which I did, and then applied Thomas Moore's techniques with great success with the press when it was

---

* A small number of black students had gained admission under special circumstances. Indeed the first request was from Kaizer Matanzima, the 'president' of the 'independent' Transkei. The Minister, M C Botha, instructed his deputy Dr Treurnicht to sign the special permission, which he did with great reluctance: Botha was concerned about the success of the 'homelands' policy, Treurnicht was an arch disciple of segregation. Young Matanzima decided that a university residence was not good enough for him and he moved into accommodation usually reserved for diplomats!

needed. I learned how to avoid giving a direct answer in a tricky situation by substituting one truth for another, which was close enough to escape accusations, but greatly frustrated reporters set on sensationalism. My task was made easier by the dearth of good reporters in South Africa at the time. Many promising young journalists left the country, frustrated by the all-pervading censorship. Some were restricted by the Government. James Moulder later became head of UCT public affairs. He left to take up a chair of philosophy in the University of Natal: we found ourselves in disagreement about educational issues at times in the future.

William Duncan Baxter had left R553 866 to UCT in 1960 to establish a university theatre. Additional funds were obtained from the Department of National Education because the theatre was to be used by the university's drama department, college of music and ballet school. After some delays, the theatre was built in the grounds of Glenara. Under John Slemon's management it became a successful commercial and university theatre, although it did cause concern from time to time as theatres do often run at a loss and additional funds had to be injected. UCT was greatly helped in this regard by contributions to the Baxter Fund, which was spearheaded by Mr Hans Middelmann. He had come to South Africa from Germany after Hitler's rise to power: he could not stomach fascism or anti-semitism. He became a very successful business man and served on the university council for almost 19 years. Committed to an 'open society', he is a liberal and a remarkable man. A liberal democracy with an open society is no high-falutin theory; like all political systems it has its defects, but other paths are much more treacherous and often unjust. I often looked to Hans for guidance and support and greatly valued his advice. He told me after I had retired that when I was appointed (he served on the selection committee) he was not sure that I was a good choice – which surprised me, because at the time I had thought that Hans was an ardent supporter of mine! He generously made it clear that he thought that his fears had been unnecessary. As vice-chancellor I was a member of the Baxter board and so I attended my first of many meetings and learnt a great deal about the vagaries of theatre life. From the outset the Baxter Theatre was open to all races. There were very few such venues in the country. John Slemon, the Irish theatre manager, is a flamboyant extrovert. Outspoken, forthright and very protective of the theatre complex, he was largely responsible for its great success.

I hosted a cocktail party for the sport administrators of Bophuthatswana, one of the so-called independent states created under the homelands policy. These independent homelands were supposed to meet the political aspirations of black South Africans who would then be foreigners in 'white' South Africa! At the cocktail party, to my astonishment and considerable amusement, I was presented with a gold medal for sport! I spoke at the sportsman-of-the-year dinner on one occasion and told the somewhat surprised company of robust men and women of my sporting prowess. I hold the record for the slowest mile at the Sea Point track (it is conceivably a world record) achieved as a small schoolboy. I took so long to run the mile that I held up the programme for the school's sports day and, in spite of some teachers' efforts, I refused to stop until I had finished. I played in a school rugby team which lost every match it played, until the last one of the season which we won because our teacher was the referee and made us feel ashamed by his gross bias towards us. As a first-year student I was thrown off a golf course because of my ineptitude. The professional who did this to me was admitted to my ward as a patient years later, when I was professor of medicine, and when I reminded him of what had happened, became somewhat nervous! I received a 'blues' blazer for tennis because I had kept a promise as vice-chancellor and built new tennis courts to replace those destroyed by the erection of the education building on the middle campus. I have already referred to my cricketing career. On a more serious note I would agree that one of my failings as vice-chancellor has been the fact that I did little to promote sport at UCT – I had other priorities.

One of the first things I did on taking office was to ask Sheilah Lloyd to arrange for me to meet with every member of staff and student who was banned. South Africans were banned by the Government under the so-called Suppression of Communism Act (later the Internal Security Act) and banning usually included confinement to a magisterial area, denial of the right to meet more than one person at a time, denial of the right to publish, to teach, to enter an educational institution and often included a curfew in the evening and at night. People who had been banned were under constant security police surveillance and had to report to the police regularly. The reasons for banning were not revealed and banning occurred literally at the whim of the Minister, faceless bureaucrats and the security police. This is what had happened to Bill Hoffenberg. Two sisters, Mary Simons and Tanya Barben,* were banned. I went to see Mary in the small flat in which she lived alone in Mowbray, a suburb near to UCT, and I found her to be remarkably resilient, correctly despising the regime which had acted against her in such a despicable manner. She was thrilled with her latest acquisition, a high-fi system, which gave her much pleasure in her many lonely hours. A strong woman, she has been a close friend of Anita, my second wife, since they were students together in residence at Fuller Hall. Anita and I both delight in her friendship today. She is still on the faculty at UCT in the department

---

* Their parents Jack Simons and Ray Alexander had been banned and were in exile in Zambia.

of political studies. Her sister Tanya is a librarian at UCT. She and her husband had a small house in Cape Town and when I saw them they were justifiably upset, because they had just been visited by the security police, who had come to tell Tanya that they knew she had broken her banning order by leaving the magisterial district of Cape Town and that the consequences could be serious. A few days earlier Tanya and her husband Heinz had spontaneously responded to a newspaper advertisement for plants at a nursery in Stellenbosch, 30 miles from Cape Town. Without giving it a thought, they had driven there, bought the plants and returned home. What upset them most was not so much the open threats made by the security police, but the fact that it underlined how close the surveillance of them was. I was outraged.

I met with Laura Levitan, an accomplished student leader, banned, and with Debbie Budlender and Willie Hofmeyr in their little house in Observatory. Both Debbie and Willie had stringent banning orders including prohibitions of communicating with another banned person. This did not stop Willie from successfully proposing marriage to Debbie and, while banned, they got married. What the security police made of this is not known, but they took no action. Both are outstanding South Africans like many others persecuted in this objectionable way. Both are playing an important role in contemporary South Africa. Debbie is a gender researcher for the Community Agency for Social Equity and Willie was an ANC member of parliament.* Their marriage did not survive the strains to which they were exposed. While I was professor of medicine I had petitioned the authorities and had a Progressive Party MP, Dr Marius Barnard, raise in parliament a request for Debbie to be allowed to train as a nurse at GSH despite the banning order. Our efforts were in vain.

Graeme Bloch[†] was the son of a classmate of mine, Cecil Bloch, who became head of UCT's plastic surgery department. Graeme was adamant that I should make no approach to the Government regarding his banning order. He did not believe they had the legitimacy to impose it (he was right) and therefore in his view they should not be given the satisfaction of a direct approach by me. I did approach the Minister of Justice (quaintly titled) and the Minister of National Education and urged for the lifting of the banning orders on UCT staff and students. In deference to his request I did not mention Graeme's name. The banning orders on the people I visited expired towards the end of 1981 and were not reinstated. I have no idea whether my

---

* Willie Hofmeyer is now a special director in the office of the national director of prosecutions.
† Graeme Bloch is studying in London. His wife is Cheryl Carolus, South Africa's High Commissioner to the Court of St James.

representations had any effect.

Noreen and I went to a church service in District Six to mark the forced removal of all people of colour from that suburb near the centre of Cape Town. The Government had declared it a 'white' area in 1966, and any black person living there was forced to move to the new 'townships' on the Cape Flats, a windswept area with sandy soil frequently waterlogged in winter. All the buildings were bulldozed in District Six except for a few churches and mosques, because not even our Nationalist masters dared to desecrate holy ground, and it was in one of these churches that the service was held. The sermon was powerful and very moving.

The last week of February is the time usually set aside for the registration of new and returning students and I faced it with some apprehension. On the Sunday afternoon before the week began I was working in the garden, wearing a rather worn shirt, short khaki trousers and sandals. I was on my knees in the garden soil, digging away, when Kate Philip,* a student leader and member of the SRC (and daughter of David and Marie Philip, the publishers), ran up to me in a state of high agitation. Just below De Waal Drive, the highway which separates the upper and middle campuses, there is a summerhouse which faces a very large lawn. Students had gathered on the lawn to hold an open-air pop concert. Kate told me that neighbours had complained about the noise (not surprisingly) and that the police had arrived saying that the concert had to stop or 'they would break it up'. We ran up the hill to the concert together. I made my way across the lawn through some 2 000 students and reached the 'stage', which was a makeshift structure in front of the summerhouse, and was immediately confronted by a distraught young man who looked as though his clothes had been painted on him. The various bands were grouped closely behind him. 'You must speak to the students,' he insisted. 'There could be a riot.' I took the microphone from him and, realising that if I announced myself as the vice-chancellor I might not get the desired result, I asked the young man to give me the name of a pop star. 'David Bowie,' he replied. I had never heard of him but announced to the crowd, 'I am David Bowie.' There was an explosion of laughter and wild clapping and cheering. When they had quietened down, I said, 'People have complained about the noise and the police want to close this concert down. I want you all to go up to the rugby fields above De Waal Drive and enjoy the concert there. Please help the bands to move the instruments.' Again much clapping and then, without any fuss, everyone trooped up to the rugby fields where they enjoyed the concert. David Bowie did not perform. I must have looked a mess with mud all over my knees, but that

---

* Kate Philip is the chief executive officer of the Mineworkers' Development Agency.

was my introduction to the student body as their new vice-chancellor! The *Cape Times* carried a cartoon the next day which portrayed me speaking to woolly-haired members of the police riot squad, with musical instruments in their hands. The caption read, 'I can't promise you a rose garden, but if you'd like to play your instruments on Devil's Peak ... preferably the upper slopes,' alluding to the rose garden which used to be in front of the summer house and to the fact that Devil's Peak towers above the university.

The noise made by students can be a problem in all universities, especially if they are near residential areas. While members of the public can show great tolerance, the decibels can reach levels which are quite unacceptable, especially if the wind is in the wrong direction. Complaints about our students in this regard were often justified and we introduced rules to try and contain the problem. Citizens are more tolerant if there is goodwill towards the students, but some of our neighbours were very critical of me, of UCT and especially of our students, whom they saw as political troublemakers, and they called the university 'Moscow on the Hill.' The threshold for annoyance is very low amongst such folk. Answering the phone between one and two o'clock in the morning, only to be harangued for not disciplining students, became part of my life.

'I can't promise you a rose garden, but if you'd care to play your instruments on Devil's Peak ... preferably the upper slopes.' (Cartoon by Grogan, 1981)

Scholarship and not ethnicity
1981 (continued)

The Rag committee (a committee of students) raised money for the Students' Health and Welfare Organisation (SHAWCO), which is the biggest and most complex enterprise run for charity by students in the world. These enterprising students organise sporting events – road running and horse racing, dances, rock concerts, an annual 'chancellor's ball' and an annual 'Rag' when gaily decorated floats are driven through the streets of Cape Town with hundreds of students in all sorts of garb imploring the citizens of Cape Town to shower them with money; – there is also a Rag magazine, *Sax Appeal*. Companies, particularly those in Cape Town, but also from throughout the country, have been generous in their support of SHAWCO, which has a current annual budget of approximately R5,5 million. The steady involvement of more and more black students in the Rag procession was an indication of their feeling more and more at home in the university.

SHAWCO began in 1943 when Andrew Kinnear returned to Cape Town after being demobilised as a result of wounds sustained in the western desert in World War II. He enrolled as a medical student at UCT and, to help fund his studies, worked part-time in the ambulance service. This took him to a Cape Town suburb called 'Windermere' which did not match the beauty of the English lake district from which it took its name. It was a slum with lean-to dwellings made of corrugated iron and cardboard. He found a house where he started a weekly clinic run by himself and fellow medical students, supervised by a doctor, all on a voluntary basis. This enterprise grew and became a major student-controlled health and welfare organisation.

Sir Richard was chairman of the SHAWCO board from 1967 to 1971 followed by Professor Richard Fuggle, UCT's professor of environmental and geographical science, from 1971 to 1982. I became the chairman of the board in 1982 and remained in that position, except for a short period, until 1996 when I retired. Professor Dan Ncayiyana, a deputy vice-chancellor, is the current chair. The board has members of staff and of the community on it, but students are always in the majority. The students represent three constituencies: health, education and welfare, and the Rag (fund-raising). A full-time warden was appointed in 1958 and the first incumbent was Arnold

1981 (continued)

Mathew, a gentle, kindly man with a deep commitment to social justice. He was succeeded by Derek Livesey in 1968, who proved to be a tireless worker, devoted to SHAWCO. When Livesey retired we appointed Dr Ivan Toms, who had developed clinics in the African townships during the turbulent '80s, had been one of the leaders of the anti-conscription campaign and had been jailed for nine months (he was originally sentenced to twenty-one months) for refusing to be conscripted into the SA armed forces. He was given a very tough time in prison. Committed to primary health care, he was an energetic warden (now termed executive director) and when he resigned to become Director of Health Services in the Cape Municipal Council, Glen Trunan was appointed and is the current incumbent. A quiet young man, he, too, is committed to achieving social justice.

SHAWCO employs 15 social workers and provides extensive social services, nutrition, senior citizen and general community centres, a place of safety for children, and mobile health clinics which go to the poorest areas in the community. The students have consistently been in advance of their elders in introducing change into SHAWCO. They were amongst the first to emphasise community involvement in the affairs of the organisation and to press (successfully) for community representation on the board, and to insist that the purpose of SHAWCO was to empower poor people so that SHAWCO's services would eventually no longer be needed in a particular area. The students' relationships with those living in the African townships in the '80s was so good that when they were a virtual war zone and no other vehicles could enter, the SHAWCO vehicles moved freely through the areas bringing food, shelter and clothing. Only once was a SHAWCO vehicle attacked during a period of two or three very turbulent years. On a number of occasions Derek Livesey, the then director, was reluctant to agree to the students going into the areas because of the risks this entailed. I overruled him on almost all occasions, not without anxiety, but with the conviction that SHAWCO's track record minimised the risk, and in the knowledge that the need was great. Once my son John (while a student) was driving a SHAWCO van with food and clothes into an African township when he was stopped by the police who refused him entry. He called me on the car phone and I argued with the police, insisting that the students be allowed through. The police maintained that it was not safe, but the students and I believed that they did not want the food and clothes to reach the destitute people. Of course there was a risk, but I persisted and eventually the students went ahead, distributed the goods, and returned safely.

Before the council meeting on the afternoon of 4 March 1981 I asked Len Abrahamse to have lunch with me at Glenara. This was the first of the lunches we shared before every council meeting, when we discussed not only the council agenda but other important issues facing the university. I found these lunches invaluable. Towards the end of 1990 we were joined by Ian Sims, the deputy chairman who was to succeed Len as chairman on 1 March 1991, and Ian and I continued the practice until I retired. Ron Reid, the deputy chairman, joined us. Ian Sims and his wife Joanne are New Zealanders who have settled in South Africa. He is a former chairman of BP Southern Africa and a director of companies. A hardworking member of council, he was the natural successor to Len. Our experiences together were not as intense as those I shared with Len because South Africa in the nineties was quite a different place. However a good university is always at the cutting edge of change and the advice of the chairman is invaluable for a vice-chancellor. Ian worked hard as the chairman of council.

When the Cape Technikon became fully fledged as a tertiary institution, its council membership included a member nominated by UCT, and Professor Folb, the UCT professor of pharmacology, performed that role at my request. It soon became clear to him that the technikon had no intention of admitting black students if it could be avoided, and he and I decided to press the technikon council on the issue. He could get nowhere.* I told Dr Shippey, the rector of the Cape Technikon, that UCT would not have a representative on his council because of the technikon's racist policies. In the new South Africa there are significant numbers of black students enrolled at that institution and Dr Shippey's successor is an African.

I first met Mr Mendel Kaplan when I was deputy principal (planning). He and Sir Richard had planned a Jewish centre during the late 1970s and the Isaac and Jessie Kaplan Centre for Jewish Studies and Research was opened on 5 December 1979, established under the terms of a gift by the Kaplan Kushlick Foundation to the University of Cape Town. I was involved in the closing discussions prior to its establishment. From its inception the Centre has been engaged in research and teaching and functions as a co-ordinating unit in the university. It also invites distinguished scholars to give Jewish-content courses within established departments and continues to strengthen the university's library book holding. Mendel Kaplan also made it possible to create a Chair of Jewish Studies. Mendel Kaplan, at one time chairman of the Jewish Agency, was brought up in Cape Town and is a graduate of UCT. The driving force behind the Cape Wire and Gate company, now a multinational organisation, he has imaginatively promoted Jewish studies in a number of universities and elsewhere. He is a generous and dynamic man, and I have the greatest respect for his integrity and his vision.

---

* In fact, while the technikon purported publicly to approve the admission of all races in its submission to the President's Council, it accepted a quota of a maximum of 5 per cent of its student body being black. This was unacceptable to Folb and myself and he resigned.

Some years later Julian Ogilvie Thompson, the chairman of De Beers at the time, had phoned me to say that the company wished to mark its centenary with a gift of R1 million to the university and would like it to be used for 'bricks and mortar'. (An equal amount was given to the University of Stellenbosch to establish a chair of human rights.) Julian Elliott, the university architect and planner, estimated that we could build a two-storied building on a good site with the donation and Ogilvie Thompson agreed that we should proceed with plans for a building to house the Oppenheimer Centre for African Studies.* At this stage I phoned Kaplan to inform him of these developments and asked if it would be possible to house the Kaplan Centre in the same building. He immediately consented and offered to donate R0,5 million. Coincidentally Ogilvie Thompson was the guest speaker at a graduation ceremony later in that year and Elliott and I made use of the opportunity to show both him and the chancellor, Mr Oppenheimer, where we planned to put up the building. It was a breezy morning and Julian Elliott unrolled his plans and briefly explained his vision. Ogilvie Thompson turned to Oppenheimer and said that Rhodes had started De Beers and had given the land for the campus of UCT and he wondered if they should not do more. Mr Oppenheimer readily agreed and the donation was doubled on the spot! Later that afternoon I phoned Mr Kaplan and told him of this. He agreed that more accommodation should be provided and increased his own donation to R1 million. The Anglo American Corporation and the De Beers Company were substantial donors to UCT under the successive chairmanship of Harry Oppenheimer, Gavin Relly and Julian Ogilvie Thompson. The companies and their chairman's fund are very important and generous supporters of many enterprises in South Africa. This is a reflection of the vision and leadership of Harry Oppenheimer and his successors. Len Abrahamse would often quote, 'As is the king, so are the people.' Mr Oppenheimer was very generous in his support of UCT in his personal capacity.

On 20 March 1981 I was installed in the Jameson Hall as the sixth vice-chancellor and principal of UCT. I was seated in the front row of the audience and, as part of the proceedings, was later led up to the stage where Mr Oppenheimer duly declared me installed. I was then gowned and gave an address, and that concluded the matter. What I remember most vividly is sitting in the front row of the audience at the beginning of the proceedings, surrounded by television and other cameras. I found it most disconcerting and embarrassing.

My published address carried on its cover 'Towards Sanity and Goodwill;

---

* The Centre had been founded in 1976.

Scholarship not Ethnicity'. After a short historical introduction the address dealt with matters of most concern to a university – quality teaching and research, emphasising at the same time that 'the university must be international in the sense that it seeks to add to knowledge in a fundamental manner without guiding or limiting research in any way.' I endorsed the view that the university should recognise its role as an African and a South African institution with a responsibility to be alert to regional issues and regional problems. This applied both to undergraduate teaching and to research related to problems of the sub-continent, but did not imply that there was a lesser place for work on fundamental or international problems. I reviewed the work of the university and its role in Africa:

'A university in Africa must accept the task of fostering and preserving the mutually enriching mixture of traditions and values that make up our African heritage and culture, and must set itself to helping to solve the pressing socio-economic and other problems around it. Its graduates, educated in the universal ethos and trained in rationalism, will certainly be able to tackle these problems vigorously and must be encouraged to do so by the emphasis given to them by their teachers in course work, lectures and tutorials, drawing not only from our universal experience, but also from local factors in which the teacher should be actively involved.'

The gross inadequacies of the educational system for Africans were underlined and the commitment of the university to increasing access for Africans, and making their studies successful by means of academic support programmes, was described.

'I am saying that it is not enough merely to call for the opening of universities and the repeal of The Extension of University Education Act No. 45 of 1959, but that universities must also be prepared to make special efforts to ensure that as many students as possible succeed without any lowering of existing standards. Education is in crisis in this country and the opening of the universities is but one of the solutions. It has been said that this might change our character. On the contrary, it will strengthen our universality. The mingling of minds, the free access to knowledge and the educational strength and diversity in the student body have in our own experience, and in the experience of universities throughout the western world, proved to be sources of enrichment and strength. The character of a university is determined by scholarship and not by ethnicity. I might add that what is true of a university is true for society in general. Differences between people should be used to enhance their contributions to society by bringing them together in a spirit of mutual respect. It is strange, to say the least, that just as the black staff in the hospital kitchen at Groote Schuur Hospital can live on the premises, but not the black nurses, so in universities black staff in residences are allowed to live on the campus, but not black students. The problems that black students have with regard to adequate housing, are enormous. Sanity and good will must prevail here.'

The academic boycott was becoming an issue at that time and this, too, was referred to in the inaugural speech. It seemed to me that boycotting those institutions which were actively opposing apartheid and were suffering badly because of its imposition on them, was wrong:

'I am troubled by attempts by some to impose an academic boycott on this country's universities. This would seem to me to be the negation of everything that the university holds dear. Surely the exchange of ideas and the mutual search for truth can only help to solve problems in a reasonable manner, whereas isolation can only aggravate and increase the risk of unacceptable solutions. I do not believe that any political consideration should be put as a hindrance to the advance of knowledge or to the education of the young. I am reminded of the example of Einstein who was threatened, together with his fellow Germans, with an academic boycott after World War I. The nuclear physicists tried to make an exception in his case, but Einstein would have none of it. Knowing that his colleagues were to be barred because they were German nationals from the fourth Solvay congress on physics, Einstein declined even to receive an invitation. He said to Madame Curie: "It is unworthy of cultured men to treat one another in that type of superficial way, as though they were members of the common herd being led by mass suggestion." It is surely incredible for the scientific world to have held a congress on physics in the 1920s without Germans like Max Planck. Individuals may decline to associate with other groups because the values that such other groups hold are repugnant to them – that is a personal choice – but it is quite another matter when organisations try to interfere with the movement of scholars. Academic boycotts are certainly not in the interests of the furtherance of knowledge or the search for truth.'

The speech went on to deal with the dangers of censorship and of the infringement of the freedom of speech and the association of individuals:

'Scholarship is also damaged by any infringement on the freedom of speech or association of individuals. Acts against members of the university community, staff and students alike, which silence them, make their publications, scholarly or otherwise, prohibited in this country and prevent them from teaching or doing their research without them being charged with or found guilty of any crime, are totally unacceptable and threaten every scholar and citizen in this country. There can be no freedom to explore the truth in a society which has such laws on the statute books and it is freedom, not licence, that the university seeks. The right to seek the truth to the full without fear or favour, is what a university is all about. Bannings and arbitrary arrests without habeas corpus strike at the heart of a university and of civilisation itself.'

I dealt with the importance of a broad education and the avoidance of overspecialisation resulting in too narrow a view of life, and I also emphasised the valuable role of the student in the university.

'The students' representative council is an elected body representing the students. Despite the impression given by some newspaper reports, the record of the SRC at UCT is a very good one. If members of the SRC never did anything controversial, if we always found ourselves in agreement with the student leadership, would they be acting as we did, or as our parents did as students? I very much doubt it. I don't believe we would want it to be so. About ten years ago the SRC made it clear that they believed all UCT students should be able to take part, both as players and spectators, in sport on an equal basis and particularly so at Intervarsity. They were supported by the rugby club and by the university as a whole, but integration in sport was then thought of as radical. So much so, that UCT was widely criticised for adopting what some regarded as an unpatriotic attitude. Because our requests were not met (and here we were very much a lonely voice in the wilderness) Intervarsity had to be cancelled and was reinstated only after a period of years when wiser councils prevailed. Now, of course, the wisdom of the SRC and the university's approach is clear to every citizen in this land, and it seems such a pity that this lead was not followed at that time. I cite this example as one which illustrates that student and university attitudes, unpopular at the time, may prove to be wise in later years. UCT's SRC is affiliated to NUSAS and it is right and proper that students should form themselves into larger organisations so that they can have a voice as a corporate group. I would hope that all students from all the universities in South Africa would be able to find some way to link themselves together in an organisation which could reflect the idealism of young people and explore the options they see desirable for future generations without outside interference and always with a sense of responsibility.'

The speech concluded with the university's need to meet the challenges of the future. It ended with this sentence: 'I believe that with the harnessing of the spirit of adventure and energy which is in UCT, the university will play its full role in helping to ensure the prosperity of our country by seeking the truth fearlessly, by applying knowledge wisely, and by having graduates able to meet the future with intellectual integrity.'

I was making it absolutely clear that I rejected racism in society in general and in the university in particular. There is no doubt in my mind that in this I had the overwhelming support of most of the people at the university and of our supporters in the community. The same would have been true of other English-speaking universities at the time, but in particular the University of the Witwatersrand under the leadership of Professor Sonny du Plessis. It had also been the case under our predecessors, Sir Richard Luyt, and Professor Bozzoli. We were really continuing a tradition. The Afrikaans-speaking universities in South Africa supported the Government, as did the majority of white South Africans. There is no doubt that the university responded positively to the call to strengthen its efforts in overcoming the imposition of apartheid on its activities, as it did to the emphasis on scholarship and research. It underlined the importance of being unequivocal in goals and values.

At 08.00 in the morning of my installation as vice-chancellor I had spoken at a journal club at the hospital, where I had continued working as a part-time specialist physician in the department of medicine, with care of patients and teaching of post-graduate students. (I declined to accept payment for this work. Such payment would have come from the Cape Provincial Administration, which was responsible for the salaries of the non-professorial staff in the medical faculty in terms of the joint agreement between the university and the Province and I did not want to be beholden to the provincial government in any way.) At the journal club I reviewed articles which had appeared in a number of journals, for an hour. This meeting occurred on a weekly basis with various members of staff presenting at differing times of the year. I continued working as a part-time specialist throughout my period as vice-chancellor and for a number of years acted as a part-time head of 'firm,' the department being divided into five 'firms', each responsible for about forty beds. I found I was able to divorce myself from the administration of the department completely and was able to decline very firmly to make any comment about the department of medicine. Any other attitude would have undermined my very able successor, Professor Solly Benatar, who has taken the department from strength to strength. Solly is a very energetic and dedicated physician who, after training as an anaesthetist, qualified as a specialist physician in respiratory medicine. His qualities of leadership have enabled the department to weather a number of storms, many of which were related to the apartheid system. He has achieved an international reputation in the field of ethics, not only in medicine, but in ethical issues in society as a whole.

I successfully encouraged the deputy vice-chancellors to keep in touch with their academic disciplines wherever possible. In my view this enhanced their abilities as university administrators.

On 26 March the United States Ambassador asked me to meet Mr George Soros. He arrived by taxi and asked the taxi to wait for him. (My personal assistant, Sheilah Lloyd, was concerned about the cost to him of keeping the taxi driver waiting!) George Soros told me that he had been very successful in his investments and that he now wanted to be a philanthropist; that it was impossible for him to gain access to Eastern Europe and that he didn't think he could achieve anything in the Middle East. He said he had travelled down Africa and through South Africa and wanted to hear about the University of Cape Town. I told him of our vision of increasing access for black South Africans, particularly Africans, despite the official Government policy, of how black students had to apply to a Cabinet Minister for a permit to allow them to study at UCT, which was regarded by the Government as a white university. I explained that it was not so regarded by us. I told him about opening our residences to all students, irrespective of race, and that thus far there had been no action taken against us by the Government. Finally I explained that the African students were largely poor and unable to pay their academic and residence fees and in 1981 the total cost for each student was R2 500.

I had spoken at length and something about Soros's intense quality of listening fired my enthusiasm. Apparently it was infectious because he then said that he was impressed with what we were trying to achieve at the University of Cape Town and he would like to support 100 students. I was astounded. I cautioned him that the support would have to be for four years because it was almost certain that the students would take more time to get a three-year bachelor degree. He said he was quite prepared to support 100 students for four years. I did some mental arithmetic and realised that this amounted to a very large sum of money. The next day I asked Len Abrahamse to check whether Soros was indeed involved in investment in New York and Len reported back that Soros was a first-class human being and that there was no question about his bona fides! I took these precautions because I had never heard of him and nor had anybody else whom I asked in Cape Town! In 1981 he was not well known and indeed George Soros insisted that his first philanthropy should be entirely anonymous.

George Soros honoured all his obligations and eighty students received R3 000 each the following year, amounting to a total of R240 000, the cost per student having risen from R2 500 to R3 000 per annum. He supported them through to graduation. We indicated to him that the students would be selected on merit and that they would all be black, and he was happy about the selection procedure. Soros had been very impressed by Karl Popper when he was a student at the London School of Economics, and we both thought it would be most appropriate if these fellowships could be named after Karl Popper, and so they were.

An Open Society club was formed and other donors were encouraged to make funds available to it for student bursaries. In addition the university allocated extra funds from its own budget for undergraduates. In 1981 there were 104 African students at UCT. The figure in 1982 rose to 168 and a lot of those additional students would not have been there but for the generosity of Soros. It should be noted that in 1957 there were 29 African students at the university out of a total of 4 782 students, and that the number dropped to 3 in 1969 because of the Extension of Universities Education Act. There were 230 Indian students and 959 coloured students at the university in 1981.

Soros visited Cape Town and the university again in 1983. He decided to go to the Students' Union to speak to some of the students there. He did not want anyone to accompany him and told me afterwards that he had joined a group of students saying to them, 'I suppose you are what people here would call "coloured"?' The response was a taunt, 'You can call us that if you like, "Whitey"!' He was surprised to find that some students – almost certainly Muslim students – supported the Ayatollah Khomeni. He and I were however quite clear that the fellowships were for black students granted according to merit and need, and that political or religious affiliations played no role in the selection process.

By 1985 there were 339 African students at the university. Soros did not continue supporting black students at UCT because he felt that their numbers were not increasing fast enough. He did, however, support MESAB * which specialised in supporting the training of black health professionals in South Africa.

There is no doubt that the university was enormously encouraged by the generosity of George Soros in 1981 and that it strengthened our resolve to admit steadily increasing numbers of Africans to the student body. He subsequently told me he was sorry he had not continued to support black students at UCT.

Early in April 1981 I for the first time chaired an inaugural lecture by a new professor. Professor van der Westhuizen, a scholar of medieval English, gave his address in the evening. During that day I started bleeding from a duodenal ulcer. The symptoms that I had had led me to suspect the existence of duodenal ulcer and it became quite clear to me that the bleeding was active. I went ahead and chaired the inaugural lecture. To my surprise nobody commented on the fact that I was extremely pale. After the lecture it is customary for the lecturer and the audience to share some refreshments and during this period I went down to the toilet in the lecture theatre complex, where I lost consciousness because I had another major haemorrhage. I drove home and went to bed and fortunately the bleeding stopped during

---

* MESAB is an organisation which raises money to fund students in the health-care professions.

the night. I said nothing to anyone and took the precaution of taking antacids and relying on the normal intake of iron to restore my haemoglobin, which is what happened. It was only years later that I told a close friend Professor John Terblanche, the head of surgery, what had happened because I thought perhaps somebody should know. But I kept it to myself because I thought that if it became known that I had had a major bleed from a duodenal ulcer, the university would conclude that it was possible that I could not stand the stress of being vice-chancellor. I did not believe this to be the reason for my gastrointestinal haemorrhage and certainly did not want others to speculate on the matter. While I was at some risk, this was tempered by the fact that I was close to our teaching hospital and that I am, after all, a physician.

I chaired my first meeting of the university senate. Senate consisted of all the full professors of the university, representatives of associate professors and non-professorial staff, and all the executive officers, and student observers. It is the highest academic decision-making body in the university and in my view plays an important role in university affairs. In the past, senate meetings had tended to last a long time. While I wanted to ensure that all matters were adequately discussed, I didn't think that it was valuable to allow meetings to go on for up to five hours. The minutes of this first meeting show that it started at 14.00 and finished at 15.30. This was possible because I had enforced an existing rule which stipulated that members of senate could speak only once to any matter, and I made it clear that though we should deal with matters thoroughly it should not be in a drawn-out manner. It was my impression that the majority of senate appreciated this approach. During my years as vice-chancellor I found senate to be a great support. Senate met five times a year and was always a somewhat daunting task for any chairman.

A Mr Jerome Marshall was appointed as an administrative assistant on 1 February 1981. In April an official in the staff office sought to establish his pension number with the Associated Institutions Pension Fund in Pretoria. He was told that Mr Marshall already had a pension, and gave the number. The staffing official recognised that the code of the pension number meant that Marshall had a police pension and phoned the pension fund again to ask for confirmation of the number. When he volunteered it was a police pension number, he was told that no such number existed! An official in the staff office then spoke to Marshall, who denied that he was a policeman. I asked to see him and claimed to have incontrovertible evidence that he was a police spy and said that I would expose him. He jumped out of the chair and crawled on his hands and knees to the telephone connection behind the desk. After examining that carefully he partially dismantled the telephone

1981 (continued)

and started looking elsewhere in the room. After he had satisfied himself that there were no listening devices, he sat down once more. (I could have told him that very occasionally my office was screened for 'bugs'.) He then confessed to being a police spy and was overcome with remorse. Apparently he had been recruited while a student and had been on the police pay-roll for years. He alleged that there were a number of spies on the campus and that the police actively disrupted student meetings and sabotaged the cars of student delegates going to NUSAS meetings. (There had been a number of accidents.) He was a weak reed and I knew that once he was in the hands of his masters in the security police he would crumble and deny everything, but I was anxious to get him to repeat his allegations publicly. I asked Len Abrahamse to see him to make an assessment. Marshall repeated his story to Len, who agreed that he would never stand up to the police or to cross-examination. I told Marshall there was no place for police informers on the campus and that he was not welcome. He left UCT forthwith. At the mass meeting called to protest against the presence of a police spy on the campus, I made clear my total rejection of such action by the police. I concluded by saying :

> 'There is no place for police informers on this campus. They are not welcome. We are concerned, at the University of Cape Town, about the development of the whole person, about students and staff reaching their full potential, about stretching people intellectually to the utmost. The presence of informers in our midst threatens this high endeavour. Academic freedom, the free exchange of ideas, and individual student and staff rights are infringed by the presence of security policemen masquerading as students or staff on this campus. For those informers who remain, I have this message. We shall speak clearly and in as simple a language as possible in the hope that you may understand what we say. We have nothing to hide. It is indeed sad that it is necessary to have to draw the university's and society's attention to the sorry state of affairs, but there can be no compromise, and we will not tolerate this abuse of police powers. Our duty to the university and to society in general compels us to make our position clear.'

The matter was prominently dealt with by the press. It was not to be my last brush with police spies. Interestingly, in 1978 while a student and a spy, Marshall had taped some freedom songs and had insisted on putting them in the SRC safe. Within hours the security police arrived, asked for the safe's keys, found the tapes and interrogated Marshall – all to strengthen his cover!

The students' representative council (SRC) had a number of sub-committees, one of them being the Edcom committee which dealt vigorously with inequities in education. The wages committee which dealt with equal vigour with the racially skewed incomes of South Africans was another. The members of both those sub-committees were harassed by the security police. I gave them as much support as I could. Dr Frank Bradlow, well-known expert in Africana and a man with a great interest in history (Edna, his wife, is a very accomplished professional historian), was a tireless worker as a member of the university council. He chaired the Bradlow commission, looking at student governance in the university. The report of his commission was approved and included recommendations which allowed for student observers on the university council (the legislation did not allow for membership at that time) and for the reorganisation of a number of student committees and student governance as a whole.

A member of the SRC came to see me with a proposal that they should form a gay and lesbian association. I supported the proposal and the gay and lesbian association (GALA) was duly formed and its constitution approved by the university council. This was not without risk. Prejudice against homosexuality was rife at the time and, since it was illegal for consenting adults to engage in homosexual acts, people were prosecuted for doing so. I was fully aware that the formation of GALA could confirm our critics in their belief that UCT in general and I in particular, were not acting in the best interests of South Africa. I knew that a number of parents would be very critical of this development and might discourage their children from coming to UCT or perhaps that they would insist they leave. All student societies are listed every year and this information is sent to all students and parents. I rather hoped that most parents would think GALA had something to do with swimming and this might have been the case because there has never been a query from any parent about it. The association proved to be an effective one, promoting a more liberal attitude to human sexuality and advancing a spirit of tolerance.

Each year I entertained SRC members to a braaivleis (barbecue) where I was the cook. I became well known not only for my skill in cooking steak and sausages, but also for cooking bananas on an open fire. When the staff association was embroiled in an internal conflict which could not be resolved I invited the executive of this association to a 'braai' where my culinary skills and a liberal supply of beer and wine resolved the issue. My cooked bananas were again in evidence and, as a consequence, the executive committee gave me a certificate affording me the title of 'Braaimaster Extraordinaire' and honorary life membership of the Ancient Order of the Burnt Banana.

The Morris Mauerberger Foundation was created by Mr Mauerberger before he died, and received a major injection of resources through his generous bequest. He had looked particularly to Sir Richard Luyt in drawing up

1981 (continued)

the Trust and my first meeting as a director on 25 May revealed the value of the work done by the Foundation. Down the years the Foundation enabled the university to create, in partnership with the Province, full chairs of cardiology, neurosurgery, ophthalmology and nursing. The foundation also gave substantial amounts as bursaries to medical students and supported research in a number of university departments. Mauerberger had wanted to favour UCT as a South African beneficiary of his bequest. The Foundation supports bursaries at other universities, particularly the University of the Western Cape and the Peninsula Technikon, universities in Israel and much else besides. It was chaired for many years by Mr Mauerberger's son-in-law, the late Mr Solly Yach, who was succeeded by his very able and intelligent wife Estelle, who has proved to be a most effective chairperson of the Foundation.

The twentieth anniversary of the establishment of the Republic of South Africa was 'celebrated' by holding a republic festival on 31 May 1981. Early in 1980 the director of the opera school had sought permission for the school to be involved in the festival and Sir Richard Luyt had ruled that UCT should follow the stance adopted towards the 1971 festival, i.e. that any member of staff or student wishing to participate may do so but that the university as an institution would not do so. In October 1980 the local director of the festival wrote asking the university to enter a float in the festival float procession. The acting vice-chancellor, Professor Maurice Kaplan, replied to say that entering a float was inappropriate and asked for other suggestions. No reply was received.

Universities were asked through the Committee of University Principals to mount a photographic display in Durban. UCT agreed to participate, provided that it would be responsible for its own exhibit. This was not guaranteed and UCT did not participate. In the same month the sports council of UCT was asked to give permission for the use of its sports centre. Assured that the festival games did not form part of the republic festival, consent was given. When the programme was published clearly linking the games to the republic festival, the sports council withdrew its permission to use the centre. I supported the decision. The overwhelming feeling at UCT was that the republic was not something we wished to celebrate and certainly that was my view as vice-chancellor.

In the week before the republic festival the SRC held a number of protest meetings in the Jameson Hall at one of which four or five students at an emotionally charged moment unfurled republic festival banners in the upstairs gallery. There were scuffles and university officials intervened. No one was injured, but the banners were thrown down into the main hall. One was torn and burnt and the same was done to another outside. On the previous day the national flag had been burnt at a republic festival protest on the campus of the University of the Witwatersrand, and the radio and television (State controlled) and Government-supporting newspapers claimed the national flag had been burnt at UCT. I issued a statement pointing out what had happened and stating that the university was a place for debate and rational discourse, for study and reflection and that anyone found guilty of violence, including burning items deliberately, would be disciplined. The next day I was phoned by the Minister of National Education, who expressed his concern at these events. I referred him to my public statement. Two days later we received a written request from the Director-General of National Education asking the university to set out in detail its attitude to the republic festival and the festival games. The Minister issued a press statement in which he said that 'the Government cannot accept that universities, as public institutions very substantially financed by government from public funds, refuse to make available their facilities for official national events, and that they fail to exercise effective discipline against students who wilfully insult and degrade national symbols of great emotional value.'

The university's response was to confirm UCT's stand, viz. that the university upheld the right of those who wished to stage the republic festival, but also recognised the right of those who wished to oppose the festival. It indicated that disciplinary procedures were already underway where appropriate, and drew attention to the autonomy of the university and the grave implications of the reference in the director-general's letter to sections 25 & 27 of the Universities Act, which purported to empower the Minister to attach conditions to the granting of subsidies to universities and to withhold subsidies where the conditions were not complied with. (This was the first salvo from the Government in this matter of financial support. Ultimately the matter was resolved by the Supreme Court in the late 1980s, as we shall see.)

Len Abrahamse, as chairman of council, and I were summoned to Pretoria to meet with the Minister of National Education, Dr Viljoen, and the Minister of Finance, Mr Owen Horwood, in the Union Buildings. Professor D J du Plessis, the vice-chancellor of the University of the Witwatersrand, and Dr Niko Stutterheim, chairman of their council, together with the vice-chancellor and chairman of the council of the University of Natal, were also summoned to meetings with the same ministers in Pretoria. The representatives of each university were seen separately. Len and I had a very frank discussion with the two ministers. Len was superb. He put it very clearly to the ministers that the policies of the Government were unacceptable and meant that from the point of view of universities and other educational institutions they were not in the best interests of South Africa and those whom these institutions were trying to educate. He pointed out that citizens should have the right to protest in any way in which they wished, provided that the protests were peaceful. I fully supported my chairman. It hadn't escaped us that the Minister of Finance was there. There was a clear message being given to us that if we didn't toe the line the Government might start imposing financial penalties as had been hinted at in the director-general's letter.

After a very tough conversation during which neither Abrahamse nor I gave any ground, the meeting broke up. Len and Gerrit Viljoen stood talking together on one side and Minister Horwood took me aside to consult me professionally! He had been a patient of mine in 1960, when I was in practice as a specialist physician and he was a senior lecturer in economics at UCT, and he wanted some reassurance from me about his health. I found it amusing that a Minister who had been rattling his sabre at me a few minutes before was now looking to me to help him in this way. Of course I gave him professional advice, but the relationship between us changed quite dramatically. We heard no more from the two Ministers about this matter. Owen Horwood, the Minister of Finance, had been the vice-chancellor of the University of Natal. He and Senator Trollip were two token English-speaking members of the Cabinet.

At that time I was the disciplinary officer of the university, with a student found guilty of a misdemeanour having the right to appeal to the university court. I found one student guilty of burning the bunting and fined him R75 (US$17). He was the only person against whom any evidence could be led. This resulted in much criticism from the student body because the rule he had broken was that he had 'brought discredit on the university in the eyes of reasonable men'. (Women were not mentioned in the rule in 1981!) They queried who the 'reasonable men' were. My point was that burning anything in protest on campus was wrong, but the students had a point. On May 28 four students who had taken down some republic bunting in Adderley Street (Cape Town centre's main street), were arrested and gaoled and charged with malicious damage to property and theft. They had intended to adorn their residence with it. It was plainly a prank and I managed to secure their release. This illustrated the over-reaction of the law-enforcing authorities in the emotionally charged atmosphere of the time. The episode also illustrates how important it was for UCT to stand firmly by the principles it believed in while at the same time trying not to be so confrontational as to provoke an overreaction by Government. It was a tricky balancing act.

On 29 June Andrew Boraine, the president of NUSAS, was banned for five years. He was a second-year BA student at UCT. The Government did allow him to complete the course for which he was registered and, for that purpose only, he was allowed on UCT's premises. I issued a public statement condemning his banning and the council expressed its full support for what I had said. Andrew Boraine is the son of Dr Alex Boraine who was then a Progressive Party member of parliament. I fully supported NUSAS and what it was trying to achieve and, indeed, had become an honorary vice president of NUSAS and a patron of the Friends of NUSAS (FONS), which raised money for the student body. The students in NUSAS actively worked against the apartheid policies of the SA Government and Andrew Boraine's* only 'crime' was that he was clearly opposed to racial discrimination. The Government did not give reasons for banning its citizens.

The university was proud to know that Allan Cormack[†] had been awarded the Nobel prize for Physiology and Medicine in 1979. He visited the campus in 1981 and was presented with a gold medal by UCT. His award resulted from his work on the development of computer-assisted tomography. A graduate of UCT and a former member of the faculty, he was the brother of Amy Read, the wife of the then registrar, Len Read.

The Centre for Conflict Resolution board is chaired by the vice-chancellor. It had started out as the Abe Bailey Institute for Interracial Studies and was a company registered not for gain, closely associated with the university but not officially part of it. This was for political reasons both within and without UCT. When the funds became available to establish the institute in 1968 there was much manoeuvring in the university, with various players trying to establish an activity in their own particular area of interest. Outside consultants were called in and the institute was the compromise solution. Such disputes and negotiations in a university take up a great deal of time and reflect the parochialism that can so easily surface. The external political reason was to enable the institute to engage all parties, including Government departments, in its work, and being at a distance from the university certainly helped its cause with the Government! Professor H W van der Merwe was the director and under his leadership the institute (later the Centre for Intergroup Studies before assuming its present name) did outstanding work. Van der Merwe succeeded in bringing together a wide range of people with diverging political views. At the 1971 conference, when student leaders representative of all student groupings met, the delegates included Johan Fick, president of the Afrikaanse Studentebond (ASB), Steve Biko, president of the SA Students' Organisation (SASO) and Neville Curtis, president of the National Union of South African Students (NUSAS). There was mediation in the 1976 upheavals, an international conflict-accommodation conference in 1984, a nationwide series of courses in mediation and conflict-intervention in 1989, and much else besides. In the early 1980s Van

---

* Andrew Boraine is now the City Manager of the Cape Town Metropolitan Council.
[†] Allan Cormack died in 1998.

1981 (continued)

der Merwe would report verbally to the board on his contacts with the ANC and his attempts to achieve dialogue between that organisation and other South Africans.

The Centre's present mission is to contribute towards a just peace in South and Southern Africa by promoting constructive, creative and co-operative approaches to the resolution of conflict and the reduction of violence. Under the leadership of the present director, Laurie Nathan, it continues to make important contributions. Laurie was the second SRC president with whom I worked, and he courageously opposed conscription and the military action being undertaken by South Africa in the 1980s.

Alan Pifer, the President of the Carnegie Corporation, visited Cape Town, and we renewed our friendship. He was to prove to be a great friend of the university. A quiet man of great integrity, he has an in-depth knowledge of South Africa and has visited the country many times, holding discussions with South Africans from many walks of life. He became a close and valued friend. We first met at a cocktail party at Glenara when I was vice-chancellor-elect. He was astounded to hear that I predicted that when I retired, the majority of the student body at UCT would be black. I almost achieved that goal. In 1996 more than 50 per cent of the first year students were black and within a few years my prediction will prove to be true. In 1981 there were 11 038 students at UCT of which 9 719 were white, 959 coloured, 256 Indian and 104 African. In 1996 when I retired there was a total of 15 423 students of which 8 336 were white, 2 126 coloured, 915 Indian and 4 046 African.

Fund-raising
1982–1984

The university received a valuable donation from Shell South Africa which made it possible for it to enter into an agreement with Uluntu, a black utility company, to have the first option on the letting of accommodation at an Uluntu development in Guguletu (a black township in Cape Town), which would provide residence for 42 students. Both the donor and the university strongly opposed racially segregated student residences (and indeed our residences had been opened) but some off-campus accommodation was necessary to cope with growing numbers and such off-campus accommodation for black students had to be in a black area in keeping with the Group Areas Act. The university did not want to own such accommodation in a black area because it would be entrenching the Group Areas Act to which it was opposed.

In June 1980 the Cabinet had requested the Human Sciences Research Council (HSRC) to conduct an 'in-depth investigation into all factors of education in South Africa with the aim of establishing principles for an education policy which would allow for the realisation of the potential of all inhabitants of South Africa, promote economic growth and improve the quality of the life of all inhabitants.' The HSRC was requested to make recommendations on a programme for making education of the same quality available to all 'population groups'.* This was four years after the 1976 riots in Soweto and all that followed on those events. The report of the main committee, chaired by Professor J P de Lange, Rector of the Rand Afrikaans University, had been handed to the Minister of National Education in July 1981 and had been tabled in parliament together with an interim memorandum containing the Government's provisional comments in October. The Government asked for reaction from the public to be submitted by the end of March 1982.

The main committee had reached consensus on eleven principles which included 'equal opportunities for education including equal standards for every inhabitant; education shall afford positive recognition of the freedom

---

* A Government euphemism for the racial groups it had classified in law.

of choice of the individual, parents and organisations in society; education will be directed in a responsible educational manner to meet the needs of the individual as well as those of society and economic development, and shall take into consideration the manpower needs of the country. Formal education would be the responsibility of the state provided the individual, parents and organisations in society have a shared responsibility, choice and voice in the matter,' and 'education shall afford positive recognition of what is common as well as what is diverse in the religious and cultural way of life and languages of the inhabitants.' Given the politics of South Africa, the last principle could be read in a number of ways, particularly to support segregation.

Importantly the commission recommended a single ministry of education and a single department responsible for all education, together with a South African Council of Education, representative of all the peoples of South Africa and of the interest groups amongst the providers and users of education. This council would advise the minister and create an infrastructure for research into education; initiate negotiations on research and collaboration to evaluate matters at a mass policy level; and obtain as a statutory right such information as was necessary to perform its functions of advising and reporting. The Government published an interim memorandum accepting all eleven principles on which the committee had agreed, but making it clear that it remained committed to the existence of different education departments for the different population groups; to the policy that each population group should have its own schools; and to the principle of mother-tongue education. It said nothing about the recommendation that there should be a single ministry. It reaffirmed the Government's support of 'The principles of the Christian character and broad national character' of education. The Government did not appoint an interim council or a South African Council of Education, but the Ministers of National Education, Internal Affairs and Education and Training were asked to function as a committee and to consider the implications of the report.

The university welcomed most of the principles enunciated in the De Lange Report, in particular the commitment to equality, freedom of choice and shared responsibility for making educational decisions. We believed that, taken as a whole and implemented, the principles would provide far-reaching changes and considerable improvements to the South African educational practice. Nevertheless, we warned against any attempt to use these principles to justify separate but 'equal' institutions or systems in which decisions about educational provision for unilaterally determined population groups were taken unilaterally by the white group. If they were, or could be used to do this, they would be inadequate principles and would not ensure equality of education for all the inhabitants of South Africa.

The university argued that the Government's already decided points of departure were in fundamental conflict with the eleven principles. We found them to be based on educationally irrelevant criteria, a failure to appreciate the diverse nature of South African society and a failure to understand that separate educational provision could not produce an equitable educational dispensation and would therefore be rejected by the majority of the population.

UCT expressed the view that access to public educational facilities should be subject to criteria that were educationally relevant; race, colour, creed and sex were not such criteria. With regard to educational management, the university strongly supported the proposal that there should be a single ministry of education. The report made the fundamental observation that policy guidelines for the achievement of equal, quality education would have to include the principle that 'no person will on educationally irrelevant grounds be debarred from available educational opportunities from which he might benefit' and in the report it was stated that ' ... differentiation ... on the basis of race or colour ... cannot be regarded as relevant'. The report therefore implied that equality of education and racially segregated public schools, universities and other educational institutions were incompatible and the university expressed itself as being in complete agreement with that position. The university also supported, without reservation, the proposal that *priority* be given to 'the granting of the right to councils of autonomous educational institutions in higher education to decide who should be admitted as students.' The university expressed the view that a clear statement of (public) national strategy and plan for education was crucial to restore credibility and to establish the Government's bona fides. The De Lange report, though inadequate in certain respects, represented the most comprehensive and constructive study in the history of South African education up to that point. The implementation of the broad thrust of the report in the view of the university could result in improvements in the quality and acceptability of the South African educational dispensation, but the university pointed out that its implementation, which was an urgent necessity, depended to a significant degree upon the political will of the Government of the day and we were not optimistic about that.

English-speaking universities met in Grahamstown to discuss the De Lange report at a conference from 4 to 6 February 1982 organised by the 1820 Settlers' Foundation. I presented a lead-in paper and emphasised, inter alia, the need for education to be non-racial.

There was a remarkable degree of unanimity at the conference. All agreed that university councils should decide who should be admitted and that the permit system should go. There had been rumours of its being replaced by a quota system and the conference ruled that such a system would also be unacceptable. The conference fully supported the recommendation of the HSRC commission that race was an irrelevant factor in education and was unanimous in its view that there should be only one department of education and that the proposed SA Council of Education should be created along the lines suggested by the HSRC report. There was general agreement that the subsidy (grant) system for a university should not be so tightly linked to student numbers as in the past and should make provision for bridging and upgrading programmes for under-prepared students from disadvantaged backgrounds and for continuing adult education. The delegates generally accepted the recommendations, but were split as to whether the reforms were relevant to change or would allow the Government to 'streamline and modernise apartheid'. The meeting called for an immediate implementation of the De Lange report, pointing out that the changes could only be partially successful until total political and social change had taken place.

A second conference was held in Bloemfontein in March. There were 1 621 delegates and 400 observers and it was titled a '*Volkskongres*' (People's Congress) on education. Those attending were overwhelmingly Afrikaans-speaking and white. Many of the motions passed at the congress rejected the principles put forward in the De Lange report. The most significant proposal was that 'Control at all levels of education management for whites, in any educational or political dispensation, will stay in their hands, non-negotiably, and that all co-ordination machinery remains subject to this.' This motion was passed by 96,67 per cent of those present (0,81 per cent were 'unsure,' 1,54 per cent against!). The Government's interim memorandum was accepted by 87,6 per cent. Such an outcome was hardly surprising given the policies of the Government and the people attending the congress. Dominee (Pastor) D J Viljoen, chairman of the organising committee, outlined four non-negotiable criteria which governed the Afrikaner's approach to education: 'Christianity, group identity, mother-tongue instruction and parental decision-making.' Professor Carel Boshoff, chairman of the Broederbond, rejected one ministry of education for all 'population groups' outright – each 'population group' should retain control over its own education system. There were some lonely voices: Professor J L van der Walt asked for a rethink of Christian National Education (one of the cornerstones of the apartheid regime's policies) which 'was often suspected of having the aim and outcome whereby Afrikaners ensure for themselves a good position in the land, but whereby others are kept deeper in a situation of oppression.'

The conclusions reached at the English and Afrikaans congresses respectively were poles apart. The *Volkskongres* reflected a commitment to racism by supporters of the Government.

The Government did move towards the creation of a quota system and this occupied a great deal of my time, particularly in 1983. It did not create a single department of education; a South African Council on Education was not established; it did not repeal the Group Areas Act; and, indeed, recommendations of the HSRC commission were greatly watered down.

While at the Grahamstown conference, John Reid and I learnt of the death of Neil Aggett in detention. I had known him as an undergraduate medical student at UCT. After qualification, Dr Aggett became very active in the trade union movement and had been repeatedly harassed, banned and detained by the South African Government. He had now died in detention. In an affidavit before he died, Aggett had described how he had been tortured. At that time more than forty people had already died while being detained without trial. All members of the conference attended a dinner that night at the 1820 Settlers' Monument and the keynote address was given by the Honourable Justice J H Steyn. He spoke about the problems facing South Africa and dealt specifically with the problems raised by the security legislation. Chief Justice Rabie had submitted a report suggesting modifications to the security legislation to improve the situation for detainees and Judge Steyn praised the Chief Justice for his efforts and his recommendations. In the view of both Reid and myself the Chief Justice's recommendations did not go anywhere near far enough, and when the assembled guests gave Judge Steyn a standing ovation for what in other respects had been an outstanding address, John Reid and I sat with our hands on the table. This did not go unnoticed by a number of people at the dinner and on the following Monday morning Judge Steyn phoned me to ask me why we had done that. I told him that we had heard of the death of Aggett in detention on that day and we simply did not believe that Rabie's suggestions were adequate. He, of course, had not known of Aggett's death and was very upset by it. He did believe that the Chief Justice's suggestions might help to some extent.

On that Tuesday John Reid and I as well as the SRC president addressed a protest meeting at the medical school about Aggett's death. After drawing attention to the iniquities of the security legislation in South Africa and to the torture and death of people in detention, I quoted from Pastor Martin Niemöller as follows:

'They came for the Communists and I did not speak up, because I was not a Communist;
Then they came for the Jews and I did not speak up because I was not a Jew;
Then they came for the trade unionists and I did not speak up because I was not a trade unionist;

*Then they came for the Catholics and I did not speak up because I was a Protestant;
Then they came for me – and by that time there was no one left to speak.'*

The students held a protest meeting against detention without trial and the death in detention of Aggett. The student newspaper described that I 'stood thoughtfully observing the crowd for half an hour before leaping onto the stage to deliver a forceful attack on Section 6 of the Terrorism Act, "an Act that no civilised parliament would support".' I was reported as referring to 'those who cannot be here, not because they have been tried in a court of law, but because they have been incarcerated under Section 6.'

The organiser of the African Food and Canning Workers Association, Mr Oscar Mpetha, 74 years old, ailing with diabetes and with an amputated limb and imprisoned, sent a message to the meeting describing Neil Aggett as a 'man of the people'. Oscar Mpetha was subsequently admitted to Groote Schuur hospital where the members of the medical school successfully kept him as a patient for months on the pretext that he required special care, in order to prevent him being incarcerated in prison.

A meeting of staff and students at the medical school condemned the attitudes of the SA Medical Council and the Medical Association of SA towards detention. Professor Peter Folb stated that the medical profession shared responsibility for Neil Aggett's death. The SA Medical Council had condoned the treatment meted out to Biko' and 'was doing nothing to give effect to its own resolution 18 months before to change the detention laws in order to ensure the safety and well-being of detainees'. The Medical Association of SA was also criticised for showing 'no public signs of concern'. Professor Frances Ames told the meeting that the suffering of Biko and Aggett should concern the medical profession as a whole. When the report of the Rabie commission was debated I called on South Africans to speak up. 'The damage caused by the excessive police power which Section 6 conveys causes too great a wound in the fabric of our society. Let us do away with it.'

The NUSAS theme for 1982 was 'Campus action for democracy'. NUSAS was certainly under attack. Nick 'Fink' Haysom,* the current NUSAS president, was banned for two years, the banning being enforced ten days after his release from a period of detention without trial. No reason was given for either restriction. Fink Haysom was a former UCT SRC president and a founder of the Western Cape Parents' Detainees Committee.

The Carnegie Corporation of New York, under the leadership of Dr David Hamburg, had decided to initiate a second enquiry into poverty and development in South Africa. Fifty years earlier the university had been heavily

---

* Fink Haysom is now a distinguished lawyer who worked in the office of President Mandela.

involved in the first enquiry. The resulting report had aroused widespread concern about the impoverishment of a large number of 'poor whites' in South Africa. The second enquiry was to focus on the poverty amongst blacks. It was proposed that a network of professional working parties would be set up to study the influence of poverty in fields such as education, health and law, and it was hoped that the programme would stimulate a wide range of research in many South African universities and initiate projects which would all be brought together at a conference on poverty and development at the university in September 1983. The council fully supported the proposal.

David Hamburg asked the university to house the project so that it could be protected from the Government which was (correctly) expected to be critical of it and I chaired the management committee of the enquiry. Francis Wilson directed the project and involved many researchers from a broad cross-section of South Africans. He invited Dr Mamphela Ramphele* to play an important role in the study and they co-authored the publication which resulted. It was titled *Uprooting Poverty: The South African Challenge* and was acclaimed as a major contribution to the documentation of poverty in Southern Africa. The subsequent conference was well attended by people from throughout the country and by Dr Hamburg and other officials of the Carnegie Corporation. It highlighted the plight of so many black South Africans and was strongly criticised by the Government.

A Johannesburg businessman told me that Africans could not do engineering because they could not think in three dimensions! This statement increased my determination to enrol more Africans in engineering and John Wilson, the chairman of Shell South Africa, was a great help. Shell provided funds for bright African students for a post-matric year at prestigious white schools, whereafter they enrolled for engineering at UCT, their full costs again being met by Shell. They also took part in the academic support programme. The enterprise proved to be a great success. When the first Africans qualified as engineers at UCT John Wilson and his wife Ruth hosted a dinner Shell gave on the campus for them and for their parents, paying all the expenses of their travel to and from the campus. At that dinner I met the parents of the most outstanding student, who had qualified as a civil engineer with distinction. They came from northern KwaZulu where they lived in a mud hut and had never before travelled on a tarred road or seen an aeroplane. They were immensely proud of their son. Towards the end of

---

* I had first heard of Dr Ramphele when she was banished to a remote area in the Transvaal. Through Francis Wilson I sent her a microscope and a diagnostic set to help her at her clinic. I also intervened to try to get her permission to do a post-graduate diploma at the University of the Witwatersrand.

the dinner the father of another graduate made a short speech. I did not understand his language but his emotions were clearly communicated. Shell continued financing African students in engineering over a number of years.

Between 1980 and 1996, 243 Africans had qualified as engineers at UCT. Fifteen of them obtained masters degrees and one a doctorate. We received substantial support for these students from Anglo American, AECI, Sasol, Eskom, Iscor and other organisations.

On 12 May 1982 I addressed a public meeting in the Selborne Hall which is in the city hall in Johannesburg. The subject was solitary confinement and I pointed out that there was no doubt that solitary confinement such as that experienced by detainees held in South Africa under Section 6 of the Terrorism Act might result, and frequently did result, in serious psychological changes, which impaired the detainee's ability to arrive at the truth, and to convey that truth to the interrogators. It therefore followed that such confinement could prevent justice being achieved. It might result in temporary insanity. It was also clearly contrary to the Tokyo Declaration and therefore completely unacceptable to the medical profession in South Africa. It had to cease. A few years later, in 1985, Don Foster, a senior UCT psychologist, and Diane Sandler, published a report from UCT's Institute of Criminology on torture in South African prisons. Dirk van Zyl Smit, the director of the institute, endorsed the work and sent me a copy. When the report appeared it was vigorously criticised by the Government and the Nationalist press. Foster and Van Zyl Smit stood their ground. I gave my full support to the work and said that the conclusions were correct and the data compelling: there was widespread torture in South African gaols. I was roundly criticised for this. An ex-judge president of the Cape, Judge van Zyl, castigated me in the local press. Subsequent events proved Foster and Sandler right but very few white South Africans believed it at the time. We were up to mischief again, in their eyes!

I was away from South Africa from 13 May to 16 June on a visit to West Germany, Britain, the United States and Israel. This was one of many journeys to many parts of the world to raise funds, predominantly for the support of black students at UCT, and to ensure that university leaders elsewhere understood UCT's mission in a very hostile environment. In Israel Noreen and I were the guests of Mr and Mrs Richard Sonnenberg and apart from the enormous pleasure we took in their company, we enjoyed their generous hospitality and were able to visit all the institutions of higher education in that country. Our visit included alumni reunions in a number of countries. We visited universities in West Germany and Britain and in the United States. I met with a number of university heads and discussed our problems and my determination to increase black enrolment significantly at

UCT.

It was during this trip that I first met Bill Bowen, then president of Princeton University and now president of the Andrew W Mellon Foundation in New York. Of all the university presidents I saw in the United States from the early 1980s he was the man who impressed me most. He showed a deep insight into the problems of South Africa and the particular problems facing the University of Cape Town, and that meeting was the beginning of a firm friendship and of consistent support by him for the university, as we shall see. A highly intelligent, compassionate man, he is making major contributions in many fields both in the United States and overseas as president of the Andrew W Mellon Foundation.

While in the United States I also met with Alan Pifer to discuss the establishment of the UCT Fund in that country. Alan, who has a deep interest in South Africa and an encyclopaedic knowledge of it, was enthusiastic. Hans Middelmann had given me an introduction to the Standard Charter Bank in New York and one of their members of staff invited an accountant and a lawyer, Mr Whitney Gerard, to the luncheon where I could discuss my proposals with them. At the beginning I sensed that they could not see any good reason why Americans should donate money to a South African university, but as I continued talking and spoke of the mission of the University of Cape Town and what the institution was trying to do to achieve equality of opportunity at university level, their attitudes changed. Whitney Gerard took me back to his office where he introduced me to the senior partner. I had suggested to Len Abrahamse that we should try to establish this fund in the United States and some time after this luncheon Len Abrahamse and Len Read met with Alan Pifer and Whitney Gerard in New York, to discuss the general feasibility of raising funds in the US. Alan emphasised the difficulties he foresaw but said it was worth a try. Len Abrahamse asked Alan Pifer to head up the fund and he agreed to do this on a strictly voluntary basis. Alan was already committed to two other projects, having recently retired as president of the Carnegie Corporation of New York. Nonetheless he put an enormous amount of work into the project over the next ten years.

Whitney Gerard proceeded with the incorporation of the University of Cape Town Fund Inc. in New York State, following which application was to be made to the internal revenue service in Washington for federal tax exemption under the provision of section 501(c) (3) of the federal tax code. After the application went in, several weeks went by without so much as an acknowledgement by the tax-exempt organisation branch of the New York attorney general's office. As more and more time passed it became clear to Alan and Whitney that, unless they put on some pressure, incorporation would not be granted. Alan wrote a strong letter of protest to Daniel Kurtz, the assistant attorney in charge of the tax-exempt organisation branch, saying that it was an entirely legitimate cause and at least deserved the courtesy of a response. This occurred quickly and a hearing was set up for 13 September 1983 at which both Alan and Whitney testified. At the conclusion of the hearing Mr Kurtz turned to his colleagues and asked them with some asperity why they were opposing the application. I was told that they were clearly embarrassed and did not answer, whereupon he turned to Alan and Whitney and informed them that he approved the application and that the certificate of incorporation would follow in short order. This came through on 5 January 1984, no doubt after more foot-dragging by his colleagues. The problem, of course, was simply that the case had to do with South Africa. With the support of officials in the Reagan administration application was then made for federal tax exemption, which was granted in record time! These difficulties indicated the problems which lay ahead for a South African institution trying to raise funds in the United States in the 1980s. Whitney and two of his colleagues constituted an interim board and on 16 January 1984 elected a permanent board of nine directors, with Alan as chairman and treasurer and Whitney as secretary. At the first directors' meeting, apart from Alan Pifer and Whitney Gerard, those present were David Meachin* who became vice-chairman, David Dyer (known to John Reid), Gordon Parker and Alec Walt, both alumni and both friends of mine. Charles Hamilton, Bernard Auer and Caroll Leevy[†] could not attend. Len Read and Leon Dempers, the director of the UCT Foundation, were present as observers.

Len Abrahamse and I attended the second meeting on 30 May 1984 and fund-raising strategy was discussed. Cheetah Haysom, an alumna, joined the board and at the next meeting Wayne Fredericks,[Δ] Sol Marzullo[§] and Charles McGregor[∞] became directors. Anne Moran was appointed as executive director. She had been a development officer at three colleges and universities and was enthusiastic, energetic and very successful. Anne was very ably assisted by the ever cheerful Beryl Dittmer, who together with her husband Erik Dittmer has remained a firm friend. Margaret Touborg succeeded Anne and became the president of the fund in 1989. She has been very successful and efficient and has brought her own brand of quiet humour and professionalism to the office. Over the years a number of distinguished

---

* Chairman of the house committee when I was warden of University House.
[†] Caroll Leevy had been the president of the international association of liver diseases when we had the international liver meeting in Cape Town, and is a good friend.
[Δ] Adviser to Carnegie Corporation.
[§] Mobil Oil.
[∞] UCT alumnus. His late father was a member of the UCT council.

Americans served on the board of directors. The current 19 members are Vincent Mai, Alan Pifer, Whitney Gerard, Charles Hamilton, Wayne Fredericks, Charles McGregor, David Meachin, Maurice Tempelsman, Alice Ilchman, Colin Campbell, Margaret Touborg, Malcolm Barlow, John Spencer, Steven Pfeiffer, Kofi Appenteng, Robert Irwin, Akosua Evans and Barbara Finberg.

The UCT Fund Inc. is completely independent and its primary aim is to raise funds for black students. In the first year of operation the fund received US$209 180. Since its inception in 1984 it has raised some US$17 million, the vast majority of the funds being used for the financial support of black students and for the academic development programme and other programmes to promote black advancement, including the purchase of a block of flats, Liesbeek Gardens, made possible by a challenge grant by the Kresge Foundation. The balance to purchase the flats was made up by a number of donors including the Anglo American organisation and Shell South Africa. Individuals, corporations and foundations in the United States including the Mellon, Rockefeller, Kellogg, Ford and Mott foundations, the Carnegie Corporation of New York and the Rockefeller Brothers' Fund gave generous support over the years. The bulk of the funds went to UCT but funds were also raised for other South African universities including the Open Society's Scholars' Fund. This granted financial aid to black students at five universities (Cape Town, Rhodes, Witwatersrand, Natal and the Western Cape). The Open Society Fund allocated over $100 000 to students at UCT. Alan Pifer, the distinguished founding chairman of the UCT Fund, retired in 1992. He had been a tower of strength and worked tirelessly to raise funds for the promotion of non-racialism at the University of Cape Town. To mark his retirement the fund established, through a gift from Edna and Caryl Haskins, an endowed research fund which allows for an annual award to be presented to a member of staff of the University of Cape Town for research which has demonstrated relevance to the advancement and welfare of disadvantaged people in South Africa. We were very fortunate in obtaining the services of Mr Colin Campbell, president emeritus of Wesleyan University and president of Rockefeller Brothers' Fund, to succeed Alan Pifer as chairman. Under Colin's wise leadership the fund continued to flourish. He stood down and was succeeded in 1999 by Vincent Mai, a distinguished banker who is a UCT alumnus.

Following on our success in the US, which I visited once or twice a year for fund-raising purposes, UCT started a charitable trust in the United Kingdom in 1990. The first three trustees were Sir Aaron Klug, O.M., Nobel Laureate and currently president of the Royal Society, Sir Leonard Hoffman, a high court judge (now Lord Hoffmann, Lord of Appeal) and the late Louis

Walker (a former chairman of Shell South Africa), all graduates of UCT. Mrs Sibylla Tindale was appointed as part-time consultant to the trust and has worked with great vigour and professionalism since 1991 when the trust began its work in February of that year. Her contribution has been exceptional. From 1 April 1991 to 31 March 1997 the trust raised £4 718 175. Sir Raymond (Bill) Hoffenberg, Professor Geoffrey Jowell, Nicky Oppenheimer, Irene Menell and I also became trustees. Lord Annan and Lord Quirk, vice-chancellors of London University, Sir Eric Ash, rector of Imperial College and Gareth Roberts, vice-chancellor of Sheffield University, were particularly helpful to me. My introduction to Noël Annan was memorable. It was at the time of the rationalisation of the London medical schools and Annan had asked Lord Flowers to chair the reviewing committee. As I approached the senate house I saw the graffito prominently displayed 'F- flowers'. Noël Annan greeted me with the enquiry as to whether I had seen the graffito. I couldn't deny it. 'The problem with medical students', he said 'is that they can't spell. They meant "pluck".'

Lord Sainsbury (John) has been an outstanding and most generous supporter of UCT. The Linbury Trust donated £1 million for financial support of black students and currently funds black students to do part of their doctoral studies at the universities of Bristol, Sheffield and Oxford. The Rhodes Trust, Glaxo-Wellcome, the Reuter Foundation, the Garfield Weston Foundation, the Wolfson Foundation, Allan Gray and many others have been very generous in their support.

I have been consistently impressed by the generosity of donors in the USA and Great Britain, and Anita and I have been privileged to meet so many fine people. Fund-raising visits had their lighter sides and their surprises. Of the latter none astonished me more than the senior administrator of a West Coast US university who, expressing fear at the growing numbers of Asians enrolling in his university, asked me for my advice! I told him that I had not fought racism in higher education for so long only to tell him how to apply it. Apparently his greatest fear was that the Asian graduates allegedly did not have a tradition of giving to their alma mater in later life!

Of the former, one amusing incident occurred when I was in Washington DC. I was staying at the British Embassy as a guest of Sir Robin and Lady Renwick, the British Ambassador and his wife, and I was driven in the embassy's Rolls-Royce to my first appointment in a predominantly black part of the city. The chauffeur was quite concerned about my safety! Margaret Touborg was in a taxi heading for the same appointment. The taxi driver asked her what her occupation was and she told him that she worked to help black students at UCT. At that moment the Rolls-Royce crossed at the intersection ahead of them and the taxi driver exclaimed, 'Well, that dude there don't do nothin' for black students!'

We were very active in South Africa and the University Foundation had been established for this purpose in 1961. By 1981 the UCT Foundation had an endowment fund of R11 509 596, which allowed a grant of R1 105 000 to the university in that year. In the ensuing years the endowment fund rose considerably, mainly because of the wise policy of the investment committee. While I was vice-chancellor most donations were tied to specific purposes. I hope UCT will be able to build up a significant endowment. In 1996 when I retired, the fund stood at R120 133 000 and the university received a grant of R8 500 000 from the Foundation in that year. A significant part of the increase in the endowment was the result of wise investment policies followed by the investment committee, which is currently chaired by Ken Geeling. The Foundation has been ably served by trustees and governors down the years. When I retired the trustees were the Hon. Mr Justice P H Tebbutt (chairman), Mr I J Sims, CBE (deputy chairman), Mr E P H Bieber, Mr T N Chapman, Mr A Z Farr, Mr K L G Geeling, Mr G N Krone, Mr M H Hales, Mrs I Menell, Dr M A Ramphele, Mr D R Susman, Mr B J van der Ross and myself. There are 31 distinguished governors.

UCT had an on-going fund-raising programme. In addition, we launched the Education for the Future Campaign with a target of R97 million. The campaign realised over R120 million. During that campaign I made visits to many donors. At one of South Africa's leading banks I was told by their chief economist that the bank was following the advice of the World Bank and was concentrating its donations in the area of primary education. The chairman and the chief executive of the bank looked on benignly while the economist torpedoed my efforts to get a major donation. I wrote to the World Bank and asked them for the evidence on which the policy was based. I read the references the bank sent to me and the only convincing evidence I could find was one study from Thailand. The study showed that if Thai peasant farmers received a primary school education the yield of rice per acre increased. Later I visited the World Bank in Washington and gave a seminar on the role of UCT. A vice-president of the bank was in the chair. At the end of the seminar I told the story about the South African economist and the result of my enquiries and asked for the basis of the World Bank's policy of favouring primary education and not emphasising tertiary education (or secondary for that matter). The chairman started to hum and haw but a member of the bank interrupted him and said that I had been very open and frank with them about UCT and South Africa and they should in turn be honest with me. They then confessed that the policy had been based on flimsy evidence and was under review. The bank has subsequently modified its policies.

The universities in South Africa receive a general state subsidy based on a formula which involves both student enrolments and their success. The formula is designed so that the funds of the university are based upon the changes which occurred in the year before the subsidy is granted. The present Government is changing the structure of the subsidy. In nominal rands the general state subsidy for UCT increased from R71,6 million in 1985 to R195,75 million in 1995. However, the rate of inflation over the same period consistently outstripped the increase in funds. The state subsidy fell as a percentage of net general operating budget revenue, from 75,3 per cent in 1985 to 56,9 per cent in 1995. When all revenue is included, for example the revenue of the graduate school of business and externally funded financial aid, the state subsidy as a percentage of the gross general operating budget revenue in 1995 was 47,8 per cent. The fall in revenue from the State, which is a major source of revenue for all South African universities, has in real terms over the ten-year period put serious financial pressures on the university. In addition to this, the value of the rand plummeted in the mid-1980s and fell further during this ten-year period, so that equipment, books, journals and many other requirements which have to be purchased offshore greatly increased in cost and further strained the university's finances.

Using the consumer price index, the Government subsidy in real terms fell by 15,9 per cent between 1985 and 1989. The international economic sanctions and the poor value of the rand and the unsatisfactory state of the South African economy in general resulted in the Government cutting the subsidy after it had been calculated, on a regular basis in the second half of the eighties. These cuts ranged between 16 and 28 per cent in any one academic year. As a result of the serious financial position, university fees increased to a much greater extent than was desirable. Between 1984 and 1990 there was an average increase of 18 per cent per annum with a range between 12,5 and 22 per cent per annum. In the 1990s the increase was either at or slightly below the level of inflation. The fee increases in the eighties made the financial burden for the students much greater and was of particular concern to us with regard to black students, most of whom did not have the financial resources to meet these costs. Our emphasis on fund-raising for student financial aid was a part of UCT's response.

In 1981 academic fees and living costs totalled about R2 200 and the university's total bursary, scholarship and loan fund budget was R4,2 million. In 1996 the annual cost for students was R24 000 to R25 000 and the total amount allocated for student financial aid was R38,9 million. By that time 2 700 students were receiving financial aid, the vast majority of them black students. This represented 22 per cent of the undergraduate student population. In addition, R2,8 million was allocated for merit scholarships. The source of the funds for student financial aid was a mixture of donations both from within and outside of South Africa and included funds allocated by the university from its general operating budget. The large allocation of funds to student financial aid from its own hard-pressed budget demonstrated the university's commitment in this area. In 1993, for example, despite an overall deficit of R15 million, the university allocated R7,65 million to student financial aid. Universities not admitting black students did not have these financial pressures. UCT also established a special arrangement with the Standard Bank of South Africa whereby the bank loaned money to students even though the students were not able to give the usual sort of guarantees which a bank insists upon, the university standing ultimate guarantor for the loans. Because the bank was charging a high rate of interest (1 per cent below prime), the ceiling put on those loans was R3 000 in any one year. I urged the Government to introduce a national student financial aid scheme and Jan Steyn, who was the chief executive of the Independent Development Trust (IDT) at the time, heard me speaking on the radio. He arranged a meeting at the IDT with all interested stakeholders and as a consequence the IDT allocated money for student financial aid, first doing so in 1992 when UCT received R3,45 million. This grew into the Tertiary Education Fund for South Africa (TEFSA) to which the Government makes major annual contributions, but the need remains greater than the money available.

UCT developed a financial aid package whereby a student would receive a R3 000 loan, plus a contribution from parents, depending on their income; and the student would have to earn R2 000 from work inside or outside the university; the balance of the financial need was given as a bursary. Up until 1996, the university was able to give financial aid to every student who was registered in the university and qualified for financial aid through a means test. By 1995 over R20 million was available for student financial aid from outside agencies, including private donors both in South Africa and overseas. As I write, the new Government has still not established a policy for student financial aid. In 1997, together with economists and actuaries[*] and with the aid of the Mellon Foundation, I drew up a comprehensive policy document in this regard and gave it to the department of education, but as yet they have not announced their policy. This is a great pity and means that the arrangements remain *ad hoc*. Fortunately TEFSA continues to operate very efficiently, so the need is being partially met.

Students who can get sureties are able to secure loans from commercial banks. In 1996 in the entire higher education system, R553,6 million of loan funds were made available in this way. Not many black students have access

---

[*] Sean Archer, Amanda Fitschen, Robert Dorrington, Jan Coetzee, Robert Segall and Jeremy Wakeford.

to these funds. In the same year the total amount of financial aid allocated to higher education from all other sources was R554,9 million.

Mrs Dorothy Mullins, a Cape Town philanthropist, made a donation to the university which enabled us to buy the Glendower Hotel. It has 120 bedrooms and is situated on the Main Road close to the university. I was anxious to acquire the hotel as a back-up, should the university be challenged for having black students in residences. The Government, in its wisdom, had declared that 'international hotels' would be open to all races and it was my strategy that, if confronted, I would tell the authorities that the Glendower was an international hotel and black students were accommodated there. They were, of course, dispersed throughout all the university residences, but I thought that this argument would buy time with the authorities. Fortunately my scheme was never put to the test. The hotel proved to be a valuable purchase in terms of land acquisition. The university was subsequently able to buy a block of flats adjacent to the hotel through a donation by Shell South Africa, giving us additional rooms for black students. Mrs Mullins also made generous donations supporting the department of electrical engineering in memory of her late father.

Quotas and dreams
1983–1984

Problems erupted on the Fort Hare campus in May 1983. The students were vigorously opposed to apartheid in higher education and in society in general and believed that the university administration was unsympathetic to them and was undemocratic in its approach to the university. Lectures were boycotted and there had been episodes of violence. Two mass meetings were held on the UCT campus during May in support of the Fort Hare students and a day-long boycott of lectures was held in solidarity with those students. The Fort Hare students had been particularly incensed by rumours of an award of an honorary degree to Lennox Sebe, president of the so-called independent republic of the Ciskei and a collaborator in the separate development policies of the SA Government. There had also been rumours that he was to be offered the chancellorship of the University of Fort Hare and that the university's name was to be changed to the University of Ciskei.

The students of Fort Hare returned to lectures by the end of May and the 22 students detained by the police were released on bail. However, a second boycott of classes followed, the issue this time being the mid-year examinations. The residences had been without electricity for more than three weeks, disrupting the students' studies. The problems continued at Fort Hare and a breakdown in negotiations resulted in more than 50 per cent of the student body (2 000 students) being unable to continue studying. Many students had been evicted from the university property and there were more than 1 000 students stranded at the railway station.

UCT informed the parents' committee at Fort Hare that those students unable to continue studying, and who qualified for admission to UCT, could be accepted at UCT. A small number of students successfully accepted the offer. We also acted to help a Fort Hare senior lecturer who resigned, after the university council found him guilty of having committed acts prejudicial to the administration, discipline or efficiency of the university and of having failed to obey a lawful order of the rector. He was appointed in a temporary post in the department of surveying at UCT to help him while he decided on his future.

Fort Hare's rector, Professor J H Lamprecht, had indicated that he might sue the UCT students' representative council for defamation. This arose from articles in the SRC press. I wrote to Professor Lamprecht asking him whether he intended calling for an independent public enquiry into the events at Fort Hare University, a step which I strongly favoured. The police presence on the Fort Hare campus aggravated the situation. The UCT council issued a statement in which it noted with deep concern that nearly half of the student body of the University of Fort Hare had been unable to continue studying at that university during the second half of the year. While not having all the facts at its disposal, the council of UCT believed that the matter was of such importance to university life in South Africa that a judicial commission of enquiry should be appointed to look into the relevant events on the Fort Hare campus. The UCT council believed that it was not unlikely that such a commission of enquiry would find that a major contributing factor was the Extension of University Education Act of 1959.

Professor Lamprecht sent a confidential report to the University of Cape Town council, but refused permission for it to be distributed to the student representatives on council. I was unimpressed by it and did not change my view that a commission of enquiry was necessary. The council shared that view. Lamprecht was furious with me and with the university council for what he regarded as interference in the affairs of the University of Fort Hare, and refused to speak to me after this event. He correctly identified me as the person who had encouraged the university council to act in this way. I had no reservations about the action I had taken.

As further signs of repression, the Government deported a student, Mark Kaplan, to Zimbabwe and denied a passport to Graeme Bloch, a full-time teaching assistant in economic history, who had previously been banned while he was an undergraduate student. The university council issued a strong statement condemning the actions by the authorities.

I had always been interested in the Charter 77 Group in Prague in Czechoslovakia. Working under enormous difficulties they had organised a university in their homes and had defied the repressive actions of the totalitarian communist state in which they lived. Dr Julius Tomin had been a leading member of the group and had gone to work in Oxford. I invited him to come to the university and he was the guest of the university's Institute for Advanced Studies in Philosophy. He had devoted himself to classical studies and in critically reliving the past he had applied his mind and energies to improve the lot of the people of Czechoslovakia. Tomin delivered the 1982 T B Davie lecture* and the subject of his address was 'Academic freedom in a repressive society – reflections upon an experience of an East

---

* The annual TB Davie lectures symbolised the university's determination to see academic freedom restored.

European country'. It was a privilege to meet him and to get to know him.

In November Jack de Wet, the dean of science, brought Jan Rafelski to see me. Jack regarded Rafelski as a brilliant theoretical physicist and he certainly had a very impressive record; I do believe he is an outstanding scholar. Subsequently Rafelski was appointed to a chair of theoretical physics at the university and, following on De Wet's urging, the university created additional positions in order to develop a strong school of theoretical physics. We were lucky to recruit Professor Viollier and Professor Cleymans and later Professor Domingez to the group, and they soon became very active. They attracted a large number of post-graduate students and I was very pleased with this development. However, as the months went by, it became clear that there was conflict between Jan Rafelski and some of the members of the physics department who had been there for some time and were respected in the university. The differences became acrimonious and in the end the issue which was used to bring matters to a head was the question as to whether quantum mechanics should be taught to physics students in the second year, the third year or at honours level. When the head of the department and the dean of science were unable to find a solution and all other attempts had failed, I was forced to intervene and the first thing I had to do was to find out what quantum mechanics is! I therefore did a crash course over a weekend. I then interviewed all the parties and made a ruling which seemed to settle the matter for some time. However, the tensions between Rafelski and other members of staff continued and he left the university when I refused to meet the additional requests which he was making. I don't think that Jack de Wet, who was in retirement when these matters came to finality, ever forgave me for allowing Rafelski to leave. The remaining theoretical physicists at UCT continue to make important contributions to knowledge.

The Vista University Act was passed and created a university with multiple urban campuses exclusively for Africans. Students other than Africans could be admitted with the minister's written permission. The university was asked to nominate a member of the council of Vista University, but we declined because it was perpetuating apartheid in higher education. I phoned Dr Hartzenberg, the deputy minister concerned primarily with the legislation which brought this university about despite our protests, to protest forcefully once again against its creation and there were strong words between us on the telephone. The following day Dr Treurnicht launched the Conservative Party with Dr Hartzenberg as its deputy leader. It was the last act that Dr Hartzenberg piloted through parliament before becoming a leading member of the extreme right wing in that house.

1983–1984

Tragedy struck our family on 19 February 1983. My wife Noreen had been depressed for some time, but her suicide that day was unexpected and a great shock. The children and I were devastated. At a time like that everyone close to the person who dies examines his or her conscience to see what role they might have played in the tragic event. I was quite clear that the children were in no way to blame and my first concern was to make that absolutely clear to them. I phoned my old friend, the professor of surgery, John Terblanche, and told him what had happened and he was at the house within five minutes.

I have had to ask myself whether the energies and time I put into my career as a trainee in specialist medicine, as a specialist and particularly as professor of medicine and then as deputy principal and as vice-chancellor had meant that I had neglected Noreen and that that had played a role in her suicide. I will never know for sure whether that was the case or not. I had thought about this from time to time while she was alive, but did not think that I was not giving my wife the love and attention which she had deserved, but as I look back on it I am forced to conclude that it is possible that I fell short.

The memorial service was moving. It was conducted by the Reverend Michael Norman, a blind minister, in St Stephen's Church in Pinelands, and the church and the church hall were filled to overflowing by members of the university community and the city, and by people from the coloured and African townships, because Noreen had been very active in providing a soup kitchen for the poor, in the African Scholars' Fund which provided financial support for black schoolchildren, and in the then fledgeling Read Organisation which provided books for black schools. Read has become a major source of books and other materials for those schools and still plays a very active role in South Africa. Black and white came to mourn her passing and the memorial service was a great source of strength for the children and myself. Len Abrahamse came to console me the day after Noreen died and I felt it only right to assure him, in view of my position in the university, that there was no hint of scandal involved. I remember his kindness and his saying to me, 'Well you never know, you might get married again,' but I thought at the time that was a very unlikely possibility. Suicide is something from which a family does not recover completely.

In the interests of the family and the university I believed that I should get into the swing of things as quickly as possible, which is what I did, and I remember going to the Rag ball on 8 March where I crowned the Rag Queen, as tradition demanded. In later years this event fell away because of the rejection of symbols such as Rag queens. That was a particularly difficult evening, but I managed. I went to the university Rag on 12 March. This is one of the fund-raising events for SHAWCO and the students make colourful, decorated floats which go up and down Adderley Street, the main street in Cape Town, twice, on a particular Saturday morning, with the citizens of Cape Town throwing money on the floats. My son John entered a private float. He had turned his small car into a large beer can and took part in the Rag procession. I thought that this represented a remarkable resilience on his part because, like his sister, he had been very upset by the loss of his mother. His car developed a flat tyre at the far end of Adderley Street on the first pass of the procession and I could see something was going on at the end of the road, from my position on a balcony of a shop where the committee and members of the university staff were gathered. I was very anxious in case a member of the public had run out in front of his car and had been injured, and was very relieved when I discovered it was only a puncture that had caused the difficulty. He and his friends rapidly changed the wheel and were soon back in the procession.

In 1983 the Government decided to develop a large African township on the Cape Flats about 25 miles from central Cape Town. It was to be called Khayelitsha, and now has a population which must exceed half a million. The township consists entirely of shacks made of corrugated iron, wood, sacks and plastic of various kinds. The officials surrounded the entire proposed site (it extends over a much larger area now as a result of the inhabitants' initiatives) with a very high fence topped with barbed wire, and built very high concrete towers surmounted by powerful lights which were on all night. It reminded me of a concentration camp. There was one entry and exit point. (There are now many.) The students wanted to send a SHAWCO mobile medical clinic there on Monday evenings as there were no health facilities in the area. The authorities were reluctant to agree as the students were regarded as 'mischief makers'. After all, they came from that centre of revolutionary activities, the University of Cape Town! I phoned the authorities and they agreed SHAWCO could send the mobile clinic, but insisted that it remain just inside the gates next to the administrative board's office which was built there. I decided to go with the students on the first visit, as the supervising doctor. We parked the two vehicles next to the administration building. One vehicle was equipped with examination cubicles and the other served as a dispensing and waiting room. The first small houses and shacks had been built about two miles from the gates. We sat and waited for the patients, but none came. This was hardly surprising because of the distance we were from the houses and because we had little opportunity to advertise that we were coming. We used one of the SHAWCO vehicles to fetch the patients. We saw a large number of patients, some quite ill. Early the next morning I was phoned by a very irate official who said that as we had not stayed exclusively next to the administration building, we would not be allowed to go again. I told him what had happened and that, if he persisted in his attitude, I would go to the press and expose their callousness. The mobile clinic went regularly thereafter without interruption and does so to this day.

A major threat to the university in 1983 was the University Amendment Bill, which sought to replaced the Government-controlled permit system with a racially determined quota which universities would be required to administer. It was strongly condemned on the occasion of its first reading in parliament by the vice-chancellors of the University of the Witwatersrand, Natal and Rhodes and by myself. I had initiated this united opposition of the bill, acting on behalf of the university's academic freedom committee.

I called a university assembly in the Jameson Hall on 3 May and I compared the proposed quota system, inter alia, with the quotas imposed by the Nazis and Stalinist Russia, and rejected the notion outright. About 2 000 students and members of the university's staff filled Jameson Hall and another 400 people were on the steps outside hoping to be able to push their way into the crowded hall. A motion to reject the quota system and calling on the university to ignore any quota imposed, should the bill be passed, was unanimously approved. The chairman of council, Len Abrahamse, and the chairman of the council of the University of the Witwatersrand, Dr Stutterheim, saw the Minister of National Education, Dr Viljoen, and urged him not to proceed with the Quota Bill.

The vice-chancellors of the University of the Witwatersrand, Rhodes and UCT issued a statement condemning the proposals. I unsuccessfully called for a special meeting of the Committee of University Principals (CUP). At an unofficial meeting convened at Glenara, Professor Mouton from the Orange Free State was the only head of an Afrikaans university to attend. The meeting rejected the quota proposals.

During May and June I had lengthy meetings with Dr Viljoen on three occasions, and wrote to him protesting against the proposed bill. The council of the University of the Western Cape also expressed its opposition to the bill, but the Afrikaans universities were silent. Indeed, most of them supported the bill saying it was 'a step in the right direction'. I sat through the entire debate in parliament while the bill was under consideration. I knew the Minister of National Education from the time when he had been rector of the Rand Afrikaans University and I fixed my eyes on him whenever he spoke. Our glances often met. He knew of my implacable opposition to the bill. During the week of the debate, the board of the South African Broadcasting Corporation held a cocktail party at the Arthur's Seat Hotel in

Sea Point. Professor Mouton was also chairman of the board of the broadcasting corporation, and I was invited to the cocktail party. The entire Cabinet was there as well as many other politicians and leading members of the professions and the business world. When I went up to speak to Viljoen everybody moved away so that the two of us were isolated in the middle of the room with about a ten to fifteen foot radius around us in which no one stood. They probably assumed that we were arguing about the bill. In fact, after my initial remark saying that he knew very well where I stood on the bill and his acknowledgement of that, Viljoen and I discussed other matters.

John Reid had been closely identified with the university's and my opposition to the bill. As acting vice-chancellor on an occasion when I was away from the campus, he spoke out forthrightly against the bill and condemned it. In the event, the bill passed the third reading in July and the Minister of National Education asked to see me. He said that the State President had signed the bill into law and that it was now an Act of parliament, but that the Government would not enforce the law, with two exceptions in the case of the University of Cape Town. They would not allow UCT to enrol African students in the department of land surveying or in the faculty of medicine, because they wanted to protect the department of land surveying at the University of Fort Hare and the training of medical students at the Medical University of South Africa (MEDUNSA). He argued that this was necessary in order to prevent all the best African students from coming to UCT. I told him that universities are not protected by such means. I also asked him why the Government was not enforcing the legislation. His reply was that they had come to realise how strongly I and the University of Cape Town and other universities opposed the bill and what an adverse effect it would have on the country's international image. I pointed out that it had taken him and the Cabinet a long time to realise that, given our outspoken opposition to the legislation over so many months. To my knowledge this was the first time that the National Government backed down on enforcing legislation of a racist kind. It did illustrate that one could have some influence on them. At this time the threatening or abusive phone calls became much more frequent. Len Abrahamse insisted the university place a guard at my house at night for a short period because of the intensity of the abuse.

There was not only trouble with the Government but also with the students of the university, and sometimes there was a connection between the two. Students were angry when Professor Robert Schrire, head of the department of political science, invited first Minister Pik Botha (Foreign Affairs) and five days later Minister Piet Koornhof (Co-operation and Development, i.e. African affairs) to give lectures in his department. Botha's visit received little attention from the students during his visit, but the head of the department was censured in the students' newspaper, *Varsity*, for arranging the 'untimely and insensitive' appearance of Botha on the campus at a time when students and staff were resisting the Quota Bill. Koornhof incensed some of the students by trying to prevent the publication of extracts of his speech. Schrire had given Koornhof his assurance that the lecture would not be published and had informed the *Varsity* reporters of this undertaking, saying the Koornhof lectures were 'off the record'. However, Nic Borain, the editor of *Varsity*, was intent on publishing a broadsheet dealing with the lectures. When I spoke to him, referring to Professor Schrire's agreement with Dr Koornhof, he replied that the *Sunday Times* were planning to run the story two days later and *Varsity* was not prepared to be upstaged by the *Sunday Times* (a major national newspaper!). There was plainly a dispute and I needed to establish how firm an assurance had been given to Koornhof. I gave Borain an instruction not to publish until I had established the facts of the matter. *Varsity* did print the broadsheet and eighteen members of the *Varsity* staff were required to appear before the university court, charged with defying an order from the vice-chancellor. My actions were vigorously criticised by the students and I now think that I was wrong in giving Nic Borain an instruction not to publish when it was clear that he would defy that instruction. The wiser course would have been for me to advise him not to publish – as opposed to instructing him – and then to deal with the matter subsequently at a lower key.

Ironically, Koornhof was speaking about possible reforms to the South African Government's racist policies; perhaps that was why he was so anxious they shouldn't enter the public domain. Senate and council, in an important policy declaration, reaffirmed support for freedom of speech and association on the campus and the right of academics to invite any person to take part in any academic programme. Any restriction on or denial of this right would impinge upon academic freedom and would limit or deny freedom of expression. The declaration also reaffirmed the right to dissent against such invitations or views expressed, provided that the expression of such dissent in no way limited the freedom of expression or speech. I pointed out that these principles were fundamental to open and free enquiry and discovery and therefore to the very nature of a university. The committee on freedom of expression at Yale put it very well in 1975, stating that 'a university must do everything possible to ensure within it the fullest degree of intellectual freedom. The history of intellectual growth and discovery clearly demonstrates the need for unfettered freedom, the right to think the unthinkable, discuss the unmentionable and challenge the unchallengeable.' This was the beginning of a number of attacks on the right to speak on campus. These occurred against the background of draconian denial of human rights by the Government.

Honorary degrees were usually conferred at the mid-year graduation ceremony. Amongst the recipients in June were Dr C F Beyers Naudé, a banned, prominent theologian, church leader and civil rights activist, and Mr R S (Dick) Sonnenberg, the chairman of Woolworths for 25 years, and a member of the university council for more than 14 years. I was very fond of Mr Sonnenberg, who was committed to UCT and its values and had generously supported the university. Permission had to be obtained from the Minister of Law and Order for Dr Beyers Naudé to come to Cape Town to receive the honorary degree, because his banning orders restricted him to a magisterial district in Johannesburg. Consent was given for that and Dr and Mrs Naudé stayed as guests at Glenara. He is one of South Africa's most outstanding living sons and had courageously spoken and acted against apartheid at great personal cost. It was customary for one of the honorary graduates to make the graduation speech and I sought permission for Beyers Naudé to do this since the terms of his banning order prohibited his speaking in public, but the request was denied. As a consequence I gave the speech and in my speech I spoke of dreams I had had the night before. I described the speeches given by each of the honorary graduates and described my dream about Beyers Naudé as follows:

> *In my fourth dream Dr Naudé was addressing this congregation. He spoke of man's understanding of God, faith and compassion, of forgiveness and reconciliation, of the importance of love of one's fellow man, and of the dangers of bigotry and ideology. He spoke as a man of God who had turned his back on ideas of racial exclusiveness and had seen so clearly the dangers apartheid had for the Afrikaner people – his own people – as a Christian community, to say nothing of the dangers it held for the rest of the people of South Africa. On a campus such as UCT's, students of diverse cultural and other backgrounds should grow together, should exchange ideas and debate the fundamental problems of life and society. Out of that free exchange of ideas new directions and enterprises may arise. Any legislation or manoeuvre that keeps people apart, especially idealistic and energetic youth on university campuses, is an impediment to progress and to present and future peace. If, as some say, apartheid is dead, the funeral is taking an awful long time.*
>
> *When I woke from my dreams I realised again that there were those who would not let Dr Naudé speak. Why should that be? I asked myself. What could be so dangerous in the spoken or written word of such a man? And then it came to me; someone, somewhere, was afraid of ideas, afraid that the fatal flaws in our society might be exposed with such force and eloquence that the folly of pursuing them would become obvious to all. But I was not depressed when I awoke; on the contrary, I was exhilarated, because as long as South Africa produces men like our four distin-*

guished honorary graduates, there is hope for us all.

Shortly after the ceremony Mrs Helen Suzman phoned me and told me that I had been naughty. She said that I was really pushing my luck to the limit with the graduation speech. The reply was that one couldn't possibly be prosecuted for talking about something which one dreamed, because dreams occurred during sleep and were not under voluntary control! The call was in fact to offer congratulations!

In August Helen Joseph, the doughty anti-apartheid campaigner, delivered the T B Davie lecture in Jameson Hall. Her subject was 'The doors of learning and culture shall be open'. I quoted from the Freedom Charter publicly during the meeting, which greatly surprised the student leaders since it was illegal to do so. Helen Joseph was given a standing ovation.

The students and staff continued to feel the wrath of the Government. Pete Hathorn, one of thousands of students who faced conscription in 1983, was one of many who resisted. He was the first to do so for political reasons, drawing links between his stand and resistance to apartheid. He received the maximum sentence of two years' imprisonment. On review a month later it was reduced to one year. Graeme Bloch, then a lecturer in economic history, had his passport application refused for the third time, probably because of his involvement with the detainee parents' support committee.

But there was an important development in my personal life as well. In April 1983 Professor Lamar Crowson* had made an appointment to come and see me in my office. Lamar was professor of music and a distinguished concert pianist with an established international reputation. He was a true maestro. He said he had come to see me to invite me to dinner on a Saturday evening. At that time I didn't accept any invitations on Saturday evenings that weren't absolutely obligatory to attend, because I was trying to keep the weekend free to spend time at home. But because he had taken the trouble to come to see me personally in my office, I didn't feel that I could refuse him and so I accepted. When I got there I met his wife Estelle, who is a cousin of F W de Klerk, and F W de Klerk and his wife Marike were amongst the guests. The other guests were Dr Raymund van Niekerk, who was then director of the national art gallery, Dr Reeve Sanders, who was chief medical superintendent of Groote Schuur Hospital and a distinguished UCT alumna, and Anita Louw, a friend of our hostess, who was a lecturer in the department of cultural history of Western Europe at the university. At the dinner party I did not feel that it was polite for me to launch into an attack on De Klerk and he plainly reciprocated. It wouldn't have been difficult to find things to fight

---

* Lamar Crowson died in 1998.

about! Indeed, at that time, I was in the middle of the very public and vigorous campaign against the Quota Bill and was certainly well out of favour with the Government of which, of course, De Klerk was a part, as a member of the Cabinet. However, Anita Louw felt no such constraint and launched into a vigorous attack of De Klerk and the Nationalist Government at the dinner party to which he responded with equal vigour. I was impressed by her. De Klerk later claimed that he played cupid for Anita and me.

Raymund van Niekerk gave a brunch at his home, which was adjacent to the national art gallery, the following month and invited me to come. It was then that I met Anita socially for the second time. I had met her the previous year when we visited the department of cultural history, and I was told subsequently that when we left the department, I said to those with me that I was impressed by her and by the vigour of her approach, and that I thought she was a good member of staff. I was strongly attracted to Anita and invited her to dinner. In the course of the following month it became clear to both of us that we wanted to spend our lives together. Some time later we went to have dinner with the Crowsons and I told Lamar that Anita and I had decided to get married. He said that he was pleased that we had settled our differences. I enquired what the differences were and he told me that I had questioned the confirmation of her appointment as a lecturer and that she had been very annoyed about it, and that he had invited us to dinner together on the first occasion to try to resolve the difficulties between us. I was astounded, having no recollection at all of being involved in Anita's confirmation as a member of the faculty. Anita thought I had known about this all along and assumed that I would have realised why she had been very critical of me as vice-chancellor, and had told people in the faculty of arts that I had 'liver on the brain', and that no physician should ever be the vice-chancellor of a university because such people didn't have a broad view of things.

When I got to my office the next morning I asked Sheilah Lloyd if she could get me Anita Louw's file and she promptly put it on my desk. She had obviously been expecting the request! And indeed, the year before, Anita's confirmation had come up and the head of the department and the dean had both recorded that she was excellent at teaching, research and administration and unanimously recommended her confirmation in a tenured post. At that time confirmation was virtually automatic at the university and I had decided to end this and so when Anita's documents crossed my desk I decided the time had come to do something about it and I wrote back to the dean and said, 'I need evidence for the statement that you make about the excellence of Anita Louw.' The dean and the head of department were astonished

– nothing like this had ever happened at the University of Cape Town before, and so there had to be a survey of student opinion and other members of staff had to give their views and in the end the Louw report came back confirming the excellence of her work. I then signed the document and added a note saying that this was an important matter and I was glad we had taken trouble with it, because indeed Miss Louw was likely to be with us for a long time. Little did I know what I was saying!

At the beginning of 1984 fifteen black students had individually approached Nic Borain, now SRC president, all saying that they could not pay their fees. They had been under the impression that once they had gained admission their fees would be paid by the university. Some of them had arrived without money for accommodation and living expenses, and without help would have to leave the university. I ordered the release of R20 000 from university funds to be allocated to 60 students and subsequently additional funds were found. None of the students were forced to leave and so discontinue their studies. Borain issued a statement which read, 'I think we should be grateful for Dr Saunders's speedy action; however, I believe UCT will not be able to uphold this principle in the long term. In coming years more black students will become eligible for admission to institutions like UCT and there will be a point at which the university won't be able to subsidise the growing numbers who apply for assistance.' I was determined to postpone that day for as long as possible.

Black students' real problems with regard to accommodation were brought into sharp focus when a group of fifty students put up tents on the lawn in front of the Jameson Hall to protest against the lack of accommodation. For a number of years we had made every attempt to meet the needs of black students. We had obtained accommodation in a vacant building at the city hospital, but with further development of the hospital this accommodation fell away. We had opened our residences to black students, but could not accommodate all black students in this way. All possible areas in the Peninsula had been searched to obtain additional accommodation for black students, and accommodation was arranged at Baker House, the Athlone Hotel, the Kensington Inn, the Hotel Reo, at the Methodist Church hostel, at the Lutheran youth centre and in private homes. Also UCT had bought the Glendower Hotel. In January 1984 Mr Albert Thomas was appointed with a brief to help black students find accommodation. He and others gave an enormous amount of time and attention to this problem during the early part of that year. They met with an *ad hoc* committee elected by a mass meeting of black students to discuss their accommodation and transport problems and agreed to investigate the possibility of arranging a bus to route through the areas of maximum need, terminating on the campus.

Soon after the tents were put up in protest, the students' representatives were asked to contact the ten students who were allegedly experiencing difficulties and ask them to give Mr Thomas their names and addresses, indicating what their needs were. Surprisingly no students responded to that request. He went to see the students in the tents but they had not formulated their demands. Later they came forward with them:

'We, the black students of the University of Cape Town, realise that the present accommodation crisis is part and parcel of the suppression and exploitation of the black working class in this country, which is one of land dispossession, hence KTC, Crossroads and Winterveld.* The squatting action is the result of no positive response on the part of the UCT administration to repeated demands to assume full responsibility for the accommodation and provision of transport for black students. Given the above, we here resolve to persist in our present form of action until such time as our short-term demand is met. Our short term demand: that UCT administration provide immediate and adequate accommodation on campus for those black students without accommodation, suitable for study purpose, and noting that other black students are accommodated far from campus, we therefore demand that transport be provided for them. Our long term demand: that UCT administration provide accommodation for all its students. The UCT administration should note that the above is but one of our most pressing grievances at this campus.'

The protesters were warned that a contract had been signed with a company to convert the centre of the University Avenue into a pedestrian mall (these costs were met by donations from alumni) and that within three days the contractor would come onto the site where the tents were. They were asked to remove the tents. The seriousness of the situation was stressed. When asked to advise me of anything which might to done to solve their problems, they suggested that the managers of all the hotels in the vicinity should be told to give students accommodation at low rates because, they said, not all the hotel rooms were occupied! Professor Reid and I visited the students and spoke to six of them, including a member of the committee. I instructed them that they had to leave the site before the contractors arrived on the next Monday morning. I was interested to see that they had been watching television in a tent. When we returned that evening most of the students were holding a general meeting in a large tent on the grass. The meeting was interrupted to allow the committee to talk with us and I gave an instruction to each member of the committee personally, and through

---

* Places where squatters lived.

them collectively to all the students concerned, that they were to leave the site on the Monday morning, and warned that if they did not do so they would be liable for any costs incurred.

On the Monday morning the contractor arrived on the site and set up a small working hut on the lawn opposite to the one where the students had their tents. The students tried to prevent the hut from being set up and immediately erected additional tents on the lawn where the contractor had started working. At considerable inconvenience the contractor proceeded. He was very co-operative in adjusting his programme to avoid critical delays, but if the tents had stayed up a few days longer it would have been impossible for him to fulfil the contract on time.

The traffic committee met, and after extensive negotiations with the City Tramways, a bus route was established providing transport from some of the black townships to the campus. This service was initially operated first as an experiment, to assess the need, but ran for a number of years. The protesting students were asked to request all students who had acute accommodation problems to see Mr Albert Thomas before 16.30 on that Monday afternoon. Only one student came to see him before the deadline. A small number came forward afterwards and were immediately helped.

The students placed an obscene poster in a prominent position. They had also put up a number of banners denigrating the university, and of course the press had given great prominence to the fact that there were tents on the university campus because students could not obtain accommodation. After fifteen days the students removed the tents. The following week eleven students received registered letters indicating that they had to answer disciplinary charges. In a show of solidarity 400 students marched to the Bremner Building where some tried to climb up some pillars in order to reach the first floor. One of the glass doors at the entrance to the building was shattered and eventually entry was forced through a side door and protesting students poured into the building. They were unruly and aggressive. I was in Pretoria on official university business and Professor John Reid was acting as vice-chancellor. He discussed the problems again with the steering committee. The students then left the Bremner Building after giving Professor Reid a list of 206 students who they claimed had also been involved. Similar charges were sent to those students.

These students next declared that they rejected the university council and its authority, that they rejected the rules for students and that they rejected the disciplinary procedures of the university. I pointed out to them that if they carried that attitude to its logical conclusion, then the results would be most unfortunate. It was also emphasised that throughout the time that the tents had been on the campus, there was accommodation for four additional students at Malangu Park flats and that four of the protesters were actually living there and did indeed have accommodation. Donald Carr, who had not been involved in any of these matters, presided over a disciplinary hearing at which 217 students allegedly guilty of offences during the protest were to appear individually to answer the charges against them. Nearly 500 students arrived for the hearing and a spokesman stated that the 'student body' had resolved that they would not appear individually. Donald Carr was only prepared to conduct the hearing on an individual basis. When it became clear that it would be impossible to proceed with the hearing, Donald made a statement to those present: 'I say to all the students involved in the recent protest, that if during the remainder of this academic year or during the next academic year any of you is in breach of Rule 8 for students, i.e. if you break that rule in the future during that time, you may be fined and will be suspended from the university pending further disciplinary action. We have a list of 217 students allegedly so involved, and those are the people who were to have been here today.'

A copy of Donald's statement was sent to every student concerned and I issued a statement that any student who wished to write to me indicating that he or she wanted his/her name removed from the list should do so, giving the reasons why that should be so, and that the matter would be treated in the strictest confidence and there would be no fear of victimisation by other students. A large number of students did write indicating that they had had no involvement in the events that had taken place. We knew that only about 50 students had been involved. The outcome was very unsatisfactory from the disciplinary point of view and resulted in a review of all disciplinary procedures.

The leader of the protesting black students was Mr Victor Steyn and the student movement which had organised the protest was the Azanian Students Movement (AZASM). Victor Steyn was subsequently involved in a number of other student protests. On one occasion the front page of the *Cape Times* carried a dramatic picture of him wielding large wirecutters to cut through a wire fence during a protest which took place on the Cape Flats against the tricameral parliamentary elections. A few years later he was excluded from the law faculty because he had not met minimum academic requirements. I intervened on his behalf because I believed him to be an able young man and a leader with considerable potential. The dean of law managed to persuade his colleagues to readmit Victor, although they did so with great reluctance. Unfortunately he was not successful the second time around. When I intervened on his behalf I told Victor that I was reminded of the experience of the deputy chairman of council, Mr Justice Marius Diemont, who had been expelled as a student by the then vice-chancellor,

Sir Jock Beattie, because he had called a mass meeting without the vice-chancellor's permission! (Things were different in those days.) Beattie had told him to pack his bags and leave. While he was packing, the registrar arrived and advised Diemont to see Beattie again, saying he thought Beattie was relenting. Beattie did give him a second chance and said, 'Be sure you do the same when you are in my position.' Diemont had related that story when he had acted in a similar way when he was presiding at a university court. Years later Victor told me that the whole event had been a drive for membership by AZASM and an attempt to gain prominence on the campus. He confessed that there had been no acute accommodation problem!

Later in the year a workshop on conflict accommodation and management in South Africa was organised on the campus by the Centre for Intergroup Studies. Chief Mangosuthu Buthelezi, the leader of Inkatha, had been invited to deliver a lecture and thereafter to participate in a panel discussion with Dr Alex Boraine, MP, Mr Wynand Malan, MP and Dr Ntatho Motlana. In the early evening, a group of about 200 students arrived at the venue and filled the back of the lecture theatre. They carried placards, sang and chanted and were addressed by the SRC president, Mr Nic Borain, who read excerpts from an honours thesis containing sworn affidavits by students of the University of Zululand about violence on their campus the year before. Other student leaders also addressed the meeting, relating incidents of violence on that campus which they alleged had been carried out by Inkatha. Chief Buthelezi, who had not yet left his hotel, was informed by Professor Reid, who was acting as vice-chancellor in my absence overseas, of the situation and decided not to appear. Professor Reid then cancelled the session and requested the other speakers to leave. The council established a committee to look into the matter.

The committee found that in view of the fact that it was very difficult to identify the students who entered the lecture theatre and that Chief Buthelezi had not come, that their behaviour had not up until that point broken any rules of the university, and that those who addressed the meeting did so after it had been announced that the meeting was cancelled, it was unlikely that any prosecution of any student in the university court would be successful. Indeed, John Reid had already taken the decision not to prosecute students. He had the sole authority to decide whether or not to prosecute when I was away from the campus. The university council issued a statement affirming the right of freedom of speech on the campus, but also the right to dissent. This was again one of a number of battles to try to ensure the right for all points of view to be heard on campus.

A new students' organisation, the National Students Federation (NSF), was launched with the purpose of providing a 'moderate' alternative to

NUSAS. They claimed they 'intended to maintain a moderate presence on campuses and promote changes, patriotism and the involvement of students in attempts at peaceful, evolutionary change in South Africa.' The first chairman stated that the NSF 'does not uphold apartheid' and would provide an alternative to the 'radical campus politics ... the left-wing dictatorship of NUSAS'. On the UCT campus the movement affiliated to the NSF was the Moderate Students Movement (MSM). The organisation seemed to me to be anything but moderate and was widely regarded as being right-wing. We strongly suspected that the NSF was aided and abetted by the police, and indeed a few years later it became public knowledge that they were helped and funded by the security police. The security police actively tried to subvert the actions of members, and destabilise the campuses of the English-speaking and black universities.

In our search for more accommodation, particularly for black students, we bought the Groote Schuur residential hotel and Consolata House, and through a very generous donation by the chancellor, Mr Harry Oppenheimer, were able to plan for the next university residence, The Woolsack. This was to be built around the old historical building, The Woolsack, which was designed by Sir Herbert Baker at the request of Cecil Rhodes. Rudyard Kipling wrote some of his poems there. The house was allegedly haunted because the original architect of the university, J M Solomon, committed suicide there. It was alleged that his suicide was in part due to failure to achieve all he had wanted to in the design of the campus because of a lack of funds. The pavilions containing the student accommodation extend down from west to east, with the Woolsack in the centre, and were built with a design similar to a student residence at the University of Virginia, one of whose alumni was Edgar Alan Poe. This was fitting because the original campus was inspired in part by the architecture of the University of Virginia.

Earlier in the year Anita and I were married in the garden of Glenara, and after a very short honeymoon we were both in full swing in our work. She was a lecturer in the cultural history of Western Europe, which was a course that investigated the history of thought and ideas from the point of view of philosophy, the visual arts, history and other disciplines. Carrying a full teaching load, she certainly found life very hectic during that first year.

Anita has been a wonderful support to me over the years. She has never complained about our hectic, demanding and overcrowded schedule. A scholar in her own right, she was a popular undergraduate and postgraduate teacher. She had also been a successful art critic. She put her stamp on Glenara, giving full expression to her sense of style and taste. Ever the thoughtful hostess she ensured that the table at Glenara was of a high standard. With her life-long involvement in fine art, she proved to be a wonderful teacher and allowed me to develop a keen interest in art. During the many periods that we received abusive phone calls, Anita and I agreed that we would not mention them to each other but ignore them completely. From the age of 93 to 98 my mother lived with us at Glenara because her eyesight had deteriorated badly, and nothing was too much for Anita to ensure my mother was comfortable and happy. Towards the end of 1984 it had become clear that, for a number of reasons, Anita should resign her post in the department of the cultural history of Western Europe. It was a painful decision for her but the right one at the time, and so after the supplementary examinations early in 1985, she left the department.

Anita's late father Dr Appie Louw was a UCT medical graduate who worked as a country general practitioner and was the complete doctor who did internal medicine, obstetrics and surgery – major and minor. He flew his own plane to visit patients. An expert marksman, he was also a notable sheep and game farmer. I admired Appie's fearless honesty. He died in 1990 and I miss his warm friendship and support. Her mother Stephanie, apart from supporting her husband, qualified and practised as a lawyer, ran her own gift shop and is an accomplished artist. I knew Anita's brother Stephen long before I met her. He had been my registrar in the department of medicine and was doing post graduate research in Edinburgh when Anita and I met. He later became professor of geriatrics at UCT before emigrating to the United Kingdom.

I spoke at the prizegivings of a number of schools and my theme was a consistent one, urging the school children to work hard and to make the most of the opportunities that they had. All the schools were privileged white schools and I made it clear that the sort of education they received had to be available to all South Africans and that the schools should be integrated. On one occasion, while I was speaking, about 20 parents walked out of the hall. I went on speaking without interruption while this was going on. The headmaster apologised to me afterwards, but I indicated to him that such things were bound to happen in a very prejudiced society.

A torrid year 1985

1985 proved to be a torrid year for the university and for me. An indication of things to come was the arrest in the early hours of the morning of 8 March of eleven UCT students who were alleged to have attended an illegal gathering in November 1984. A group of students had formed a poster demonstration on the university rugby fields following on the detention of Kate Philip, the president of NUSAS. One of the students arrested was Christine Burger, the president of the SRC, and another the daughter of Advocate Farlam (later Judge), a senior advocate in Cape Town.

I was awoken early that morning by Andy Durbach, a young woman lawyer who had been called to represent the students. We went to the magistrate's court in Wynberg where the students were being held in the police cells. We went down into the police cells, reassured students that they would be adequately represented and that we were confident they would be let out on bail. I expressed my outrage that they had been arrested. Apparently police video cameras had been used to identify them. Some of the students were doing professional courses and were worried as to whether they would be able to practise their professions on qualification. Indeed the police had been telling them that they would not be able to do so. I reassured them and told them the police were engaged in misinformation. I stayed in the magistrate's court with Andy Durbach and the hearing was remanded to a later date. They were released on bail of R150 each. We had arranged for the deputy registrar of student affairs to have the money available for any student who could not afford the bail. We often took such action both for staff and students, taking care that the funds did not come from the money we had received from the Government. I publicly expressed my objection to the fact that the students had been arrested and to the way in which the arrests had been conducted. The mother of one of the students had said that ten policemen had come to arrest her eighteen-year-old daughter.

My protests received a lot of publicity in the press. Brigadier Kotze, divisional head of the Cape Town C I D, came to see me and admitted the police used inappropriate force. He said the police believed I had forbidden them to enter UCT property and that consequently the arrests had been made off campus. I asked him, if that was the case, why were the arrests made in the early hours of the morning and with such a show of force. I pointed out that the police weren't welcome on the campus when the students or staff were going about their business or were involved in peaceful protest but only if they were combating criminal activity such as robbery or assault. The Brigadier gave me an undertaking that ordinarily no police action would occur on campus without notifying me beforehand, unless time did not permit this in an emergency. As we will see, the police did not always keep this undertaking but my attitude did act as a relative deterrent to them. He told me that the police held warrants of arrest for about 100 students on the same charge.

This highlighted the question of what the university's response should be, should a police officer approach the university with regard to a member of the university for whom a warrant, a summons or a subpoena had been issued for an arrest. The university's policy with regard to providing information to a third party, including State authorities, had been determined some years earlier and was reviewed in the middle of 1984. In terms of this policy the university had decided it would release the address of an individual if such a warrant or summons or subpoena had been issued, but that the person concerned would also be informed immediately by the university. This policy had been decided in consultation with the student leadership. It had been decided upon because in terms of the law, the university was obliged to give the information. In the event neither I nor any other university official was approached by the police regarding any other student. Eventually the charges against the students were withdrawn. At an emergency meeting of the Students' Representative Council a resolution was passed to thank the university authorities for the 'high level' of support shown for the arrested students. 'The prompt and vocal response to the arrests clearly showed the outrage felt by the campus,' and that those arrested 'derived great strength and courage from this support.'

Shortly after this I was asked to see the Minister of Education and Culture in the House of Assembly (Own Affairs), Mr J C (Stoffel) Botha (our nickname for him was 'Stifle' Botha). When I saw the Minister in what was called the Verwoerd Building* it was clear to me that he really had nothing to say. After about ten minutes he said that his friend, the Minister of Law and Order, Mr Louis le Grange, wanted to talk to me and that he would take me to him. We went to a very large office, replete with South African police flags and the South African national flag and large photographs of P W Botha,

---

* Now 120 Plein Street.

who was then the State President. Having introduced me to the Minister of Law and Order, Stoffel Botha left. Le Grange asked me what he could do for me. I replied saying that it was not a question of what he could do for me, but what he wanted to say to me because he had asked for the meeting, not I. He then discussed the recent events concerning the arrest of the students in the early hours of the morning and said that he had discussed the matter with the divisional commissioner and Major Odendaal, the head of the riot squad. He had indicated to them that he was very unhappy about what had happened. He said, 'I am not going to do what you want me to do' and I said, 'Why not?' and he said, 'I will never criticise the police in public. I will never undermine the police.' I told him that that was exactly where he was wrong; that if the police did something wrong, it was his responsibility to say so publicly to ensure that the police did not abuse their powers, which were extensive and far-reaching. He would have none of it. He said he was issuing a statement which would show his displeasure. It was a very weak one and certainly would not have caused any policeman to think twice. A few days later, during a funeral at Uitenhage in the Eastern Province, the police opened fire and killed several people. It was a major tragedy. Minister Le Grange lied in Parliament in recounting what had happened. He and the country were reaping what he had sown.

There were sporadic student demonstrations on the campus, but matters really came to a head after the declaration of a state of emergency, which was imposed from midnight on 20 July in thirty-six magisterial districts in an effort to curb the rising protests throughout the country. Later the state of emergency was lifted in six of these districts, but in October it was extended to another eight, including the Cape Peninsula where many violent protests were occurring. The South African Defence Force was employed widely in the townships to try to control the protests against the Government. This was exactly what I had predicted when I met the generals in 1980, when they had told me that this would never happen.

The student protests were met by the use of force by the police. In one of the first such incidents the students were peacefully marching down Burg Road next to Glenara where Anita and I lived. I happened to be in Johannesburg on that day and the police charged the students and beat them with whips and batons. The gates to our house were open and Anita had run down to see what was happening in Burg Road. When she reached the gates, a large armoured police vehicle, called a Casspir, was about to reverse into our drive so as to be able to change its direction and drive up the road. Anita immediately closed the gates so that the vehicle couldn't turn. A fuming police major approached her and demanded that she open them again but she refused to do so, telling him that he and his men had no business to be doing what they were doing to the students, who were only protesting peacefully against injustice.

Just after lunch the next day the students were again protesting, holding placards at the edge of the rugby field as it overlooked the main highway, and I heard that a large police presence had arrived on the other side of the highway. This was also university property. I ran up to the site as the policemen were both running through the passage under the highway, which would take them onto the rugby fields, and scaling the walls to run across the highway. I managed to catch up with the major in charge and told him to stop what he was doing, that I would speak to the students, and that the whole matter could be settled peacefully. He was incoherent with rage. He had completely lost control of himself and had no control over his men. The students fled as the police rushed towards them, and ran up the steps into university buildings, where they dispersed. I phoned the divisional commissioner of police, gave him the name of the police major and told him the man was not fit to hold command, that he wasn't capable of controlling his own emotions and certainly was not capable of handling men in an emergency. There was a long pause on the telephone and the commissioner then said he agreed and he would take him off command. The major was replaced by a series of police officers with whom I had to deal in similar circumstances. Most managed to control themselves, but they also showed no compunction in charging and assaulting students. On a few occasions I was able to resolve the matter peacefully, usually by getting the police to go out of sight and then persuading the students to disperse. As long as the police and the students were within sight of each other, a violent end to the confrontation was probable. The students would provoke the police by shouting slogans. 'Botha is a terrorist' particularly incensed them. The police, in turn, incited students by waving their whips and making a show of their side arms, shotguns and rifles.

About one month later 1 500 students and staff gathered in the Jameson Hall. The original idea had been for them to drive to Athlone Stadium, the starting point for a march to Pollsmoor prison to demand the release of Nelson Mandela. When they learned that the stadium had been closed off, it was decided to march to Groote Schuur, the State President's residence. I addressed the meeting and pointed out the dangers of marching, because they would meet with a very determined police response. My rhetoric did not impress the students. As I walked through the emptying hall my son John came up to me and told me that, despite my advice, he was joining the march. I told him not to do so, but he did. More than 2 000 students, led by a group of 40 staff members in academic gowns, then marched from Jameson Hall carrying portraits of Nelson Mandela and banners calling for his release. They moved along University Avenue and off the campus onto Woolsack Drive, which is a public highway. Just beyond a pedestrian bridge they were confronted by the police. The marchers halted. I intervened, going up to the senior officer in charge to tell him the marchers wished to hand a petition to the State President and that he should accept the petition on behalf of the President. He refused. I walked back to the marchers to discuss the position and they indicated that if the officer accepted the petition, they would march back to the campus and disperse. The police were well armed. I returned to the officer and told him not to be a fool, that policemen should be peace officers and that his aim should be to ensure the whole matter ended peacefully. He said that he had to act because the protesters were breaking the law. This became a frequent refrain on such occasions. Repeating that he had to accept the petition, I said, 'What you do with the petition afterwards is your business, but for God's sake accept it.' He duly received the petition and the marchers had turned round and started back towards the campus when someone rushed up to me to tell me that Professor Phimister, professor of economic history, had been arrested. I ran up to a police colonel and told him that he was crazy to allow his men to arrest one of the professors as this would certainly result in violent protest on the behalf of the staff and students. He took me to a car in which Phimister was sitting and asked if he could release him into my care. I readily assented and a very relieved Ian Phimister joined me. The police had enormous powers and could have detained him indefinitely without trial. During the march three students at a bus stop were nearly arrested because it was illegal for three people to gather, as this constituted a demonstration. The students managed to convince the police that they were in fact waiting for a bus!

The grass verge in front of the indoor sports centre of the university overlooking the main highway was a favourite place for protest. Numerous protests against the state of emergency, detention without trial, apartheid legislation in general and against censorship and other matters were held on that site. I frequently negotiated with the police officer in charge to establish the boundary of the university. It was a movable feast. Sometimes it extended slightly onto the road, at other times a few feet up the grass verge, my aim being to confuse the officer in charge as much as I could and to get him to agree that the protest could continue as long as it happened on university property. These negotiations usually bought a fair amount of time.

On more than one occasion the police closed off the highway, causing a major traffic diversion and annoying the citizens of Cape Town. Sometimes I believed it had been done deliberately to make the student and staff protests even more unpopular with the general population than they already were.

One morning, towards the middle of the year, I was working at my desk when the deputy registrar of student affairs ran in to tell me that a large contingent of police was waiting just below the highway and that a large group of students was marching down across the rugby fields, plainly intending to go through the tunnel under the highway, where they would come into confrontation with the police. I ran up to the police and told them to move back until I had had time to talk to the students. As students were just beginning to emerge from the tunnel the student leader said it was an unplanned march. It was rumoured that Nelson Mandela had been released from Pollsmoor prison and they wanted to go and meet him. The students were very agitated and noisy. I stopped them and said that I would establish from the police what the true position was. The police response was one of incredulity. They stated quite clearly they would use force to stop the students. I told the students that the police had no knowledge of Mr Mandela's release and suggested they return to Jameson Hall until the facts could be ascertained. To my immense relief the students turned round and marched back to the Jameson Hall where, after a number of speeches and confirmation of Mr Mandela's continued incarceration, they dispersed.

One afternoon there were numerous armed police vehicles on University Avenue and on the concourse in front of Jameson Hall. A large group of students was at the southern end of University Avenue, singing and marching towards the police. About a dozen policemen were drawn up across the road facing the oncoming students and a police officer went up to the sergeant in charge of them and said, 'Fire tear gas at them.' As they raised their tear gas pistols I stepped in front of them and ordered them to lower their arms. They did, much to the astonishment of their sergeant, who then asked me what I thought I was doing. I replied that it was unnecessary to shoot tear gas at the students. The officer shouted at the sergeant, who again ordered his men to cock their weapons and once again, as they raised their pistols, I instructed them in as loud and authoritative voice as I could muster to lower their weapons and again they obeyed. (South African police have a habit of obeying direct, vigorous orders.) The sergeant was puce with rage, as was the officer who came up to tell me that I was breaking the law by giving the police instructions. While this was happening, the student group filed past the police and down the other side of University Avenue. The police took no action against me.

In my direct dealings with the police in the midst of student protests I tried to keep as calm as possible and to defuse the situation in the police officer's mind. I remember walking up to a police colonel in the pouring rain in the midst of mayhem and saying to him that it was my birthday and this was hardly a way to celebrate. His body language immediately changed and one could talk rationally to him after that. On nearly all occasions when I rushed about trying to restrain the police to ensure a peaceful outcome to a student protest, I was greatly assisted by the deputy vice-chancellors and deputy registrars and members of the administrative staff. They were stalwarts and remained consistently calm and collected, giving me very wise advice. They frequently had to handle very difficult situations on their own. I cannot speak highly enough of them for the way in which they dealt with these matters.

During one of the tense confrontations between chanting students and belligerent, heavily armed police two young African students, immaculately dressed in track suits and the latest sports shoes, casually wandered down a path immediately in front of the students, idly swinging their squash rackets as they laughed and chatted with each other. It was an almost surrealistic experience. I had a similar sense of dislocation at other times. For example Anita and I went to a glittering reception, immediately after I had visited a woman student imprisoned in Pollsmoor prison.

Because of the events which had been unfolding in South Africa during the first half of the year, I was persuaded to issue a mission statement, which I did on 15 July 1985. I had been reluctant to do so at first because I wasn't sure that mission statements had much value. (I have come to realise that I was wrong.) I knew just how difficult it would be to get a mission statement which was acceptable to the entire university. It would certainly take months to move it through all the university structures, so in the end I agreed to issue it in my name so that we would not have to waste many months getting agreement on the final wording. Coincidentally the statement was issued the day before the state of emergency was declared on 16 July, and I was doubly pleased, therefore, that I had acted and that I had received such good advice from Len Abrahamse, from my deputies and from Hugh Amoore, the registrar. The statement included a rejection of racism and racial segregation, set the goals of the highest possible standards of teaching and research, stressed the need for academic freedom and the role of the university in the community.

On 14 October 1985 the chancellor, the chairman of the university council, the chairman of the staff association, the president of the students' representative council and I issued a further statement after the declaration of the state of emergency in parts of the western Cape. We described the atrocities occurring around us and called for the lifting of the state of emergency, the abolition of apartheid, the release of all political prisoners, the withdrawal of troops from the townships and restraint by the police.

In November and December the crisis in education deepened, particularly in the coloured schools of the Peninsula. We made clear that the solution could lie only in a new constitutional dispensation for South Africa, one which satisfied the legitimate political aspirations of all and ensured equal provision of education in a single educational system. The school boycotts and disturbances continued throughout South Africa in the coloured, African and Indian schools. Carter Ebrahim, the Minister of Education and Culture in the House of Representatives (for coloured people), closed the schools as a result of the boycott, and there was a great deal of violence in and around them. About 360 000 coloured pupils were involved. According to the Department of Education and Training (African education), 674 275 African pupils at 207 schools were affected by school boycotts in 1985. Some 230 secondary schools out of a total of 323 registered secondary schools were affected. Altogether 294 African schools were damaged at a cost of R7,8 million. There were protests and police action on many other campuses as well as that of the University of Cape Town.

On 1 October Ebrahim issued a notice in the Government Gazette, banning meetings of any pupil or student organisation on school or college campuses and giving himself extensive additional powers. Professor van der Ross,* the rector of the University of the Western Cape, Mr Franklin Sonn,† the rector of the Peninsula Technikon, and I were outspoken in our criticism of Carter Ebrahim and of the Government's actions in the schools, with particular reference to the closing of the schools, the use of force and draconian regulations to try to secure a 'normal' school environment. This was plainly not the way to achieve that result. As a consequence, we were called to meet with the State President, Mr P W Botha, at the Union Buildings in Pretoria. We were ushered into a large conference room. Mr P W Botha was in the chair and was accompanied by Mr F W de Klerk, Minister of National Education, Dr Gerrit Viljoen, Minister of Education and Training (African education), the Reverend Allan Hendrickse, Premier of the House of Representatives (a House elected solely by coloured voters) and Mr Carter Ebrahim, Minister of Education and Culture in the House of Representatives, Mr Louis le Grange, Minister of Law and Order, and Mr Nel, Deputy Minister of Information. The three of us sat facing this array of apartheid rulers. The meeting began with P W Botha haranguing us for our outspoken criticisms of Government policy and in his characteristic way, wagging his fingers at us. He told me that he knew all about me and what I was up to. Each of us made an opening statement criticising what was going on in the schools and emphasising our objection to their closure and to the way in which the Government was approaching the problem, indicating that

---

* South African Ambassador in Spain.
† Until recently South African Ambassador to USA.

the only solution lay in fundamental change. While we were talking, Dr Roux, who was the director-general in the State President's office, obviously fell asleep and leaned on some buttons which were close to him. Suddenly, part of the wall started moving and revealed a whole array of recording and video apparatus. He rapidly woke up and shouted '*Jammer, jammer, jammer!*' (Sorry, sorry, sorry!) at the top of his voice, pushed another button and the wall slid back. This didn't seem to phase members of the Cabinet present. Shortly after that, Richard van der Ross asked if he could keep detailed notes of the discussion and P W Botha replied by saying he could keep any record he liked, because everything was recorded anyway.

In my statement I emphasised that the only solution could lie in fundamental political change and that the Government's immediate response to the crisis in the schools was inappropriate. I said that I was not one of those who believed that the schools should be made ungovernable, referring to the cry echoed by some of the protesting students. Botha asked Carter Ebrahim to reply. He said that the closing of the schools had been a great success, because ever since they had been closed there had been no violence in them. He then said that it was interesting to hear that I thought that the schools should be made ungovernable. I interrupted him saying that I was astounded to be misquoted within such a short while of making a statement in the room and that what I had said differed absolutely from Ebrahim's version. Botha turned to me and told me to be quiet, and to give Carter Ebrahim an opportunity to speak! When Ebrahim had finished I indicated that the reason why the schools were quiet when they were closed was because the children were in the streets and that there was now mayhem in the streets, and that I simply could not follow Mr Ebrahim's logic. It became apparent during the meeting that all the decisions regarding coloured education were allegedly the sole authority of the majority party in the House of Representatives, and that the National Government ministers claimed that they could not influence those decisions. I thought it was so much poppycock. A number of the ministers, including Botha, tried very hard to persuade us that they were doing their best, that matters would be resolved and that the only way to deal with violent protest was with a very firm response by the security forces. Botha and Louis Nel, the Deputy Minister of Information, who was responsible for Government propaganda at the time, were particularly keen that we should issue a statement to the effect that the meeting had contributed towards a better understanding of Government policy. We indicated that we weren't prepared to do so and Mr Botha became more and more cross with us. In the end somebody recommended that the meeting end, but that Mr Nel and some of his officials stay with us to discuss a statement that could be issued. Botha and his colleagues left and for a while Nel continued trying to persuade us, but we refused to be moved.

On 16 October Professor Jakes Gerwel,* who was then rector designate of the University of the Western Cape, and I went to New York to attend a meeting convened by a group of presidents of leading United States foundations and universities. We discussed the problems in education facing South Africa and they were most anxious to know how they could be of assistance. We suggested that the emphasis should fall on bursaries for black students at those South African universities which were publicly opposed to apartheid, in addition to the visits by US academics to the campuses and vice versa. Jakes and I were enormously encouraged by the support we received from our colleagues in the United States.

During the year Professor Jean Meyer,† president of Tufts University, had written to the heads of all South African universities, including myself, indicating that he understood that we were 'State universities' and were probably doing something to alleviate the problems in South Africa, but asking why we weren't doing more. I replied informing him of what the University of Cape Town had achieved and of the very difficult circumstances under which we had done so. Jean phoned me saying that he hadn't realised what was happening at UCT, that he was very impressed and asked me what he could do to be of help. 'You can raise funds for the financial aid of needy black students' I said. 'Only at UCT?' he asked. 'No,' I said, 'for all the universities openly opposing apartheid.' And that is exactly what Jean did. The universities and colleges of New England got together and raised funds from their own universities by approaching their trustees, staff and students. These funds were sent to the Universities of the Western Cape, Witwatersrand, Natal, Rhodes and Cape Town through the UCT Fund in New York and were termed Open Society Scholarships. Jean remained a staunch supporter until his untimely death.

On August 8 about 500 students arrived at the Bremner Building and the chairman of council, Mr Len Abrahamse, the acting deputy vice-chancellor Professor Leatt, the SRC president Christine Burger, and I left a council meeting and met the students outside the building. They demanded that the university should immediately decide to grant an honorary degree to Nelson Mandela and that it should state its attitude to the state of emergency and to the crisis confronting the country. I informed the students that there was a set of procedures which had to be followed for the granting of honorary degrees. As for their other demands I referred them to my mission statement and my statement to the student body, which clearly indicated our attitude.

* Later Director General in the office of President Mandela.
† Jean Mayer died on 1 January 1993.

Two days later about 400 students again marched on the Bremner Building. This arose out of the boycott of lectures called by an ad-hoc students' action committee, mostly led by students from SOYA (Sons for Young Azania) and AZASM (the Azanian Students' Movement). As they marched down the hill they were singing 'We are marching on parliament.' They gained entrance into the building and I met with them and they set forward three demands: that the intervarsity rugby match between UCT and Stellenbosch should be summarily cancelled, that the administration should recognise the workers' committee and that lectures should be cancelled for a week. The current state of emergency was the reason for the first and last demand. I responded by saying that the intervarsity was a student affair and had to be taken up with the students representative council. I said that negotiations were taking place with the workers' committee and that it was not within my power to cancel lectures. The students then marched up to the SRC offices where they called for the chairman of the intervarsity committee and demanded to speak to members of the SRC. The SRC informed them that they could not unilaterally cancel the intervarsity on the demand of a relatively small number of students and that the only option available would be to hold a general referendum amongst all the students, for which there was not enough time. The situation was described by those present as 'very tense', but eventually the marchers, having rejected the SRC statement, left quietly. One or two lectures were disrupted for a short while, but otherwise all teaching activities went on uninterrupted.

In October the vice-chancellors and chairmen of councils of South African universities met in Pretoria with the Minister of National Education, Mr F W de Klerk, and four of his colleagues. De Klerk announced that parliament's approval was being sought for the fusion of the CUP and the Committee of University Rectors, which represented the black universities, into a single body. We had been urging that for a long time. In thanking the Minister I, as the current CUP chairman, indicated that the universities still hoped for a single Minister and Department of Education and urged that the constitution be changed accordingly. Walking into lunch De Klerk tried to make me understand that he believed in reform. My response was to say that deeds spoke louder than words and that he and the Cabinet simply had to act. Until some real reform occurred, I would not be able to take him seriously.

After the lunch De Klerk stressed the importance of the security situation. Voicing his belief that small numbers of people at universities were involved in fomenting revolution, he called upon the universities to assist the Government in stamping out such action. In response, I pointed out that there was a lack of opportunity to protest peacefully, that the police used unnecessary violence against protesters and that none of us were supporting violent revolution. I stressed the need for the Government to move rapidly with real, purposeful political reform. De Klerk said it was only under the present circumstances that people couldn't protest and I pointed out to him that he was quite wrong, and that the Internal Security Act had prevented protest for years. That seemed to shake the Minister, who had been shown to be ill-informed on the Government's security legislation. He also asked if we couldn't persuade the students to protest in another way, which did seem to be a rather shallow response. Professor Pete Booysen from Natal supported me as did Professor van der Ross from the University of the Western Cape, who explained why he had led a march and so broken the law. He said that if it came to a choice between the prevailing laws and peace on his campus, he would opt to break the law. He described the tumult in the coloured townships, the beating of people by the police, the disruption of family life and, pointing out that the students came from that environment onto the campus, he asked the Ministers how they thought these students felt. Van der Ross said that if there were to be a revolution it should come from within the Government, and that this should happen soon. He spoke very well.

Judge Diemont, acting chair of the UCT council, urged the Government to move faster and more determinedly than they had. The chairman of the University of Natal's council and Professor J C de Villiers, chairman of the council of the University of the Western Cape, generally supported what we had said. Significantly, Professor Cas Crouse from Vista University said that while it was true that only 5 per cent of the students were actively involved, the other 95 per cent wanted political rights acceptable to them, and were impatient. He indicated that the real problem was the disillusionment of all the black students on his campus with the current political situation. Professor Rademeyer of the University of Port Elizabeth offered a simple solution. If one constituted the students' council with a representative from each residence and from each constituency, and met with them once a month no problems would arise! Professor Lamprecht of the University of Fort Hare claimed that he could control his campus (which I doubted) but said that, although 95 per cent of the students were not actively involved, a group of revolutionaries were creating a pre-revolutionary climate. He supported what the Minister had said. Dominee Moolman, chairman of the council of the University of Port Elizabeth, spoke about the communist danger and praised the police for preserving the peace in Port Elizabeth. At the end the Minister asked us to help stamp out revolutionary activity. He said he didn't want the Government to have to 'use a sword'.

The Minister of Education of the Republic of Taiwan was visiting South

Africa and F W de Klerk invited Jakes Gerwel, rector of the University of the Western Cape, Franklin Sonn, rector of the Peninsula Technikon, Theo Shippey, rector of the Cape Technikon, and Mike de Vries, rector of Stellenbosch University, and myself to meet the Minister and his delegation at dinner at Groote Schuur, which had been the home of Cecil John Rhodes. Groote Schuur is part of a large property on which Westbrooke also stands. At that time Westbrooke was the home of President P W Botha. We were instructed to bring identity documents with us as they would be needed to gain access to the property. It was pouring with rain when I reached the gates of Groote Schuur and Westbrooke and as I drove towards them a policeman ran towards my car and pointed an automatic weapon directly at me. I stopped the car abruptly, thrust my hand into my pocket and got out my identity document and waved it frantically in front of my face, but that did not deter the policeman who continued to look most threatening and continued pointing his gun at me. I swung the wheel of my car and turned on to the verge. The policeman then lost interest in me. The gates opened and out swept a cavalcade of cars. The policeman then ambled over to me, his gun hanging harmlessly at his side and I protested to him that he had no right to deal so aggressively with me. His excuse was that P W Botha was leaving to attend a social event in Cape Town and I was in the way!

The dinner party was an interesting one. The Government side was represented by De Klerk, who was the host, Gerrit Viljoen, who was responsible for African education, Piet Clase, who was the Own Affairs Minister for Education, and Pik Botha, who was the Minister of Foreign Affairs. We had drinks before dinner and I was very embarrassed by the fact that the ministers were all talking to each other in Afrikaans for quite long periods of time, to the obvious puzzlement of the Chinese guests. At the dinner wine was liberally dispensed and at one stage Pik Botha rose to his feet with a goblet full of KWV pinotage, which is a very good wine. He looked at the Taiwanese minister, raised his glass and said 'gambay!' which apparently means 'bottoms up.' The astonished minister rose to his feet and emptied his full glass of wine, whereupon Pik Botha emptied his. His glass was repeatedly filled until he had 'gambayed' every guest at the table. Pik Botha then resumed his seat, turned to the Chinese ambassador who was sitting next to him and told him he was the best ambassador in South Africa. He then swore about the other ambassadors and said they did everything to undermine South Africa. It was clear to me that Gerrit Viljoen, who was sitting opposite me, was very embarrassed at what was happening, as were most of us. At the end of the evening Pik Botha put his arm around Franklin Sonn and me and insisted in taking us to another room where he said they had 'fired' B J Vorster!

Through all these events university life went on. No academic teaching time was lost, university scholars continued with their research and the everyday business of the university was attended to. The turbulent times added a great deal to the workload of the deputy vice-chancellors, the registrar and many other members of staff and of myself. Some students wrote their examinations in jail in November and I was able to secure educational material for some students who were incarcerated. About 1 000 students affected by township violence were allowed to defer their examinations in November to the following January and February; they had plainly had their work interfered with as either they or relatives and friends had been assaulted by the police and subjected to tear gas and general mayhem. Most candidates did sufficiently well to be readmitted to the university, but some did not. Of course we were criticised by many white citizens in South Africa for this and for the other actions we were taking. I am quite certain we were right to show leniency in this very troubled situation.

Mr Hugh Amoore, the academic secretary, was coaching Zinzi Mandela to help her complete the subjects she needed to get her matriculation exemption and university entrance qualification. She subsequently enrolled at UCT and was a successful student until she had to leave the university to join her family in the Transvaal.

I was a member of the Friends of NUSAS (FONS) and also an honorary vice-president of NUSAS, and attended the AGM of FONS in December. Richard Luyt was very active in FONS and the whole purpose was to support NUSAS in its activities. I was also president of the South African Institute of Race Relations for two years. In each of my annual presidential addresses I was strongly critical of the Government.

On his seventieth birthday Dr Beyers Naudé, who was then unbanned and secretary-general of the SA Council of Churches, delivered a major address in the Jameson Hall entitled 'My Seven Lean Years'. He called on those universities, trade unions and political groups which affirmed justice and equality for all people before the law, to establish a freedom alliance. He gave a moving account of his and his wife Ilse's suffering, courage and fortitude under a banning order served on 19 October 1977 and lifted in September 1984. He was honoured by his peers, who presented him with a festschrift compiled by leading theologians. It was a very moving occasion.

Freedom of speech & association

1986

At the beginning of 1986 I had a sabbatical for three months and, after spending some time working at home, Anita and I set off on the first of many major fund-raising trips. At the beginning of our travels we stayed over in Rome and spent two unforgettable days in Florence. Regular visits to the USA in the future offered the bonus of more such short but very rich experiences. The Museum of Modern Art became a great favourite, but on this occasion criss-crossing the US fund-raising meant it was six weeks before we could visit it or the Metropolitan Museum of Art. I had made over 60 speeches and Anita over 20 in that time.

Sir John Hanson, deputy director and later director of the British Council, and I regularly lunched at the Athenaeum when I was in London. Sir John visited South Africa on a number of occasions, had a keen understanding of the country and was a great help. Sir Martin Jacomb, the chairman of the British Council, was also very helpful. I had arranged to meet Anita outside the Athenaeum after one of our lunches and when she arrived there it was pouring with rain and she could not shelter near the front door because a television crew was busy there. After a while she went through the first set of glass doors to get out of the rain. A startled butler said that the club was for men only and she pointed to the weather, the TV crew and her umbrella which had been blown inside out. They started chatting. Through a second set of glass doors she could see the handsome hall and a fireplace with glowing coals. Deciding to warm herself in front of the fire she assured the now mollified butler that she would leave if anyone objected. An elderly gentleman came up to her and said it was unusual to see a woman in the club. They were soon talking about South Africa and he called his young assistant, a Rhodes University graduate, to meet her. We were somewhat taken aback when we left the dining room to find her there! She had not understood that the club's rules of exclusivity were so deeply entrenched, and she may be the only woman to have been in that part of the holy of holies.

I also lunched at the Athenaeum with the late Sir Hugh Springer. Sir Hugh had been a founder of the trade union movement in the West Indies, then the secretary-general of the Association of Commonwealth Universities

(ACU), after which he went on to higher office. He was very critical of the vice-chancellor of Edinburgh University, who he believed had tried to gain popularity with his students when he effectively prevented Richard Luyt from giving the keynote address at the ACU meeting in Edinburgh on the grounds that Richard Luyt was a South African. During coffee two men approached him for advice on Ethiopia. He deliberately told them they should ask me as I came from South Africa. They looked startled and backed off. I was not politically correct.

The Ebert Stiftung could not obtain a visa for a representative to come to South Africa and help the emerging trade union movement. I met with representatives of the German foundation in Paris and arranged for its man to be a research fellow in economics at UCT, enabling him to get his visa and to have an office on campus and work in South Africa.

1986 was the third successive year of African school boycotts and for some time there had also been extensive boycotts in the coloured schools in the Western Cape. Although the first state of emergency was lifted on the 7 March 1986, it was reimposed on 12 June in the same year. There were extensive disturbances, violence and unrest in the Cape Peninsula as ordinary South Africans battled to try to bring the apartheid regime to an end. These tensions obviously involved the university community. A number of students were detained for varying periods and at the end of the year one staff member and one student remained in detention. I protested publicly whenever a member of the university was restricted in any way under the emergency regulations and the laws then in force.

The cynicism of the security police was demonstrated when a Masters student was detained without trial in the security police headquarters at Caledon Square police station in central Cape Town. I had been trying to get him released or, failing that, to ensure that he could study in his cell, but had made no progress. Anita and I went on a short holiday to our house at Yzerfontein, which is a sixty-minute drive from Cape Town. From there I phoned the security police commander and again raised the question of the student's release and he told me that if I knew the reasons for his detention, I would understand why they had acted. He then said that he could not talk to me further on the phone, but that he would like to talk to me face to face. I accepted that invitation with the full intention of revealing anything that he told me to the press, and accordingly drove into Cape Town and went to Caledon Square. I was taken through a series of self-locking doors into the security police section of Caledon Square and was left in a large room with very uncomfortable chairs around the walls, all of which were covered with posters showing various forms of machine guns, land mines and bombs. I was kept waiting for about an hour and while waiting I heard the sound of chains clinking. I looked out of the window and saw a large number of prisoners, chained hand and foot, moving slowly around the central courtyard. A colonel and a major, both in plain clothes, came into the room. We sat facing each other on the upright chairs and the colonel said to me, 'Well, I don't think our conversation is necessary because we released the student last night and he has been deported to Zimbabwe.' I expressed myself forcefully to the two police officers, saying that they had known that the student had been released when they invited me to return to Cape Town from my holiday house. I asked them what they were playing at. They just smiled.

I was very impressed by the student leaders during these years. They showed great maturity and were often responsible for a peaceful end to a demonstration, failing which they usually managed to ensure that the disruptions were minimised. These young people carried a very heavy burden of responsibility in fulfilling their roles on the campus and beyond.

On one instance some 2 000 students were standing on the grass verge holding banners. The police were lined up opposite them on the other side of the road and had closed off De Waal Drive on the Cape Town side of the university. I was negotiating between Captain Dowd, who was the officer in charge of the police on the road, and the student leadership, trying to ensure that violence did not occur. A police helicopter hovered overhead. Captain Dowd told me that his instructions were to disperse the students and that if necessary he would have to use force. I asked for one more chance to get the students to move away and he undertook to take no action until I came back to him, which I said would be in about five minutes. I ran up the road and started talking to the students, but they couldn't hear me because the helicopter had come down very low and was drowning out my voice. I gesticulated to the helicopter to move, and while I was doing this, Major Odendaal, the head of the riot police, attacked the students from the rear and opened fire on them with shotguns. The students ran in all directions, were chased by the police, who lashed them with whips, arresting those students they could catch. I was beside myself with rage, marched down the road to Captain Dowd and said to him, 'You have no honour and the South African police has no honour.' He went white and asked why I said that and I told him what had happened. He immediately replied that he had had no knowledge of what the riot squad was doing and that the brigadier in the police helicopter was in charge directing operations. He was plainly telling the truth and I apologised to him but I repeated that the police had no honour. Helicopters became a symbol of oppression. Whenever I heard the police helicopter I knew that there was trouble on the campus.

There was stone-throwing on De Waal Drive on at least two occasions, with some damage to motor cars. I strongly condemned it, pointing out that while peaceful protest was a right, and that I would defend the right to engage in it with all my might, I could not support violence as part of protest. I also stressed the fact that throwing stones onto De Waal Drive put innocent motorists at risk. It turned out that on one occasion the student who had initiated the stone-throwing and had thrown most of the stones had been a police spy. We often had to deal with the problems of *agents provocateurs* on the campus.

In response to the turmoil in the country which was spilling over from time to time on the campus, I convened a university assembly on 15 August. Assemblies were also held on the same day at the Universities of the Witwatersrand and of Natal. The UCT assembly was addressed by representatives of the full spectrum of the student and staff community. We reaffirmed our commitment to non-racialism, called for an end to apartheid, the release of Nelson Mandela and all political prisoners and an end to the state of emergency. The vice-chancellors of the Universitie's of the Witwatersrand, Natal, Rhodes and the Western Cape joined me in issuing a statement on the same day, calling for a lifting of the state of emergency.

The Government seemed determined to have as many people as possible removed from the squatter camps around Cape Town and the police encouraged a group of vigilantes, called the *witdoeke* because of the white bands they wore round their heads, to attack other squatters and destroy their homes, often by fire. There were dreadful scenes during that Cape winter. The police and defence force were active in these squatter camps and there was a rumour that they were determined to destroy the KTC squatter camp. One morning I received a phone call from someone in London who asked me if I could give them the name of a South African architect who was an expert in Cape-Dutch architecture because an Australian millionaire wanted to build his stables in that style. Immediately after I had put the phone down it rang again and this time it was Margaret Nash from the Black Sash office in Mowbray asking me if I would go with some people from the Black Sash to KTC because they had information that the *witdoeke* with the aid of the police were going to destroy KTC and drive the squatters out. She thought our presence might inhibit the police. I immediately agreed. The irony of the request from London was clear to me because of the fact that so many South Africans did not even have a house to live in and even those living in shacks were under threat.

Donald Carr came as well and after we had picked up Margaret Nash and another member of the Black Sash, we drove out to KTC. We were driving along a mud road and reached a T-junction, having noticed smoke in the air from burning shacks and having passed several armoured police vehicles. At the T-junction I looked to my left and saw hordes of vigilantes running down onto the road. We turned right and drove towards the KTC squatter camp with the vigilantes running behind us. They were all well-armed with knobkieries and sticks. I didn't see any guns but I didn't have a lot of time to look carefully. As we approached KTC I saw young men gathering stones to defend their homes, women running away with their children, some pushing some of their belongings in wheelbarrows. As we passed KTC we saw numerous armoured police vehicles but no attempt was made to stop the vicious attack by the vigilantes on the KTC squatters. We drove to the nearest police station where we lodged a protest with the station commander about the fact that the police were doing nothing to stop the violence and we urged him to instruct his men to act. He denied that they were doing nothing but gave no instructions to his men. A large part of KTC was destroyed by fire that morning. Many people were injured. SHAWCO students were active in the area, bringing relief in the form of shelter, food and clothing and taking care of injured people. One of the SHAWCO vehicles was burnt. It was one of the rare occasions on which that happened to one of the students' vehicles. The whole scene at KTC, as we observed the vigilantes running down the road and the people running from them, was almost surreal. When one sees such violent scenes in a movie there is loud music and a great deal of shouting, but there was almost total silence as the vigilantes ran down the mud road and people either prepared for their attack or tried to flee.

A few weeks before this, SHAWCO vehicles had been stationed outside the Zolani Centre amidst tear gas, several armoured police vehicles (Casspirs) and about 2 000 people of the Crossroads community whose homes were being destroyed by vigilantes. Andrew Feinstein, the SHAWCO president, was asked to negotiate with the police to allow the crowd time to collect their belongings and disperse. He did so and when the crowd moved, chaos broke out as the Casspirs threatened the people, who then pleaded with the SHAWCO students to remain because their presence seemed to be the only thing preventing police intervention. The warden of SHAWCO, Mr Livesey, asked that the students who wished to stay sign a declaration saying that they were there by choice and no one was to be held liable for their death or injury. The students readily signed the indemnity and over a number of months co-ordinated relief operations. They appealed to the campus and the Cape Town community for donations to help homeless and injured people and there was an incredible response to this. The students had seen the *witdoeke* actually riding on the police vehicles. I went to see Chris Heunis, a member of the Cabinet, to protest about what was happening at Crossroads, but achieved nothing.

Our visit to the ANC in September did not endear us to the Government.

It was illegal to have any ANC publications in one's possession or to quote the ANC. A number of corporate and other leaders had held a meeting with ANC members in Lusaka. I had had contact with the ANC for some time and had met with their representative in the United Kingdom. The upshot of these contacts was that I led a delegation of UCT staff and students to Lusaka from 14 to 17 September. Jim Leatt, one of the deputy vice-chancellors, George Dall, the dean of medicine, Jon File, the academic planning officer of the university, Charles Villa-Vicencio of the department of religious studies, Mamphela Ramphele, who then held a joint appointment in anthropology and child health, and three students, Carla Sutherland, who was vice-president of the SRC, Glen Goosen, who was the president, and Chris Mzamane, the chairman of AZASO, were also in the delegation. We were joined by Professor Jakes Gerwel, the rector-designate of the University of the Western Cape, who was accompanied by the vice-rectors, Professors Durand and Reddy. Two further delegates were Professor P Mohanoe from the University of the North and Mr John Samuels of the South African Council of Higher Education (SACHED). The ANC had indicated they would like the broader delegation and not one exclusively from UCT. We kept our impending visit as secret as possible, but as soon as we arrived in Lusaka it became national news in South Africa. Once we were there it did not matter. We had worried about being prevented from going.

Alfred Nzo,* then secretary-general of the ANC, led the ANC delegation and he and I met to set the agenda. We agreed that the meeting would open with a statement by Professor Jack Simons, the head of the ANC education desk in Lusaka. Jack Simons had been an associate professor at the University of Cape Town, teaching comparative African government and law. He was a brilliant teacher and inspired many students. A communist, his integrity was such that he taught the students many points of view in approaching any subject with which he was dealing, and he did not try to impose his own political views on them. He was banned and restricted for years in South Africa, as was his wife Ray Alexander, who as a young sixteen-year-old immigrant from the Baltic states had organised an African trade union, had helped them mount a strike and had become a leading member of the South African Communist Party. They were remarkable people, who went into exile because of the continuing banning orders and restrictions placed upon them, and they worked actively for the ANC in Zambia and elsewhere.

We met in a large conference room. Nzo and I agreed that after Jack Simons's initial statement, Jakes Gerwel and I would reply. We would then

---

* Minister of Foreign Affairs in the first democratic government in South Africa. Now retired.

deal item by item with a number of issues including the structure of higher education, the ways in which one could ensure increased enrolment of African students and the means of selecting them, the role of academic support programmes, the financial problems facing students, research and governance at universities and the role of women.

Jack Simons reminded me of a lion. He had a shock of white hair, with a bald patch on the top of his head, and had penetrating steely eyes. He spoke for over an hour, using very few notes, and he was eloquent in his denunciation of the educational opportunities which Africans have had in South Africa since the formation of Union in 1910 and, indeed, long before that during British and Dutch colonial rule. He was particularly scathing about Bantu education. No one in the room was in disagreement with him in his description of the appalling lack of educational opportunities for blacks in South Africa in the past, although of course the University of the Western Cape and the University of Cape Town, the two universities representing the major parts of the delegation, were doing all they could to make a contribution in this regard and had been doing so for some time.

I described the present structure of higher education in South Africa and what was happening on campuses which were resisting apartheid and dealt with the imposition of draconian security regulations and the states of emergency. I discussed UCT's policies for ensuring steady, significant increase in black enrolment, particularly Africans, finding financial support and residential accommodation for them and developing an effective academic support programme. Jakes Gerwel spoke in much the same way, describing the role of the University of the Western Cape and the vigorous way in which the students had protested. He outlined his vision for the university as the rector-designate and made it clear that he intended to enrol large numbers of African students in the university and to turn the concept of a coloured university on its head, rejecting a university designed for the education of a single racial 'group'.

Before the afternoon session started I said I thought the chairs and tables were too far apart and that we should bring them closer together so that we could see the eyes of the whites! The debate was vigorous. At one stage Chris Hani and leading members of Umkhonto weSizwe, the armed wing of the ANC, joined the conference and told us of their activities and their determination to overthrow the SA Government. They were clearly committed and somewhat intimidating. During the last session, Mamphela Ramphele and Barbara Masekela* objected strongly to the fact that the item on the agenda which dealt with the role of women in higher education had been

---

* South Africa's Ambassador to France until 1999.

progressively passed over each time and had been moved down to the bottom of the agenda. Their very vigorous protest plainly embarrassed the ANC, who had been largely responsible for this, and the matter was promptly debated in full.

There were ample opportunities for private discussions and I know that the whole UCT delegation found it an invaluable experience. What surprised me was that there were large gaps in the knowledge that the ANC had about what was happening on campuses in South Africa. They knew the general scene but not the details. We were very impressed by the quality of the ANC delegation; by their friendliness and by their commitment to overthrowing apartheid and replacing it with a democratic Government. We were impressed by their non-racialism and were sad to realise how homesick they were. They wanted to hear about ordinary things: what Cape Town looked like, what developments there had been, what changes there had been in Soweto, in Johannesburg and elsewhere in South Africa. We brought back messages for friends and loved ones. I had taken with me lengths of dress material for the wife of the treasurer of the ANC. He was quite overwhelmed to get it from family in South Africa. Amongst the ANC delegates were Billy Modise of the education secretariat, James Stewart of the national executive, Barbara Masekela of the cultural desk and Ruth Mompati of the national executive.

We had meetings with Dr J M Mwanza, the vice-chancellor of the University of Zambia. We toured the campus and he graciously hosted a dinner for us on one of the evenings we were there. I asked him whether some of his student leaders could join us at the dinner so that we could chat to them, because we had not had much opportunity of meeting students. He agreed but in the end only his daughter joined us at the dinner. This was a disappointment for us all, and worried me.

On the last evening in Lusaka most of us from UCT went to the casino. I watched Jon File playing roulette. I hadn't played the game for a long time and I got him to explain the rules to me and then I bought some chips with a modest investment. To everyone's astonishment, including my own, I started winning. Jon File became my banker and after five or six straight wins I picked up the chips and cashed them in. I established that one could only take 50 US dollars out of Zambia and so I gave most of the balance to students to buy presents and the next morning before we left, I went to the bank in Lusaka where it took me two hours to get a 50 dollar travellers' cheque.

On the last evening we returned to the hotel quite late. I went up to my room, had a bath, got into bed and went to sleep, but at about 1 o'clock in the morning Johnny Makatini, at that time head of the foreign desk of the

ANC, phoned me. He hadn't attended the meetings. He told me he had just got back to Lusaka and wanted to talk to me. I indicated to him that we could have breakfast together, but he wanted to talk to me straight away, so I got out of bed, got dressed and went down into the lounge, which was also the bar. There was cane furniture in the lounge and fans moving slowly overhead, only one or two waiters and the barman were there. I met Johnny Makatini and we sat at a round table. He put a large buff envelope in the middle of the table. We spoke about various things and then he asked me if I would take the envelope back to South Africa. He said it contained the script of a movie on the life of Nelson Mandela which had been written by Harry Belafonte. He wanted me to take it back with me and meet somebody in the domestic arrivals hall at the Johannesburg airport, who would collect the package from me and take it to Winnie Mandela. The atmosphere and circumstances reminded me of a scene from the movie 'Our Man in Havana'! I asked him if he wanted the South African security police to read the contents of the buff envelope, because if he did the best thing he could do was to give it to me. Of all the people in the party, it was likely that my baggage and everything I had would be scrutinised the most closely. He said, 'They told me that you were intelligent,' and he took the buff envelope back and shortly after that we parted. I couldn't make out what that was all about. I woke up Jim Leatt and told him in detail what had happened so that somebody else would know of this extraordinary conversation. Unfortunately Johny Makatini died some time later. He was a very able and certainly a very charming man.

When I visited Zambia I discovered that the Crown Prince of Japan (now the Emperor) had arranged for Japan to create a veterinary school in Lusaka. I wrote to him and asked for support for black students and a few bursaries were donated. The Japanese consul-general asked me to have lunch and greeted me with, 'You wrote to the Crown Prince?' and as he spoke his eyebrows rose so far up his forehead they almost disappeared into his hair. He was both shocked and angered at my effrontery.

Shortly after my return I went to see F W de Klerk in Pretoria to tell him how valuable the discussions with the ANC had been in contributing to a better understanding of each other. De Klerk told me I was a traitor to speak to the ANC. I replied by saying that *he* would speak to the ANC, because dialogue was the only way forward. He replied that he and the Government would never do that.

Anita and I attended the splendid enthronement of Archbishop Desmond Tutu in St George's Cathedral. It was a very moving occasion. I have always thought very highly of the Archbishop, who played a key role in leading the opposition to apartheid in the '80s and early '90s. He is a true man of God. While he was Bishop of Johannesburg, I learnt that he was not supporting the university's efforts to raise funds in the United States, and I went to see him. I explained to him that the primary purpose of our fund-raising was to obtain financial support for black students. We also raised money for buildings which could accommodate the increasing numbers of African students, and for the vital academic support programme. He told me he hadn't understood the position and now that he did he would not oppose our activities. Unfortunately, for a number of years after that he continued to do so and I really couldn't understand it. Alan Pifer and others approached him but he did not change his view. I have reason to believe that he was annoyed with the university because some time earlier in the '70s, when he was under intense attack by the South African Government, he believed that the university did not give him sufficient support. I went through all the council and other relevant documents in the university's archives and couldn't find anything which explained why he should have adopted this view. Certainly Sir Richard Luyt and the university had consistently opposed the draconian actions of the Government. Despite these past misunderstandings Desmond Tutu remains one of my favourite people.

Vusi Khanyile was chairperson of the National Education Crisis Committee (NECC). He was subsequently detained without trial and held in Johannesburg. John Reid knew his qualities and I decided to offer him my special assistant's post, which was becoming vacant. Vusi had been admitted to the psychiatry wards of the Johannesburg General Hospital with a feigned mental problem to get relief from his prison cell. I made contact with the professor of psychiatry and arranged to see Vusi in consultation with him. We went into the ward and the security police guarding Vusi had to remain at a distance from us because this, after all, was a professional medical consultation! I talked to Vusi about his role in education and expressed admiration for what he had done. I told him about the post of special assistant, and said that if he was willing I would recommend his appointment to the council of UCT. Accordingly he was appointed. He was then released from prison and took up his appointment in September. He went home to fetch his family and while they were packing the police arrived and Vusi was detained without trial yet again. The family came to Cape Town and lived in a university house. Naturally he received his salary all the time he was in detention. During the few months that he was able to work as my special assistant, towards the end of 1986, he undertook his new role with vigour and was of particular help to my colleagues and me in many ways, especially during the student disturbances surrounding the visit of Dr Conor Cruise O'Brien.

Towards the end of September 1986 Conor Cruise O'Brien, the Irish academic and politician, gave a series of lectures on the campus and soon presented the university with a major crisis. A number of articles had appeared in the media in which O'Brien had been very critical of the academic boycott. He addressed a lunch-time meeting of students in the course of which he described the academic boycott as 'mickey mouse'. A group of students, particularly some of the members of the Azanian Students Organisation (AZASO), were furious and vigorously objected to his being allowed to continue to speak on the campus. The students threatened to disrupt a lecture to be given on the same evening under the auspices of the Kaplan Centre for Jewish Studies, where O'Brien was to speak on the Middle East. As soon as I heard of this possibility I met with the immediate past-president of the SRC, Cameron Dugmore,* a young man whom I liked very much indeed and for whom I had considerable respect, Carla Sutherland, president of the SRC, an African honours student in Zoology who was very articulate, and Zeko Themeli. Zeko was short in stature, not particularly articulate in a conversation in a small group, but when he stood up in front of a room or hall full of students, he held them spellbound. He was charismatic and could whip up the students into a state of high excitement.

I was unable to budge the students. They said that O'Brien had insulted their leaders, that the ANC and its allies were not allowed to speak anywhere in the country, nor were they allowed to be quoted, nor was any ANC literature allowed to be read. They pointed out that they had not acted against O'Brien until he ridiculed the academic boycott publicly, and they felt that as a consequence they thought he had denied himself the right to speak. I emphasised the seriousness of the situation, the importance of freedom of speech on the campus, of hearing the other man's point of view and debating it together, but they were obdurate. I decided to chair the meeting myself, because I felt so strongly on the right to speak. The rules recently introduced to try to deal with such an eventuality were invoked. This meant that the public could only attend the lecture by invitation and that students had to show their student cards before they could enter the lecture theatre. I mobilised as many members of our campus control as I could, to protect the lecture theatre and ensure that the lecture did take place. Our campus control was a small body of people, unarmed and with a very limited ability in situations such as this. In the event, the protesting students arrived shortly after the lecture had started and, while O'Brien was lecturing to the visitors to the Kaplan Centre, their shouting and chanting outside the lecture theatre was audible. Members of campus control contained the situa-

---

* An ANC member of the Western Cape Provincial legislature.

tion until O'Brien had almost come to the end of his lecture. Then the students burst through one of the doors. They danced on the writing surfaces and ran around the lecture theatre chanting. To their great credit the audience left in a completely orderly manner. Some of them debated the issues with the students. I made sure that O'Brien made a rapid exit through a door in the front, well protected by campus control, and that he got safely back to his hotel. I was very cross indeed.

Immediately after the disruption of O'Brien's lecture I stated publicly that no university could accept such a situation. The very freedom which all South Africans yearned for would be damaged by actions such as these. Professor David Welsh of the department of political studies, who had invited Dr O'Brien to give a five-week lecture series on siege societies, said that if UCT could not prevent such student action, it should either close or cease calling itself a university.

The next day a lecture which O'Brien was to have given to the first-year students in political studies was disrupted. During that morning he left for Johannesburg, as had been his original intention. I held further discussions with the student leadership during the day. I strongly criticised what happened, but it was clear to me that they would not allow O'Brien to speak on the campus again. I phoned O'Brien in Johannesburg and explained the position to him saying that I couldn't guarantee his protection on the campus and did not think he would be able to speak and that if he tried to do so, violence was likely to result. (I was unable to call the police because of previous actions by them on campus, and their total unpredictability once they were there. They were correctly seen as the agents of the apartheid state. I had to rely entirely on our small, unarmed, campus control personnel.)

O'Brien agreed that it would be better if he didn't return to lecture on the campus. This event split the university. There were those who argued along the same lines as the students had done. On the other hand, there were those who felt very strongly that freedom of speech was a fundamental part of a university, and that if it couldn't be ensured, the very existence of the university as an institution of higher learning was threatened. The students marched to the Bremner Building in protest against O'Brien. There were meetings of many university bodies, including the academic freedom committee, faculty boards, various groupings on the campus and a stormy, very long meeting of the university senate, which was divided on the issue. Towards the end of that meeting, which was heated and tense, one or two of the members called upon me to indicate where I stood but I declined because, although I believed it was fundamentally wrong to deny O'Brien the right to speak, I knew that if I threw my authority behind those insisting that O'Brien should be allowed to speak, I would further polarise the university. At that stage I saw my primary task as that of keeping the university together. I believed that the failure of O'Brien to be allowed to speak on the campus was an 'imperial defeat', recalling the words of Winston Churchill, when the battleships the *Repulse* and the *Prince of Wales* were sunk off Malaysia. This 'imperial defeat' was one battle lost in what I believed was going to be a long war and we had to persevere and win the war while ensuring that the university emerged intact in a new South Africa. Some battles would be lost along the way but I hoped that, with victory, freedom of speech would be restored to the university. The senate passed a resolution, making it clear that students who disrupted academic activities should forfeit their right to attend the university. A motion recognising academic freedom, rejecting the academic boycott and censuring the disruption of lectures on campus, was passed by 85 votes to 47.

The senate had been concerned with the fundamental values of freedom of thought, of speech and of conscience, values crucial to a university and the vocation of an academic, but recognised that these values and academic freedoms did not simply come to be. Values had to be recognised and upheld. Debate on their place and purpose was continually necessary if all sections of the South African community and succeeding generations were to accept and allow them. This was especially true where these and other freedoms had been systematically denied to whole communities or sections of them. One of the national newspapers carried a photograph of students in the act of forcing entry into the lecture theatre where O'Brien was speaking. The young man shown taking a leadership role was subsequently identified as a policeman masquerading as a student. The student leaders were indeed being advised by this police spy. This was another example of the dirty tricks which the security police were playing on campuses like UCT. Disciplinary action taken involved one of the students being substantially fined and others receiving strong reprimands.

There had been a wide-ranging discussion in the senate on the question of academic boycotts. An academic boycott was used by the ANC as a political tactic and the senate's overriding concern was the freedom of exchange of ideas and knowledge. This overriding concern was exemplified in the principled stands on academic boycotts taken by such bodies as the International Committee of Scientific Unions, but in this context it was recognised that a fully free exchange no longer existed, as demonstrated by the refusal of a visa to José Miguez Bonino, the Methodist theologian from Argentina, to visit UCT to lecture in the department of religious studies, and the bannings of Jack Simons and Bill Hoffenberg. The senate committed itself to strive for the removal of all restrictions on the uninhibited intercourse of international scholarship.

There was a commission of enquiry into the O'Brien affair which was duly appointed by UCT's council. Professor D J du Plessis, former vice-chancellor and principal of the University of the Witwatersrand, chaired the commission. The other members were Advocate A Chaskalson, SC* and Mr I Mahomed, SC.† I was criticised for the selection of these two advocates, but their subsequent careers have certainly justified my judgment! The report of the commissioners stressed the context in which the events had occurred, the need for a university ethic of academic freedom and identified several areas of potential conflict which had to be addressed. The commission approved of the actions the executive and council had taken and found the students' actions 'unacceptable'. The commission concluded that 'UCT is engaged in a leadership role in non-racial education which is progressing successfully. The problems of integration are being well managed and if steady progress is made with this little-understood process, UCT can be an example to all in this country.' The commissioners were critical of O'Brien's behaviour and he hotly disputed the report.

I did not have the unanimous support of council members for the way in which I handled the O'Brien affair and was widely criticised in the press. David Welsh and many others were very critical of me and of the university council for the way in which this matter was handled. There was no doubt in my mind that it was absolutely wrong for the students to have prevented O'Brien from speaking, given the critical importance of freedom of speech on a university campus and, indeed, in society as a whole. I am convinced that if O'Brien had returned to speak on the campus, and we had surrounded him with every campus control person in our employ, and had joined ourselves to protect him, and had done everything humanly possible to try and ensure his speaking, we would not have succeeded, and the campus would have been disrupted in a major way.

Another event underlined the loss of freedom of speech. I spoke in the Claremont Civic Centre under the auspices of the Progressive Federal Party. It was the first and last time that I spoke from a political party platform and I did so because speeches off campus were only permitted at meetings of unbanned political organisations. Such were the regulations of the oppressive state of emergency. I spoke on the need for peace.

This was the society in which the university was functioning, a society which denied freedom of speech, where the Government used extensive censorship and where the truth of what was happening around us and in our neighbouring countries was impossible to obtain. The South African

---

* First president of the Constitutional Court in a democratic South Africa.
† Second chief justice in a democratic South Africa.

army invaded Angola without the South African public's knowledge. The Government authorised it secretly, it was carried out in secret and it was some time before any member of the public in South Africa knew about it.

During the year a full recognition agreement was signed between the university and the university workers' committee, which later in the year changed its name to the University and Allied Workers' Union, and extended its scope to cover workers in all tertiary institutions. In these matters I came to meet Mr Ebrahim Patel, who had led the union negotiations at UCT. I was very impressed by him and thought that he was an able representative of the unions. He now holds a very senior position in COSATU, the largest union in South Africa, and it gives me some satisfaction to know that he had cut his 'union' teeth at the University of Cape Town.

'Wag 'n bietjie, Van der Merwe. That opstoker's official!' (Cartoon by Grogan, 1987)

Spies and disruptions
1987

In 1986 nearly 40 per cent of the students at UCT were women. The proportion of women amongst the teaching staff, though increasing, did not approach this proportion and indeed there were very few women in the senior ranks of the academic staff. In 1886, the council of the South African College, as UCT then was, decided to admit women undergraduates to the chemistry department on an experimental basis. That experiment worked so well that the council, amply satisfied with the academic prowess of those first women students, decided in the next year, 1887, to throw the gates of the college wide open in honour of Queen Victoria's Jubilee.

UCT decided to mark the centenary from 1886 to 1987 and, knowing that Anita was no longer lecturing, my special assistant James Moulder suggested that Anita should organise the programme. She was very enthusiastic. A public meeting of all women on campus was convened and a steering committee, with Anita in the chair, was appointed. The programme for the commemoration ran from September 1986 to the end of August 1987, reflecting our academic year in a previous era, and was opened by Mrs Albertina Sisulu, wife of Walter Sisulu,* in Jameson Hall, which was packed for her address. (She didn't please the feminists by emphasising the role of women in the home and their need to bring up their children themselves.) One of the most successful fund-raising events was a phantom lunch to which people were invited and asked to pay, but which didn't take place. Instead, ticket holders received a brochure containing the menu they might have enjoyed, copies of lunch-time speeches not delivered, and the notation for a short composition by Peter Klatzow† – which had, of course, not been played. The lunch was the brainchild of Mrs Wendy Ackerman, whose husband Raymond Ackerman is the founder and chief executive of Pick 'n Pay, a major South African supermarket chain. Both of them are generous benefactors to UCT and SHAWCO and to many other causes in South Africa.

During the next twelve months there were lectures on issues related to

---

* Walter Sisulu was on Robben Island with Nelson Mandela. He and his wife have both been leading members of the ANC.
† Senior academic at UCT's College of Music.

women, a function to honour women of outstanding achievement associated with UCT and a publication containing articles on the history of women at UCT, with a message of support from the Queen Mother, an honorary graduate of the university.

Anita co-ordinated the production of a portfolio of silkscreen prints in a limited edition of 25, made by staff members at UCT's Michaelis School of Fine Art. This was sold to raise funds for needy women students. She frequently needed to visit the upper campus while co-ordinating the centenary programme and, after checking with me, would use my parking bay. On these occasions, she was always stopped and questioned by campus control officers. Once she was in a great hurry to keep an appointment, waved to the officer as she drove into the bay, and ran off, pointing to the note from me displayed on the windscreen, saying she was my wife. She returned to find a traffic ticket, which fined her for entering a reserved area and parking in the vice-chancellor's bay. The ticket noted that 'she claims to know the vice-chancellor'! Plainly he did not believe that anyone driving a beat-up twelve-year-old Datsun and running away from him in sneakers could be the vice-chancellor's wife!

Father Healy, the president of the University of Georgetown, visited UCT and I asked Professor de Vries, the vice-chancellor and rector of the University of Stellenbosch, to meet with him but warned Professor Healy that, if told that Stellenbosch was a multi-racial university, he should dig deeper into the statement. Healy reported that he had indeed been told just that and De Vries was speaking about coloured, Indian and Chinese students living together in a segregated residence. That was what he regarded as a multi-racial university.

Colin Campbell,* then the President of Wesleyan University, a man of considerable ability, was committed to the promotion of a democratic society. He and I co-chaired a conference on liberalism.

A black staff association was formed, the committee consisting of senior academic and administrative staff, and I had meetings with them down the years. Unfortunately they did not seem able to reach a consensus amongst themselves on the many important issues which were raised and the association never really functioned efficiently, much to my disappointment.

Sheilah Lloyd retired in the middle of the year and she was such an outstanding personal assistant running my office that I was very sorry to lose her. She was replaced by Cynthia Williams, who had worked in the office

---

* Later president of the Rockefeller Brothers' Fund and the second chairman of the UCT Fund in New York.

for some time as a senior secretary. Cynthia was succeeded by Maggie Sükel, who was a superb personal senior secretary. She had the knack of putting everyone at ease and the ability to protect me from unnecessary enquiries. Her sense of humour was refreshing and, coupled with her energy, made her an enormous help to me. She was ably supported by the secretaries in the office.

Mr van Huyssteen, who succeeded Len Read as the registrar, retired at the end of the year. Van Huyssteen was a very conscientious registrar and he was succeeded by Hugh Amoore, whom I had, of course, known since his student days. Hugh Amoore is still the registrar of the university. He is an outstanding man and probably more knowledgeable about university administration in South Africa than anyone else. He is completely committed to UCT.

At the end of November my son John emigrated to the United States. He had refused to serve in the South African army to fight to defend apartheid, and I remember saying to him at the airport that I knew what his leaving meant to me, and knew what it meant to him, but that I entirely agreed with his action. He still lives in the United States, as do so many other young South Africans who live abroad now, having left for the same reason.

There were two meetings every year in Johannesburg attended by the chancellors, chairmen of council and the vice-chancellors of the University of the Witwatersrand and their opposite numbers from the University of Cape Town. This gave the chancellors and chairmen of council an opportunity to spend a morning hearing of the particular problems faced by the two universities, which had historical ties and had usually approached the problems of South Africa in the same way. The meetings were invaluable in anticipating problems and discussing strategies to deal with them.

In 1986 all universities achieved the same legal position with regard to the independence of their councils and were all funded on the same basis. The so-called historically black universities are now called the historically disadvantaged universities, largely because it is assumed that they were disadvantaged financially. This is to a large extent untrue. Indeed, the reverse is the case. Unlike the established universities they received larger subsidies for students and made no contribution to the costs of buildings. In the latter '80s there was a period of two years when some of them, and in particular the University of the Western Cape, had relatively low incomes because they had admitted large numbers of students at a time when the Government was not increasing its grants. It was only from 1986 that the same funding formula was applied to them. Some of them, e.g. MEDUNSA, continue to get special favourable treatment financially.

At the end of November the chairman of council, Len Abrahamse, Mr Justice Marius Diemont, the deputy chairman, Peter Bieber and George Dall, members of council, and I met with F W de Klerk, the Minister of National Education, Louis le Grange, the Minister of Law and Order, Kobie Coetsee, the Minister of Justice, and Piet Clase, Minister of Education in the Department of Education and Culture, House of Assembly, together with a general from the security police. De Klerk drew attention to the problems in the country, alleging that on some university campuses 'radicals' were pampered and 'moderate' students were given no protection. He expressed concern at the fact that university administrations might be losing control of their campuses and were not disciplining students who acted incorrectly, and he indicated that the Government might have to take action. (They later tried to do that.) He said the Government was under great pressure and that they had constituted a Cabinet sub-committee to report back to the Cabinet.

Len indicated very clearly that the university was very much in control of the campus and put the recent and past events in perspective by referring to what was happening in the country as a whole. I did the same. I indicated that the freedom of speech which they alleged they wished to protect, and other freedoms were being considerably encroached upon by the state of emergency and other legislation. I told Le Grange that if in trying to protect freedom of speech he destroyed it, he would not be doing anyone a favour and I proceeded to give him some examples of that happening. De Klerk raised other points, alleging that universities were wasting the tax-payers' money, that some of the staff were inciting students to be subversive, that the general public and Government had these perceptions, and that the student protests were illegal. I disagreed strongly with him. We were then told that there was a perception that I might be advocating civil disobedience. I asked them to prove that allegation. We did not yield. I told them that matters such as these did not require 'a sledgehammer' and they should leave it to the universities to look after their own affairs.

I had an extraordinary visit from the Director-General of National Symbols. He came into my office with a number of parcels and a flag-pole. He said that the State President, Mr P W Botha, wanted the promotion of national symbols. He presented me with a full-size national flag (and the pole) and a small flag for my desk. He also gave me two large copies of the preamble to the constitution which created the tricameral parliament, and a lapel pin of the national flag. Finally he said that P W Botha knew nothing of it but he wanted me to have a large portrait of the president. I managed to keep a straight face, thanked him and sent him on his way. I went into Hugh Amoore's office with all the paraphernalia and collapsed laughing. We put the flag-pole complete with the flag in Jim Leatt's office late that after-

1987

noon, put the small flag on his desk and stuck the large posters on his wall. He had ten minutes to get rid of the rubbish before meeting with the student leadership the next morning.

Christmas Day that year remains vividly in my memory because at the table for some 25 or 30 people we included Nombelela Khanyile and the three children. Two of them were quite small and when I proposed the Christmas toast, including one to absent friends, I could hardly speak with emotion because I looked at these three children and their mother and I knew that Vusi was in detention in the hands of the police, never having been charged, tried or found guilty of any offence.

Over the Christmas holidays after the O'Brien affair I was swimming in the surf at Plettenberg Bay when Helen Suzman came bounding up to me and, with the waves splashing over us, told me in no uncertain terms how wrong it was that O'Brien had not been able to speak. I calmed my friend down and tried to explain what had happened. It was vintage Suzman.

The turbulence on the campus continued in 1987. On 20 March SANSCO (SA National Students' Congress, an ANC-aligned student organisation representing black students) and NUSAS organised a meeting on campus to commemorate the Sharpeville tragedy in 1960. A mass meeting was held in the Beattie lecture theatre and the students then moved as a column to the plaza in front of the Jameson Hall where they toyi toyied.* This came to an abrupt halt with a cry of 'Amandla!' and 'passes' were then burnt. The crowd then moved to a meeting in a lecture theatre in the Leslie Building where speeches were made by members of NUSAS and COSATU. The students refused to leave the lecture theatre to allow a scheduled Afrikaans lecture to take place, asserting their right to remain. The lights were turned out and there was a great deal of dancing and singing in the darkness. The students defied the dean of arts, who had asked them to move to an alternative venue. A decision was taken to march to the Bremner Building and during the march several lectures were disrupted and the students from the disrupted lectures reacted angrily.

When the students reached the Bremner Building they staged a sit-in in the foyer and demanded the observance of certain dates in South African history as 'people's holidays' at the university. This was a matter which had been debated in the university. The students met with John Reid and dispersed peacefully. I met with the student leadership of NUSAS, SANSCO and the SRC and they gave an assurance that it had not been their intention for the meeting to extend beyond the time allocated, nor had they intended

---

* A toyi-toyi is a protest dance, often performed in a circle with someone in the centre leading the singing. At times it was meant to be intimidating by students.

in any way to defy the dean of arts. There had been no plan to disrupt any lectures. It was plain to me that the student leadership was not pleased that their plans went awry. Of course emotions had run very high, given what had happened at Sharpeville and given the current state of affairs in the country. I reminded the students of the findings of the recent commission of enquiry into the O'Brien affair at the university, which had clearly found that disruption of lectures by students was unacceptable, a position which I told them was certainly my own as well.

Punitive action was not called for because the student leadership disapproved of what had happened and those who had disrupted lectures could not be identified. I was certainly criticised both within and outside of the university for not acting more severely. Towards the end of the year 21 March (Sharpeville Day) and 16 June (Soweto Day) became official university holidays and the academic year was extended to take account of them. UCT was roundly criticised for this by many white South Africans. They are national official holidays in the new democratic South Africa.

There was a division in the student leadership. NUSAS had become a white organisation, SANSCO a black organisation. Black students would not get involved in university structures. At that stage they would only take part in the academic activities of the university. This was a source of concern to us, but its roots lay in apartheid and in the fact that the majority of the students and staff were white, and the black students frequently felt alienated.

We had more problems on the campus at the end of April and in the run-up to the election for the (whites only) House of Assembly in early May. John Reid, Jim Leatt and I met with the SRC and discussed all the issues involved. Jim and I went to the police in Wynberg, where the district commissioner had his headquarters, to urge them to stay off the campus and to let demonstrations pass off peacefully. The police agreed, provided that their presence did not become imperative in their view and I told them that if they weren't there, everything would go off peacefully. On the same day students held a mass meeting attended by a number of off-campus organisations. The protests on the campus were a culmination of the 'votes for all' campaign which had been launched by NUSAS and endorsed nationally by SANSCO. The venue of the meeting had been kept secret until the last minute because a number of organisational representatives were in hiding. The campaign culminated in an alternative poll on 4, 5 and 6 May, asking students to vote for or against the 'votes for all' campaign. Despite my meeting with the police, asking them to stay off the campus for three successive days, the police intervened in student protests along the side of the highway. The police used sjamboks (whips), tear gas and birdshot.

Occasionally the protests resulted in the police invading the heart of the campus, and I witnessed large numbers of police with armoured vehicles drawn up on University Avenue in front of Jameson Hall. On that occasion a number of missiles were thrown at the police. I found myself dodging large bricks thrown at the police. One young woman student walked up to a policeman and slapped him in the face. She was promptly arrested. Major Odendaal, who was the notorious head of the riot police, was standing next to me slapping the ground with his sjambok when he suddenly growled, '*Kom, manne*' ('Come on, men') and ran up past the Jameson Hall into the university buildings. He charged into a lecture theatre where law students were being taught, slapping his sjambok on the floor. The lecturer propelled his wheelchair from where he was sitting and confronted the enraged police officer. A stunned Odendaal turned about and took his men out of the lecture theatre. A number of students were whipped on the campus, however.

During the demonstrations of those three days a total of 25 students were arrested and between 25 and 30 students were treated for sjambok and gun injuries. The upper campus was blanketed with tear gas, three policemen were said to have been injured – one bitten by his own dog. The whites-only election was a clear demonstration of the racism of the Nationalist Party regime and the students were right to protest against it, but that was not the view of most white South Africans and certainly it brought the university into disrepute in their eyes, but not in the eyes of most black South Africans.

I was sitting at my desk when a student rushed in to tell me that the students were marching down from the Jameson Hall and that the police were again on the campus. I ran up onto the middle campus and saw the riot squad cantering in front of me, fully armed. I ran through the police and said to the officer in charge that he should halt his men and that I would talk to the students, who were marching down about 100 yards ahead of us. I had to repeat myself several times before Captain Dowd* ordered his men to stop. I went to the students and said to them that I supported the right of peaceful protest and that in my view the police had no business to be there, but that we had to face the reality of their presence. The students were very nervous and the atmosphere was very tense. Somebody behind me suggested to me that I should tell the students to sit down, which I did, and all the students sat down. This made them less threatening to the police and certainly temporarily lessened the tension.

I then said to them I thought that a small delegation should come to meet me in my office to discuss their demands and that the rest should return to the Jameson Hall on the upper campus. The students said they would be

---

* Dowd was one of the best police officers with whom I had to deal. He seemed to dislike the orders he was instructed to carry out. In a democratic South Africa he received a deserved promotion.

attacked by the police if they did so. Again somebody behind me spoke and said, 'Lead them back yourself' and I promptly said I would do so. I told the students to form rows of eight and to link their arms, and I walked in front of them directly towards the police at a slow pace. The students followed. There were probably 1 000 of them and as we approached the police we started singing, 'We shall overcome.' The police slowly retreated backwards and started wheeling away from us and I led the students past the police, back up the hill to the Jameson Hall. I sat on the stage of the hall with the student leadership while a number of speeches were made, and I again repeated to the students my belief in the right of peaceful protest and complimented them on the orderly way in which they had behaved. A number of students started several 'toyi-toyis' in the hall and a large 'toyi-toyi' in front of me followed the usual pattern of one of the dancing students saying, 'Viva Mandela, viva Tambo, viva the ANC!' He suddenly shouted out, much to my astonishment, 'Viva big daddy Saunders!' I subsequently learned that there were police snipers on the rooftops around the area and I have no doubt that on that day there had been a real possibility of students being severely injured. I was always terrified of a Kent State situation on the campus and feared that students would be killed by the police during protests. We were very lucky indeed that this did not happen.

On a number of occasions I experienced the effects of tear gas fired by the police. It certainly makes one's eyes run and I found that it was an excellent way to cure a cold because it clears the sinuses. An Australian newspaper reporter once saw me with my eyes streaming after being exposed to tear gas and reported to his Australian readers that everybody felt sorry for me because I was crying because of what was happening to the campus!

Five security policemen raided the SRC offices, arriving with a search warrant for a pamphlet on the ANC. They confiscated copies of the originals of the SRC election posters, a copy of Natal University's *Dome*, a student newspaper which was apparently banned, and 'half the contents of a dust bin.' René Alberts, the publications officer of the SRC, was instructed by the security police to accompany them to their headquarters to obtain a receipt for the confiscated documents. She reported in the student newspaper, 'I had waited there for about half an hour when Dr Saunders arrived. When he saw me he said, "What are you doing here, students should be in lectures".' Suddenly remembering a lecture, Ms Alberts grabbed her books and hastily left. I didn't want her to go with them and that's why I indicated that she should get out of the room and disappear as quickly as possible. In the event nobody had to go with the security police to get a 'receipt'.

Because of the repeated protests by students and staff during 1985, '86 and '87, and the frequent consequential clashes with the police, and because of the fact that the university was outspoken in its opposition to apartheid, the university was increasingly criticised in the press and of course by the National Party in parliament. The same was true for the University of the Western Cape, the University of the Witwatersrand, the University of Natal and Rhodes University. There were threats from the Government with suggestions that the university subsidy from treasury would be reduced if action wasn't taken. The *Financial Mail* and some other English-speaking newspapers carried a spate of articles and editorials attacking the universities from the top administrators down to the first-year students. The Afrikaans newspapers had consistently done so. There was a lot of rhetoric about 'ruthless and intolerant Marxists' and the following quote from the *Financial Mail* of 15 May 1987 was entitled 'Tight-faced Reality'. 'So any democrat on the Wits or UCT campus, assuming there are still some, is up against two fronts: the racism of an intolerant Government, but also its counterpart, a ruthless and intolerant Marxist trend which endorses violence* ... the end of which could be the triumph of a more ruthless and tyrannical Government than any South Africans have experienced so far. There appears to be a policy of deliberate provocation of the police by student radicals, calculated to cause an overt reaction enabling them to cry "police brutality".'

The students' press wrote, 'But it is Dr Stuart Saunders's precision balancing act that is to be commended. Stuck between critics from the white community, led by the commercial and liberal press and the perceived need to continue with a programme of Africanisation of the university, Saunders's verbal defence and action can be likened to a tightrope walker high above the audience. It is this performance that so aptly brings to light the debate on the position of the university in South African society. The *Financial Mail* argues that the university can maintain a separate identity and in doing so retain its traditional liberal values, but in joining the chorus of voices that criticise the university, whether from the position of the Government or the position of the black community that argues for rapid Africanisation, the *Financial Mail* aptly reinforces the view that the university rejects the society. It is unfortunate at a time when the Government is mustering its forces to carry out its mandate for security, that the *Financial Mail* and the *Business Day* choose to lead the crusade against the university, in effect joining hands with those on the right.'

Two events occurred on the campus which did not endear the university or myself to the Government or to many people amongst the white population of South Africa. A group of about 150 mainly African students, dis-

---

* I had no evidence of this.
† A student residence.

rupted a formal dinner at Leo Marquard Hall because there had been an objection to the invited speaker, Dr Dennis Worrall, spokesman for the Government during his term as ambassador to Great Britain and also because he had refused to object to the state of emergency. I was called to the residence and found a group of students singing and dancing in the dining room. Zeko Themela,* (one of the student leaders in the O'Brien affair), was the leader of the protesters and was urging them to continue with their dancing and singing. I went to the common room where Worrall was waiting and he told me that he could see that it would be impossible for him to attend the dinner and to speak, and so he left.

The other episode arose when members of the Moderate Students' Movement arranged for Mr Tomasinqa Linda to speak on the campus. He was a former community councillor and co-president of the United Christian Conciliation Party and was alleged to have been instrumental in the setting up of vigilante groups in the Eastern Cape. My clear information was that Linda's talk would be disrupted and that he could be attacked by people in the audience who might not necessarily be members of the university community. Accordingly, I instructed the two organisers of the meeting to postpone it until we had time to ensure Linda's safety. They flouted my instruction and the meeting was disrupted. About 40 people attended the meeting, 20 of whom it was alleged came from the University of Stellenbosch. Then 50 students moved into the back of the lecture theatre chanting and singing while Linda shouted: 'You are little fascists, little howling dogs!' The SRC president Carla Sutherland informed the chair that the meeting had been postponed by me and that the continuation of the meeting was therefore in direct defiance of my orders. The chair of the Moderate Students' Movement, Lance Terry, who had been present at the meeting earlier in the day at which he had been informed of my ruling, sat at the back of the room, allegedly making no effort to stop the meeting. Linda was bundled out of a side door but his briefcase was burned.

Following on the disruption of Worrall's talk I disciplined six black students and suspended them until the end of the year and fined a further twenty R250 each. All the students appealed, as was their right, to the university court. I disciplined the two Moderate Students' Movement students, Mr L A Terry and Mr J R Peers, who had defied me and had proceeded with the meeting at which Linda spoke. When they arrived at my office I called

---

* A South African Breweries delivery vehicle was set alight during another protest on campus and there were allegations that Zeko Themela had been responsible. He was subsequently charged with arson in the Wynberg magistrate's court and fled the country before being brought to trial. The event was a public relations disaster. The SA Breweries was an important donor to UCT.

them in one at a time and went through what had happened very carefully with each one, and then asked whether what I had told them was correct. There was no way they could deny that I had formally instructed them to postpone the meeting. I then said to each one in turn that I was suspending him from the university for the rest of the year. The first student was then called back in and I asked him whether he had thought about what had taken place between us and whether he had anything further to say in mitigation. He affirmed that he fully understood the matter and I affirmed the sentence. The same happened with the second student. There was no doubt in my mind that both students were fully aware of what was going on and I made it clear to them that they had the right to appeal to the university court. The two members of the Moderate Students' Movement lodged an appeal against my actions with the Cape Supreme Court. A number of senior advocates and at least one judge told me that they were absolutely confident the appeal would be turned down, but Mr Justice Selikowitz found against me, overturning my ruling on procedural grounds, because he found that the students had not been given due notice of the charges against them and had not been able to prepare themselves for their defence.

These students did have a sense of the dramatic and one of humour. Mr Peers and his brother got into the roof of the new science lecture theatre during an address which was being given by the Rev. Allan Boesak. Boesak is a charismatic speaker and apparently he threw his arms into the air saying, 'God is on your side, and God will help you when you defy the Government ...' or words to that effect. And from the ceiling came the words, clearly, in a deep baritone, 'No I won't.' The meeting ended in uproar.

As a result of the judge's ruling I set aside the sentences imposed on both groups of students and they were all charged afresh in the university court. Sixteen students were found guilty by the university court (including both of those who had appealed successfully to the Supreme Court, which had ruled that the internal procedures of the university should be followed before the merits of their case could be dealt with by the Supreme Court). One of the students found guilty in the Worrall matter was rusticated for the remainder of the year and he was also given a suspended expulsion sentence. In all, 13 students received suspended rustication sentences and were fined. The two MSM students received suspended sentences rusticating them until the end of the year. They all appealed to the university council and none of the appeals was upheld.

Marius Diemont, deputy chair of council and a judge of Appeal, presided over both courts, at each of which I gave evidence against the students. In the case of the students accused of disrupting Worrall's evening and defying my instructions, Advocate Dullah Omar* appeared for the students. I have known the Omar family for a long time and am particularly fond of Dullah's wife Farieda. When I was giving evidence against Zeko Themela for his leadership role, Omar asked me how I could know he was inciting the other students, given the agreed fact that the noise made it impossible for me to hear what he said. I replied that I could see the expression in his eyes and face and could see him shouting and gesticulating at the students in a way that left me in no doubt as to his role. The students indicated that they wanted to speak to Omar and he called for a recess to consult his clients. They crowded around him and every now and then I heard him exclaim, 'I can't say that!' When we resumed he asked me whether I knew that Zeko's head had been burnt as a child and that as a consequence he always wore a woollen headgear. I said I did. He put it to me that Zeko's woollen hat had been pulled down over his eyes and that I could not have seen the expression in them. I pointed out that if that had been the case he would have needed a guide dog or the equivalent and that it simply was not true. It cut no ice with the judge. Afterwards Dullah apologised to me saying, 'I had to say something.' The judgment of Selikowitz had far-reaching effects on our disciplinary system, which became a very formal one causing considerable delays in getting results. It certainly frustrated me. We often had cause to remember the saying, 'Justice delayed is justice denied.'

As these events were unfolding the students uncovered a self-confessed police spy among their number. They asked to have an urgent meeting with me on the lawn outside my office, fearful that my office might be bugged. There was no doubt that my telephones were being tapped and from time to time I did have the office inspected for other bugging devices in it. Nothing was ever uncovered, but none of us had any great confidence that this excluded bugging devices. The SRC's telephone was certainly tapped and they were quite sure that their offices were monitored. They told me that a Mr Daniel Pretorius had confessed to them that he was a police spy. I subsequently saw him and he was quite open about his activities. He alleged he was seventeen years old when a department head at his school, Paarl Boys' High, asked what he planned to do after completing his matriculation examination. He answered that he intended studying at UCT. A week later he was called to a vice-principal's office where two security policemen, one of whom was an old boy of the school, asked if he would be prepared to infiltrate NUSAS and give the police information on the internal workings of the organisation.

At the beginning of 1986, Pretorius had joined the projects committee with the brief to move as far up the NUSAS hierarchy as possible and to

---

* Minister of Justice in the first democratic government in South Africa.

exploit any potential flaws in the non-racial alliance between NUSAS and SANSCO. Pretorius said he was asked to behave as militantly as possible – the police seeing any violent action on the campus as working in their own interests. The SRC received an affidavit from a student that Pretorius encouraged other people to throw stones at the police and at cars on the highway during a demonstration on the campus in the previous term, a demonstration which resulted in a number of students being arrested and others being injured by birdshot. Had he remained a spy for four years, he would have been exempted from his national service in the army. It was when he became aware of a massive pamphlet campaign by the security police that would be used to discredit the SRC elections that he decided to confess. He claimed that the South African security police were seeking to isolate me politically by deliberately sowing dissension on the University of Cape Town campus. He claimed this was part of a larger plot to alienate certain anti-Government organisations such as NUSAS, SANSCO and the UDF in an orchestrated campaign to undermine them. He said he was convinced there was an overall plot to undermine 'progressive' organisations in South Africa and he stated that I was regarded as a liberal and as an 'enemy' by the security police, that the security police would make as much use of organisations such as as the National Students' Federation (NSF), to which the Moderate Students' Movement was affilliated, as they could.

The Minister of Law and Order, Mr Adriaan Vlok, publicly confirmed that Pretorius was a policeman. Pretorius had given the police details of where members of certain organisations were hiding when they were being sought by the police. Pretorius was now in hiding himself and he confessed to being 'confused and scared'.

Some finer points of law
1987 (continued)–1988

On 4 August the chairmen of university councils and the vice-chancellors of all South Africa's universities were called to a meeting in the Verwoerd Building in Cape Town by the Minister of National Education, F W de Klerk. All the Own Affairs Ministers together with Government officials were also present. It had not escaped my notice that this meeting occurred on the day after the Linda episode. De Klerk outlined draft conditions on the award of the State subsidies, the funds universities received from the national treasury. Universities which failed to stop protests would be penalised financially. He said that the Government was alarmed by what was happening on some campuses, by the lack of control and the lack of discipline of students, by the unruly behaviour of students, and the necessity of using the police to break up student meetings. He said the taxpayers' money was being wasted and that the Government was not prepared to allow things to continue in this way. Public opinion in South Africa (he was of course referring to white public opinion) clearly supported the Government in this matter and they had had numerous protests from the public. The steps which the Government intended to undertake were outlined in a letter to the chairman of council dated the following day and was received by us four or five days later. It set out in great detail what students and staff were not allowed to do, that they should be disciplined if they acted improperly in terms of the letter including the 'disciplining of any student or staff member who conducts himself in a seditious or riotous manner within a radius of two kilometres from the perimeter of the campus of your university.' 'Unrest' or 'disruption' had to be reported to the Minister and the action taken by the university described. If the Minister was not satisfied he would penalise the university financially.

At the meeting both Len Abrahamse and I objected strongly, denied the Government's right to take such action, insisted on the right to peaceful protest and spoke against the state of emergency and its infringement on university affairs. The spokesmen from the other English-speaking universities were also opposed to the proposed action. De Klerk agreed that we should be given time to react to the draft proposals.

Writing on behalf of council to the Minister in response to these proposals, Len Abrahamse made his rejection of them unequivocal; they were designed to curb dissent. He stated that the university council viewed the conditions as ultra vires and liable to be set aside by a court of law. The objections of UCT were based on principle. Before the conditions were finalised I invited De Klerk and Len to lunch at Glenara. At lunch I told De Klerk that if the Government enforced the conditions on our income we would take them to court and he would have 'egg on his face'. De Klerk confirmed that they would proceed. The universities of Cape Town, Witwatersrand, Natal, Rhodes and Western Cape publicly rejected the conditions which were finally promulgated in the middle of October, with only minor amendments.

University assemblies were held on the campuses of UCT, Rhodes, Natal and Witwatersrand on 28 October. I was overseas to rally support and John Reid presided over the assembly and announced that the council was taking legal advice regarding the new subsidy conditions. There was a total of eight speakers and Professor Reid spoke strongly, saying that UCT had found a way to answer violence with logic and debate, with restraint and a minimum of constraint. Sometimes it would lose, but it hoped and thought that it would win in the end to provide the model to society that it needed. He said that he objected to the efforts to turn him into 'a kind of academic Casspir.'

While I was overseas for part of this time, I had discussions with Bill Bowen, then president of Princeton University and he organised for the presidents of the State University of New Jersey (Rutgers), Harvard University, Dartmouth College, the University of California, Columbia University, the University of Chicago, the University of Pennsylvania, Stanford University, Tufts University, Cornell University, Yale University, the University of Michigan and Brown University, and the chairman of the Corporation of the Massachusetts Institute of Technology to write, together with himself, the following letter to Minister De Klerk.

Dear Mr Minister

It is with deep concern that we have learned of the 'conditions' which the South African Government has placed on the subsidies for South African universities.

These conditions can only further compromise the freedom of speech and enquiry on the campuses of South Africa. You are asking the councils and presidents (vice-chancellors and rectors) to police the actions of both students and staff on and off the campus in ways that are inconsistent with universal standards of academic freedom and autonomy. To accept such conditions would be to forfeit the respect and the moral authority needed to secure their compliance.

Any university of standing must enjoy the independence and freedom required to carry out its essential mission. Accordingly, we urge you and the South African Government not to impose these conditions.

We had also received letters of support from the following British institutions: the Universities of Bristol, Surrey, Manchester, East Anglia, Salford, Lancaster, Aberdeen, Sussex, Edinburgh, Durham, Exeter, Stirling, The Open University and Corpus Christi College in Cambridge. I was unsuccessful in getting the Committee of Vice-Chancellors and Principals in the UK to support us. The chairman explained that they could not get involved in politics as an organisation. The executive committee of convocation* publicly supported the stand taken by council and senate in opposing the subsidy conditions which the Government intended to impose. Under the presidency of Judge Pat Tebbutt, convocation consistently supported me and UCT. Father Healey of Georgetown University, an Auden scholar, likened the South African Government to Auden's 'slobbering beast'.

The vice-chancellor and rector of the University of Stellenbosch, Professor Mike de Vries, echoed the view of the Afrikaans universities when he said that the new subsidy conditions did not conflict with his university's policy outline and that he could 'go along with them'.

In December the university council authorised the institution of legal proceedings to set aside the conditions. There had been a lot of debate amongst ourselves as to whether we should proceed in this way, as there had been on the other four campuses which had been protesting against the Government's intentions. In this matter the wise counsel of Hugh Amoore, the university registrar, gave strength to the arguments in favour of taking legal action, a step which I fully supported. We took action jointly with the University of the Western Cape.

UCT and UWC were represented by Advocate Seligman, SC and Advocate Jeremy Gauntlett, SC. The case was heard in February 1988. During the hearing Anita and I sat with Hugh Amoore immediately behind our two advocates. The advocates for the Ministers were being advised by senior officials from the Department of National Education, all of whom I knew and I must say they did seem somewhat embarrassed. At the outset, when I sat in the court and saw the three judges of the Cape Supreme Court in their formal robes, I was not at all confident that we would win the case, but I was impressed by the intense questioning to which they subjected the Government's counsel. At one point, one of the judges enticed the Government's counsel into admitting that while he was a student at Stellenbosch University he and other students had indulged in card games

---

* Convocation consisted of all the graduates of the University of Cape Town.

and other non-academic activities. Had they been guilty of wasting the taxpayers' money? the judge enquired.

Anita and I were in the car park outside the Bremner Building when we heard that the unanimous verdict of the Supreme Court was in our favour and that costs had been awarded against the Minister of Education. I was enormously relieved, because I had realised that had the case gone against us, my position and that of the university would have been very tenuous indeed. A victory was essential to maintain the independence of the university and to allow staff and students to protest against the iniquitous laws under which we were being forced to live.

We had raised three objections to the conditions. That their imposition exceeded the powers conferred by the legislature in Section 25 of the Universities Act; that they were so vague that they did not convey with reasonable certainty what universities were required to do to avoid non-compliance and its consequences; and that they involved unreasonably oppressive or gratuitous interference with a university's rights. A full bench of three judges unanimously found in favour of the university. In his judgment delivered early in 1988 Mr Justice C T Howie said that 'The imposition of the conditions ... was prompted substantially by the motive to achieve objects not empowered by Section 25 (of the Universities Act). The latter (motive) was an ulterior motive' which rendered the conditions ultra vires and invalid. He further found that the conditions were void for uncertainty and that ' ... placing the university disciplinary tribunals under pressure to pass or sanction sentences that may or may not, depending on their severity, stave off withdrawal of the university's subsidy, is not only an unwarranted intrusion upon a university council's powers to administer discipline, but an intolerable interference with its duty, and the accused's right to have those powers exercised freely and fairly.' The Minister's application for leave to appeal was denied by the Supreme Court in Cape Town and the Natal Supreme Court subsequently declared subsidy-linked disciplinary conditions 'to be of no force and effect'. In both cases the Government was ordered to pay costs.

Minister Clase wrote to the chairman of the university council, stating that it was the Government's view that four aims should be secured in the university:

1. the uninterrupted and undisturbed function of and study by students,

2. the functional, constructive and educationally responsible utilisation of public funds that may accrue to a university directly or indirectly,

3. the maintenance of the traditional academic standards and values of the university, and

4. the application of effective measures to maintain good order and disci-

pline to achieve the aforementioned aims.

The chairman replied indicating that the university had always conducted its business in a proper manner and that the university would continue to do so in the future. The Government announced that they would negotiate with universities to achieve the aims of the subsidy conditions they had tried to impose. We heard no more from them in this regard. In his autobiography* F W de Klerk makes no mention of his attack on the universities and the Government's defeat in the Supreme Court. His account of his political career shows evidence of a selective memory of which this is an example.

For part of 1986 and for most of 1987, Len Abrahamse had again insisted that my house be guarded to prevent any attacks on me or my family. Through all of these events, Anita was calm and unafraid. She took it all in her stride and gave me unstinting support.

Vusi Khanyile remained in detention. I had discussed his plight with Bill Bowen and Bill had arranged for Princeton to offer Vusi a Fellowship. Armed with this information, Len Abrahamse and I repeatedly wrote to the Minister of Law and Order, Adriaan Vlok, but he declined to release Vusi. I went to see him in the Verwoerd Building and I was faced with Minister Vlok, Deputy Minister of Law and Order Roelf Meyer,† the commissioner of police and the commissioner of the security police, General Johan van der Merwe, together with a number of other police officers. They sat on the other side of the table with Vlok at the head, and I sat alone on the other side of the table. Vlok had Khanyile's dossier in front of him. Every time I made progress with Vlok, the Deputy Minister, Meyer, pointed out something to him and whispered in his ear and Vlok then turned to me and answered in the negative. In my view, Meyer was clearly trying to impress the Minister and especially the generals, so that a good report would go back to President P W Botha, which could only further Meyer's political career.

I received permission to see Vusi in John Vorster Square in Johannesburg where he was being held imprisoned. I was taken by the security police into a room and Vusi was in the room next door. We could see each other through a glass panel and could speak to each other through a grille. We talked extensively about what was happening in South Africa and I brought him up to date about events at the university. Vusi was better informed than I was about what was really happening in South Africa. He told me that those in detention with him were in good spirits. They were all in individ-

---

* FW de Klerk, *The Autobiography. The Last Trek – A New Beginning* (Macmillan, 1999).
† Roelf Meyer subsequently played a key role in the Kempton Park negotiations which plotted the way forward for the emergence of a democratic South Africa. He subsequently left the National Party and started the United Democratic Movement with Bantu Holomisa. It remains to be seen to what extent it will be a political force.

ual cells, but could communicate with each other in various ways. He had rigged up a method of making tea at night. By putting a wick into fat which he had accumulated he could boil water in a small tin can on the windowsill. Fresh hot tea was then passed up and down the cells; a little expression of defiance which helped to maintain morale. I brought him greetings from his family. When we both got up to leave I discovered that there was no door handle; I put my hand up to the top of the door and pulled and it opened. Vusi had done the same and we found ourselves outside in the corridor and were able to embrace and hug each other for at least 30 seconds before pounding footsteps announced the arrival of a large contingent of security police, who pulled us apart.

Shortly after I got back to the university I walked into my office to find an envelope on my desk. There was no postage stamp and no one knew how it had arrived on my desk. The envelope contained a letter from a prisoner in another jail, far away from John Vorster Square, thanking me for going to see Vusi Khanyile. An application in the Rand Supreme Court for Vusi's release from detention was turned down.

I was frightened of possible violence between white and black students on the campus, but in the fifteen and three-quarter years that I was vice-chancellor, such an event never took place to my knowledge. So you can imagine my anxiety when John Reid ran into my office one lunch time to say that there were reports of black and white students fighting on the upper campus. Together with Jim Leatt, we rushed up to the Molly Blackburn room in the students' union building where the events were alleged to be taking place. It was at the time of Eid and what we found was a very tense situation. Members of the Students' Jewish Association were confronting members of the Students' Muslim Association. The Muslim students occupied half the hall, the Jewish students that part of the hall which was closest to the entrance. We pushed our way through the Jewish students and placed ourselves between them and the Muslim students. Three or four members of campus control were with us. There was an uproar, with each group of students shouting abuse at the other. One of the leaders of the Jewish students told me that the Muslim students were inciting them by putting up very provocative and inflammatory banners, such as one claiming that Zionism was a crime against humanity. I found one of the leaders of the Muslim students, who referred me to a guest speaker whom they had invited onto campus to address them and I asked him to persuade the students to take the banner down to defuse the situation. He refused. I repeatedly asked the Muslim students to take the banner down, but they would not. By now the situation was electric, and we were very close to violence. I instructed one of the campus control men to take the banner down, which he did without any resistance from the Muslim students. I then told the Jewish students that they could see the banner had been taken down, and that they should leave the room. Fortunately they complied. There had been some tension in the past at this time of the year between these two groups of students and I believe that the tension was often fuelled by forces off campus. A few days after this incident the Jewish students organised a meeting in Jameson Hall. The hall was packed when someone called 'Heil Hitler'. It is a credit to the students that their only reaction was to catch the man, who proved to be a stranger to the campus. In the ensuing years we ensured that there was adequate consultation between the two groups and, to the mutual credit of these students, there was no repetition of the confrontation of that day. I had enough troubles without having to deal with the problems of the Middle East.

Donald Carr retired at the end of 1987 as a deputy vice-chancellor, having given sterling service to the university, and Professor David Woods,* a very distinguished professor of microbiology, succeeded him and was responsible primarily for research and equipment.

Arising out of the report of the commission of enquiry into the O'Brien affair, meetings were held between staff and students to discuss conflict resolution, and Jim Leatt took forward the debate on the academic boycott. The university-wide debate on the academic boycott culminated in a resolution supported by senate and supported by council, opposing the boycott.

There were, of course, groups within the university which supported an academic boycott although few would publicly claim to support a total one. Some spoke of a selective boycott, implying that either people within or outside the university would decide who might or might not visit universities abroad and what institutions in South Africa might or might not be visited. It seemed to me that some sections of the university had imposed such a boycott on themselves. As is absolutely clear I had consistently opposed any form of academic boycott, believing that it was inimical to the purpose and functioning of any university.

We had further episodes of police action on the campus, including sealing off the campus with roadblocks in an attempt to stop a rally which had been called by the student leadership of the University of Cape Town, the University of the Western Cape and the Peninsula Technikon and the national student organisations to debate the coming local authority elections. The police had required students to present their registration cards

---

* Dave continued directing his research unit and, throughout his tenure as deputy vice-chancellor until 1996, remained an 'A' rated scientist. In 1996 he was appointed vice-chancellor of Rhodes University. Dave Woods is an outstanding man and proved to be a first-rate deputy vice-chancellor. I have no doubt he will lead Rhodes University with great distinction.

before they were allowed onto the campus. Many bona fide visitors and others were denied access. We took the matter to the Supreme Court in order to try, on an urgent basis, to get an order against the Minister of Law and Order, the divisional commissioner of police and others. The judge, Mr Justice D M Williamson, agreed to hear the matter at 2.15 pm. However, the police blockade was withdrawn at 1.45 pm and at the request of the counsel for the university, the judge postponed the matter *sine die* in order to allow the parties to file papers. No one was arrested or detained. A rally was held on the campus while a police helicopter circled overhead, but many potential participants were prevented from attending. Police spokesmen said the police had taken precautionary measures 'acting on information received regarding an illegal gathering on the campus.'

Nelson Mandela's birthday is on 18 July and in 1988 it was celebrated in Cape Town on a Sunday. It was raining quite heavily that afternoon when Anita and I were at Glenara having tea. Jane came in and asked what was going on on the campus. I said they were having a party in the Jameson Hall to celebrate Nelson Mandela's birthday. She said that she had seen a heavy police presence including armoured vehicles, going up the drive towards the campus. I drove as fast as I could to the campus, ran along University Avenue and found a police colonel, Kannemeyer, talking with the SRC president, Cameron Dugmore, and Farid Esack.* I told Kannemeyer that he had no right to interfere with a birthday party because it was a social event. He said it was illegal in terms of a section of the Internal Security Act. Chancing my arm, I told him that that section of the Internal Security Act didn't cover an event such as the one taking place in the Jameson Hall. In fact I was not sure of this. In that case, he replied, he would insist that the activity cease immediately in terms of the state of emergency. I replied that he did not have the power to do that in terms of the state of emergency. He then made absolutely clear to me, in very simple language, that whatever I thought, he was going to shut down the birthday party. I pointed out to him that there were women and children inside Jameson Hall and if his police went in there, there was a serious danger that many people, and in particular children, might be hurt. I asked him whether we could have some time to allow them to disperse. He gave us fifteen minutes.

Cameron Dugmore and Farid Esack had taken part in this conversation and I asked them to go back into the hall and to make an announcement saying that everybody should disperse peacefully because the police would not allow the celebrations to continue. Colonel Kannemeyer went down and sat in a Casspir out of the rain. A large force of policemen was huddled

---

* Farid Esack is now an Imam and a member of the Commission for Gender Equality.

about a hundred yards behind him, some inside vehicles and some standing in the rain. I could hear the music and singing coming from Jameson Hall. After about five minutes, I walked up to the hall and, looking in at the front door, saw balloons, streamers, people singing and generally having a good time. I became quite concerned because there were no signs of the birthday party coming to an end. Cameron Dugmore then went onto the stage and after a short while managed to get the hall to quieten down. He announced that before they dispersed, Dullah Omar would speak and they would sing the national anthem, 'Nkosi Sikelel' iAfrika'.* He asked for everybody to disperse quietly after singing the anthem. I looked at my watch and realised that we only had about six minutes left before Colonel Kannemeyer would bring the police into the hall. I knew that Dullah Omar would not make a short speech and that the national anthem would be sung to the full, so I went down the steps to the Casspir in which Colonel Kannemeyer was sitting.

I joined him in it saying that I was sorry that the wet clouds could not be blown over to Calvinia because my father-in-law had a farm there and that district desperately needed rain. It turned out that the Kannemeyer family farm was close to Calvinia and he immediately started talking about the difficulties of farming in the Karoo and the problems of the drought, etc. I then asked him whether he was related to the Kannemeyer prominent in the administration of South African rugby, and it turned out that they were related and we started talking about South African rugby, the national side and the joys of rugby football in general. This conversation took quite a long time, and while we were talking about rugby, I was pleased to hear the strains of 'Nkosi Sikelel' iAfrika' reaching us from the Jameson Hall. Once the national anthem had finished, students and young mothers with children started emerging from the hall. I looked at Colonel Kannemeyer and said that the meeting was obviously breaking up and that the crowd was leaving peacefully. I glanced at my watch. Twenty-five minutes had passed since the deadline had been given. Of course no policeman could act without the colonel's orders and I had gambled that the colonel would not give orders while he was talking about the drought and rugby football.

Vusi Khanyile continued to be in detention without trial. In August the council agreed with my proposal that the chairman of council, the chancellor and I make representation to the Minister of Law and Order and, if necessary, to the State President, to try to effect Vusi Khanyile's release, and failing that, to express our protest publicly in the strongest possible terms once

---

* This was not the national anthem at the time but was regarded as such by the students and the majority of South Africans.

again. However, Mr Khanyile's lawyers advised that it would not be appropriate to make a high level approach at this juncture. Shortly afterwards Vusi Khanyile, Murphy Morobe* and Mahommed Valli Moosa† escaped from detention and sought refuge in the American consulate in Johannesburg. They were later joined by Clifford Ngcoba, who had also escaped. The escapees were allowed to speak to the press and they insisted that detention was unjust. They stated that the object of their escape was to highlight the plight of hundreds of other emergency detainees, some of whom had been in detention for as long as 27 months without being charged. Bill Bowen contacted John Whitehead, then Deputy Secretary of State in the United States, and he in turn ensured that the escapees were given the protection of the US consulate.

The Government announced that Vusi and his companions were free to leave the consulate without fear of re-arrest. Vusi took up the fellowship at Princeton University. Murphy Morobe later also received a fellowship from Princeton University. Vusi Khanyile was promoted to deputy registrar of student affairs at UCT, but did not hold the position long before he was recruited by the ANC to head their newly established finance department in Johannesburg. He is currently a successful businessman and chief executive officer of Thebe Investments. I was sorry to see him leave the university.

---

* Now chairman of the Financial and Fiscal Commission.
† Now Minister of Environmental Affairs and Tourism.

Still on the tightrope
1987–1989

Jakes Gerwel, the vice-chancellor of the University of the Western Cape, and Franklin Sonn, rector of the Peninsula Technikon and I, together with others, held a joint press conference. We identified ourselves with a statement by various organisations representing teachers, students and parents at the schools, particularly coloured schools, in the Western Cape. We pointed out that the reaction of the education authorities to the crises in the Peninsula was a recipe for 'chaos and confrontation' which destroyed the possibility of normal school activity and undermined the meaningful educational process in coloured and African schools.

Shortly after this, Government agreed to instruct the police not to enter school premises except in the course of 'normal' duties, and pupils returned to their classes in their thousands after a short protest stay-away. But before that happened, and during the time that the black schools were closed by the Government, I was phoned one night by the headmaster of Langa High School. He asked if I would come to the school early the next morning together with others he had approached, because our presence in the school grounds might restrain the police. Hundreds of parents were going to bring their children to the school that day for registration, determined that they should have the right to be in school. He told me we were to meet in a church hall in Athlone at 6 am the next morning.

When I set out early there was a low mist over the Cape Flats and it was very cold. In the church were the Reverend Allan Boesak, one of the leaders of the United Democratic Front, the Reverend Matt Essau, an associate of Archbishop Tutu, whom he was representing, two ladies from the Black Sash and Mr Jan van Eck, Progressive Federal Party member of parliament. Graeme Bloch, who had been in detention when I took office, came to brief us. He was on the run from the security police and wore a wig and a false moustache. It was a very effective disguise. The briefing stressed that we should maintain a visible presence just inside the school gates so that any police arriving would see us before they entered the school. We reached the school at about 7 am in the morning. It was, and remained, bitterly cold and my feet felt as though they had been anaesthetised. From about 9 am until

10 am the occasional police armoured car drove slowly past the school, but no policemen attempted to enter. We stood inside the school gates and parents and their children streamed past us into the school. By midday there were hundreds of children in the school and many parents. The headmaster assembled everyone in the school yard and made a speech thanking us. At his invitation, the children and parents sang lustily. As we broke up, Allan Boesak moved amongst the pupils and I saw them trying to touch him, an expression of their adulation and of the very high leadership role that he was taking in the UDF. I did think that such adulation could be dangerous for both the children and for him. It made me uneasy.

On another occasion, Jakes Gerwel and I, together with representatives of non-Government organisations and some black student organisations, gave a press conference in one of the rooms in the cathedral hall in St George's Cathedral. When I got there, the chairs and table where we were to sit were backed by an enormous red flag emblazoned with the hammer and sickle and the words 'South African Communist Party'. I took Jakes aside and told him that I couldn't sit in front of that banner during a press conference, because it would cause enormous problems for me and the university. I pointed out that I wasn't a communist. Jakes understood, as I knew he would. He turned to the others, explained the position, and the banner was removed. We were protesting against the actions of the Government and security forces in the schools and the universities.

In the 1960s the students' representative council at UCT made it clear that all UCT students should be able to participate both as players and spectators in sport on an equal basis. They were supported by the university as a whole. Integration in sport was then thought of as radical by most white South Africans, and the university was widely criticised for adopting what some regarded as an 'unpatriotic' attitude. South African sport had correctly been shunned by the rest of the world because of the refusal of the South African Government to allow people of colour to play in national teams, and of course sporting facilities for South African blacks were abysmal. By 1988, the wisdom of the students' and of the university's approach was becoming clear and the first shift in attitude by South African whites was becoming apparent. South Africans are sport lovers and the sporting boycott certainly was effective in helping to force change. A few more years would pass before full integration occurred and I expressed the view that it was a pity that the students' and the university's lead had not been followed sooner. I thought this was a good example of how student and overall University of Cape Town attitudes, unpopular at the time, often proved to be right and generally acceptable in later years.

All students were entitled to join any sports code in the university and until 1987 the university had one set of sports clubs, each affiliated to a sports union which in turn was affiliated to a number of outside leagues. In 1987 the formation of an alternative sports union was requested by some students, mainly black, for those not wishing to play in the outside leagues where the teams were usually composed only of whites. This proposal to have two parallel sporting codes in the university was a very controversial one and it was with considerable difficulty that we achieved the establishment of the South African Tertiary Institution Sports Council (SATISCO) on the university campus, which in turn was affiliated to SATISCO nationally. The student affairs committee had recommended that the sports union should be disbanded and that an overarching sports council should replace it. We managed to secure agreement for this on the clear understanding that both unions and their clubs were open to all students, ensuring the right of freedom of association, and that the new structure would not be permanently entrenched. Every effort would be made to establish a single sporting structure in which all sections of the university student population would be willing to participate. And so, until the unbanning of the ANC in 1990, UCT had two sporting codes.

Some expressed the fear that we were establishing 'apartheid in sport' on the university campus, but I pointed out that the opposite of enforced segregation was not enforced integration, that freedom of association was critical and that the important issue was that all sporting codes and both organisations were open to all students. Both sports organisations functioned successfully and over 6 000 students participated in sport on the campus. There were separate intervarsities and the situation was far from ideal. Many of the alumni of the university were unhappy about this turn of events and I certainly came in for a lot of criticism. Soon after the unbanning of the political organisations, the sports union and SATISCO-UCT were united on campus and the sporting codes of all the universities became one throughout the country, an integration of sport in which Mr John Donald, the head of our sports administration, played a key role.

The students' representative council represented and was elected by the entire student body. A large number of student clubs and societies were affiliated to it and in 1988 one of the new affiliated societies was the black students' society, which was created to concentrate on issues particularly affecting black students. Its constitution ensured that membership was open to all students irrespective of race, as was the case with all societies and clubs on the campus. It was true that there were very few white students in the black students' society and its emergence was another sign of black students' reluctance to be involved in the traditional structures of the university at that stage. This changed after the unbanning of political organisations and the release of Nelson Mandela. The attitude of non-involvement was also related to the numbers of black students on campus.

The dean of medicine, George Dall, and I vigorously protested when Dr Kane-Berman was transferred from her post at Groote Schuur Hospital for jocularly suggesting to a local newspaper that Nelson Mandela should be president. The Administrator told us that there was 'a political cloud' over Groote Schuur, our teaching hospital, which had been a factor in the transfer. When pressed to define this 'cloud' he indicated that it referred to the actions of UCT students (there had been some student protests on the medical school campus). An Afrikaans newspaper carried an article in which a senior but unnamed provincial officer was quoted as having said, '*Politiekery by UK was een van die faktore*' (political shenanigans at the University of Cape Town was one of the factors). Dr Marius Barnard, a Progressive Party MP, took the matter up with the Minister of Health, Dr Willie van Niekerk, in Parliament. In his reply Dr van Niekerk stated that Dr Kane-Berman had unsuccessfully applied for the vacant post of dean in our medical school, trying to undermine her position. I was furious because the selection procedures for deans and for other academic staff are strictly confidential and I made a statement to the press expressing my displeasure at this break of confidentiality.

Len Abrahamse and I asked to see Van Niekerk as a matter of urgency, and when we met that same afternoon Len set out very clearly the impropriety of his making that statement. (Van Niekerk's information had come from a source in the provincial government.) I underlined what Len had said. He then turned to us and said that as I had criticised him in the press, he wasn't prepared to discuss the matter any further. We were still in the building when Len took me by the shoulders, telling me to calm down and relax, because he thought I was going to have a heart attack. I was incensed. The incident reflected the arrogance of the apartheid regime. The Cape Provincial Administration then advertised the post of chief medical superintendent and asked us to concur with the appointment of one of the candidates (not Dr Kane-Berman). The provincial administration had not followed the correct procedures in terms of the joint agreement* between UCT and themselves and the request to concur with their decision was referred back to them, pointing out their failure. Dr Kane-Berman was then reinstated.

George Dall and I had another brush with the hospitals' department. Departments in the medical school were about to occupy the new hospital and President P W Botha insisted that the wards should be segregated. Dr

---

* The joint agreement defined in legal terms the responsibilities of the university on the one hand and the Cape Provincial Administration on the other, with regard to the teaching hospitals.

Nicolaas Louw, the director of hospital services, asked to see us. I told him that I knew we shared the same ethical values and that the admitting doctor must decide where the patients should go. He agreed and said that he would speak to Mr Botha. He contacted us and said Botha insisted on segregation. We returned to Louw and again persuaded him against this. Botha remained obdurate. We saw Louw a third time and again he spoke to Botha. Then Dr Louw suddenly died of a heart attack. Dr Reeve Sanders became the acting director and Botha had problems of his own, so when the new hospital was occupied, it was fully integrated from the start. The medical staff would correctly have refused to have it otherwise.

During September Anita and I attended the 900th anniversary of the University of Bologna in Italy. Most of the universities from around the world were represented. The ceremonies closed with the signing of the 'Magna Charta' of universities, which included a commitment to close communication between them. It seemed ironical that South African university heads were signing together with their colleagues from institutions practising an academic boycott of South African universities.

I participated in a discussion on one of the South African Broadcasting Corporation's television channels on the future of universities in South Africa and put the case for a non-racial university system. It was always problematic taking part in an S A B C programme, either on the radio or on television, because the corporation was a propaganda arm of the Government and editing could easily distort what one had said. On one occasion in a live television programme I came into sharp conflict with the interviewer, a Mr John Bishop, who tried to imply that the university was not doing its business in a proper manner. I had resolved to take part in live interviews only so that my message could not be distorted. Interviewers and cameramen of the corporation often privately apologised for the way in which the news was distorted and biased.

Early in 1989 the students protested against detention without trial and the SRC president, Geordie Radcliffe,* went on an eight-day fast in solidarity with detainees who had embarked on a hunger strike. I addressed a mass meeting on the matter and said it was no surprise that detainees should resort to a hunger strike to draw attention to their desperate plight, that staff and students at UCT had been detained without trial and that I had knowledge of what this 'despicable system' did to those detained, and to their loved ones.

The students held a peaceful protest on the highway, holding placards in

---

* Geordie Radcliffe was probably the best student leader I worked with while I was vice-chancellor. She gave inspired leadership to the student body.

support of the hunger strikers and calling for the release of all detainees. Seventeen of them, including the SRC president, Geordie Radcliffe, were arrested. A group of 9 picketers outside St George's Cathedral were arrested within minutes of their arrival. Another group of 8 were held at a simultaneous demonstration in Greenmarket Square in the city, and were arrested after about an hour. They were all held for approximately 2 hours at the Caledon Square police station and were released without being charged. (They were not brought to trial.)

On a number of occasions the Mass Democratic Movement (which included the United Democratic Front) held marches in the city. These marches were usually broken up by the police, and SHAWCO stationed mobile clinics close to the route of an expected march, ready to offer first aid and emergency treatment if the protesters were assaulted by the police. I supported this action by the students because the police were often brutal. Early in September a march attended by thousands of Capetonians took place in the centre of the city. SHAWCO had a number of vehicles placed strategically at different places along the route. These were staffed by volunteer doctors, nurses and students. SHAWCO students marched amongst the protesters, wearing Red Cross armbands and carrying first-aid equipment. The police reacted with considerable violence. They used a water cannon in which the water had been stained with a purple dye to spray the marchers so as to be able to identify them subsequently and arrest them. A student climbed on top of one of the water cannons and turned it on the police. The police entered a number of the SHAWCO vehicles and arrested the doctors, nurses and SHAWCO students. They also arrested a number of SHAWCO students in the street carrying first-aid equipment and wearing Red Cross armbands. Many other people were arrested as well.

That evening, Anita and I were preparing to host the Chancellor's Ball in Jameson Hall, an important Rag fund-raising event. About half an hour before we were due to leave the house I was told that a large number of students had been arrested during this march and that my daughter Jane, one of the medical students in attendance, was amongst them. Anita and I immediately drove into town – formally dressed, Anita wearing a ball gown – and went to St George's Cathedral, where we spoke to the students and members of the public who had taken refuge there. We then drove to Caledon Square police station where the arrested students were being held and spoke with Mr Essa Moosa, a lawyer who was acting on behalf of the students, emphasising that my concern was for all those arrested, not just my daughter. (My future son-in-law Brendan was also amongst them.) At the gala occasion in Jameson Hall I had to speak to the donors, emphasising the need to support SHAWCO and indicating to them what had happened in the city that day, and under what dreadful conditions black South Africans were having to live. I had a sense of dislocation as we joined in the dancing and sat down to an excellent meal, knowing that many of our students and other citizens were in the police cells.

The policemen went into one of the large cells and asked everyone to indicate whether they were white or black so they could be segregated. Dr Ivan Toms, who was one of those arrested, shouted out that he was purple, which indeed they all were. None of them would indicate what race they belonged to: all insisted they were purple. They were charged with taking part in an illegal march and were released on bail. No further action was taken against them. I was very angry and protested against the police action to the commissioner of police and to the Minister of Law and Order. The local commissioner invited me to go to an office in Cape Town, saying that if I saw the videos of the protest I would understand the police action. He claimed that the SHAWCO students with the red crosses on their arms had been actively involved. I asked the dean of the medical school, Professor J P van Niekerk, and Professor Ralph Kirsch, one of the professors of medicine who was closely linked with SHAWCO, to go with me. We were shown into a room where there were about six policemen. A police colonel was in command and we watched a video lasting three or four minutes. It showed the protesters walking peacefully in the street with the SHAWCO students moving on the edges of the crowd, carrying their first-aid equipment. There was no evidence of violence.

When the video came to an end I waited for the next tape to be inserted, but nothing happened. It suddenly dawned on me that they had nothing else to show us. In a very disparaging tone I told them that they were incompetent, were misleading the public and that nothing they had shown us in any way represented an excuse for the way in which the police had acted. The police colonel repeatedly said that he knew nothing about it, that he hadn't been involved in controlling the demonstrations and that his role was simply to be in charge at the showing of the videos. I didn't spare him either. I issued a public statement indicating that what we had seen contained no evidence which could possibly justify the police action and that if this was an example of how the police collected evidence for the enforcement of the draconian regulations of the state of emergency, our country certainly was in peril. I also wrote a very strong letter to the Minister of Law and Order, Mr Adriaan Vlok. We must remember that police actions resulted in the death of people in detention and that torture and severe beating of prisoners and of protesters in the street happened often. The incompetence of the police and their failure to gather evidence properly has rolled over into the democratic South Africa and has resulted in the force's inability to combat crime. Police action produced a generation who viewed the police as enemies and at no time saw them as officers of peace who were there to protect the public. This has resulted in an unwillingness to co-operate with the police and is one of the reasons for the high rate of crime in democratic South Africa. The attitude of many South Africans, persecuted at the time, spilled over to the whole judicial system as well.

At the beginning of a mass meeting in Jameson Hall, Mr Malcolm Roach, the deputy registrar (buildings and services), told me that a message had been received, warning of a bomb in the hall. I announced that there was a bomb threat and asked everyone to look around their feet and under their seats for packages or anything that could contain a bomb. I then asked them to examine the person and the seat next to them, and then asked them to do the same on the other side of them, and when they had done all of that, I ran through the same procedure a second time. Since nobody identified a suspicious-looking object, the meeting proceeded and concluded without any untoward events. I must confess to being very anxious throughout the meeting. Some would criticise me for the way I handled this threat, but I was determined to show how serious we were about the protest and would not give any satisfaction to those who opposed our cause.

It was decided in the late '80s that the vice-chancellor would, at an appropriate occasion, present a medal to an individual who had given outstanding service to UCT. Among those who received medals during my years as vice-chancellor were our chancellor, Mr Harry Oppenheimer, on his retirement, Mr Len Abrahamse on his retirement from the chairmanship of council, Mr Hans Middelmann, who gave long, dedicated service to UCT, Mr Pat Tebbutt, who was an excellent president of convocation for many years, John Slemon for his superb management of the Baxter Theatre, and Dr Andrew Kinnear who had been the founder of SHAWCO, on its 50th anniversary.

The housing shortage, particularly for black students, was eased when the university was able to purchase Liesbeek Gardens, a complex with over 200 flats close to the campus. This would not have been possible without a very generous donation of R4 million from the Anglo American Corporation and De Beers and R500 000 from Barlow-Rand. The Trustees of the Kresge Foundation in Detroit made a challenge grant of $500 000 towards the purchase and the balance of the funds was obtained from a number of donors including a very generous donation from Shell.

At the University of Stellenbosch, NUSAS and the university's black students' organisation were not treated in a friendly fashion and indeed, both organisations were suspended and the president of NUSAS, a Stellenbosch University student, Leslie Durr, was expelled from the university because she had participated in a student march against racially segregated residences on the Stellenbosch campus in August 1989. University rules banned demonstrations on the campus.* She later applied to the Cape of Good Hope Provincial Division of the Supreme Court to have the rule declared ultra vires. The application was dismissed. During a visit to the university, Anita and I had the opportunity of meeting with Ms Durr, the leaders of NUSAS and of the black students' organisation and the levels of frustration which they felt were palpable.

The problems surrounding sport surfaced again during the year. A soccer fixture between one of the university's soccer teams and a team from the South African police had to be abandoned on one of the university's soccer fields, following a disruption. This occurred after a debate on the campus which resulted in the co-ordinating sports council requesting all sports clubs to place a moratorium on all sporting events involving the police and defence force teams which would be played on UCT fields. This caused a number of problems because in terms of the fixtures arranged by the Western Province Rugby-Football Union, teams had to play on their own fields as well as on fields owned by other clubs. The WP Rugby-Football Union threatened to exclude the university rugby club from its schedule of games. This was more bluster than a real threat, and never took place, but did put pressure on us.

In September the vice-chancellors of the Universities of the Witwatersrand, Natal, Rhodes, Western Cape and Cape Town were invited to a conference at Taillories in France, hosted by Dr Jean Mayer, President of Tufts University. This meeting was to see how the universities in South Africa opposed to apartheid could be helped by the international community of universities. It proved to be a very valuable meeting. The South Africans were able to explain what was happening in their country and how they were responding to the challenges they faced.†

In November and early December I joined other South Africans from both inside and outside the country for discussions in Paris sponsored by the France-Libertés Foundation and Madame Danielle Mitterrand. At this meeting members of the ANC, the Mass Democratic Movement, including COSATU, members of the business community, journalists and academics from South Africa were able to exchange views in a frank and constructive manner. The macro-economic policies of a post-apartheid South Africa were

---

* Like all Afrikaans universities then, it was a very different place from UCT.
† Two years later I went to a second conference hosted by Jean at Taillories, this time dealing with sustainable development. There was conflict between universities from the first and third worlds and I was asked to chair the final day's session because I was 'neutral', having been outside the debate in the preceding years because I was a South African!

thrashed out and, encouragingly, the policies of communist Eastern Europe were rejected. The other major issue addressed was that of human rights and there was a clear commitment to a Bill of Rights in a democratic South Africa. I had the privilege of being one of four to speak publicly at the closure of the meeting in the French National Assembly. The delegates were housed in a conference centre in a suburb of Paris and the French were very concerned that the South Africans might be targeted by the South African Government's dirty tricks brigade.* And so security was very tight and we were not allowed to leave the compound unescorted. At least that is what we were told, but it's not easy to control South Africans in that way and nearly everybody managed to slip away and spend some time in Paris away from the conference centre. There were armed gendarmes patrolling within the conference centre. When we arrived on our Air France flight in Paris, we were put into buses and escorted through the early morning Parisian traffic by gendarmes on motor cycles with flashing lights. We cut through the dense traffic like a hot knife through butter. The man sitting in front of me was a large African wearing a raincoat and a soft felt hat. He enjoyed the experience immensely, having spent many years in prison on Robben Island and never having been protected and escorted by the police in this way before.

One evening during that week I sat chatting to Alec Erwin,[†] who at that time was a leading member of COSATU. We enjoyed a fair amount of French red wine and I waxed eloquent on the dearth of proper planning in technological development in South Africa, a subject about which I knew very little, but at the time was prepared to say a great deal. When I returned to South Africa I received a message from COSATU indicating that they wanted me to organise and host an international conference on the development of a policy for technology in South Africa. If anything should have taught me to keep my mouth shut, that should have done so. The result was that such a conference was organised which proved to be a great success, the consequences of which are still apparent in South Africa today.

During one of the breaks at the conference in Paris, Barbara Masekela and Steve Tshwete[Δ] came to see me and said they understood I was going to Australia and that anti-apartheid activists there had asked if they should protest against me. They suggested that when I was planning to travel abroad I should contact them first. I replied that I was not going to Australia (John Reid was), that I did not need their help when travelling abroad and

---

* The Truth and Reconciliation Commission has confirmed over and over again that the dirty tricks brigade was capable of doing anything.
† Minister of Trade and Industry.
Δ Minister of Safety and Security.

that I had not fought against outside interference in UCT's affairs for so long to yield it to them! They immediately assured me it was not their intention and dropped the matter.

The leader of the ANC at the conference was Thabo Mbeki. He was most impressive, with an in-depth and wide-ranging knowledge of the issues under discussion. I concluded he would be a front-runner as a future president of South Africa and that has proved to be the case.

The traditional intervarsity rugby match between the universities of Cape Town and Stellenbosch took place in the middle of August. On the day of the match, students were taken in crowded, decorated buses to the Stellenbosch rugby-football stadium where they sang lustily in the stands in support of the UCT team which, as usual, lost. As was traditional I and a number of my colleagues went to watch the match. On the same day another set of buses left the university, taking students to a beach near Cape Town where they were to meet with the Mass Democratic Movement, led by Archbishop Desmond Tutu. They were intent on showing, by their presence, that blacks as well as whites should be able to play on the beach and swim in the sea. Apartheid was rigorously enforced on all South African beaches.

I was very concerned about what might happen on the beach because I knew that the police would respond in force. Indeed that is what happened, and the 2 000 people on the beach, many of them students, armed with picnic baskets and beach balls, were faced by a strong police presence. The crowd, made up of students and citizens of Cape Town, remained calm and Archbishop Tutu addressed them from the top of a van, urging them to remain peaceful and controlled. They then left the beach in a stream of buses and the students returned to the campus after a meeting at a church in a coloured township, where beach apartheid was roundly condemned.

During the rugby match an aircraft flew overhead trailing a banner telling people to vote for the National Party, the party of the apartheid Government. It all seemed so unreal to me, an illustration of how many white South Africans, and certainly our colleagues at the Afrikaans universities, were living in a completely different world to those of the majority of the citizens of South Africa. It was very sad. On reflection, it was clear to me that I should have been on the beach as well instead of following the tradition of attending the rugby match.

Together with Neal Chapman, the chief executive of the Southern Life Insurance Company, I convened the Consultative Business Movement (CBM) in Cape Town. Efforts were made to involve business in transforming South African society and arriving at a just political dispensation. I had reservations as to whether such a movement could be effective, but as events turned out, the CBM did achieve a great deal. Mine was not a significant role in these developments. The CBM organised a meeting with the MDM at Broederstroom in the Transvaal. I gave Dullah Omar a lift from the Johannesburg airport and we got lost and spent several hours driving along dark country roads late at night searching for the conference venue!

The tide turns
1990–1991

1990 began in a momentous way. The university's executive and I were all at a conference centre outside Cape Town on 2 February where we were meeting for two and a half days as part of what had become biennial meetings, planning the coming six months or year and reviewing the previous year's work. We had arranged to have a television set in the room so that we could see the opening of parliament by the new State President, F W de Klerk. He announced the unbanning of a host of organisations including the African National Congress and many student organisations. He also announced that political prisoners would be released including Nelson Mandela. We were all amazed and overjoyed. It was only four months since I had been in Paris at a meeting with the ANC and it was quite clear to me that the timing of these moves by De Klerk was completely unexpected. We went and joined our spouses and celebrated what was a foreseeable end of apartheid. Anita pointed out that exiles could now return to South Africa and that we should immediately contact Jack Simons and his wife Ray Alexander in Lusaka and invite them back to the university.

As a result, a phone call was put through to them in Lusaka that same morning and, on behalf of the university, I had the privilege of inviting them to return as visiting scholars, the university being responsible for all their travel costs and their accommodation. They were the first exiles to return home and spent several months carrying out library and archival research in the Centre for African Studies on the campus. The following Saturday I was at a hotel in Somerset West, just outside of Cape Town at a joint meeting between the MDM and the CBM. This was to take forward discussions between business and the ANC. Early in the afternoon one of the leaders of the MDM was called to the telephone and after he returned all the MDM delegates left and returned to Cape Town because Nelson Mandela was to be released from prison the following day.

Shortly after his release, I had lunch with Nelson Mandela at Bishopscourt, the home of Archbishop Desmond Tutu. I wanted to discuss with him the timing of the conferral of an honorary degree upon him by the University of Cape Town. The university had decided at the end of 1989, while he was still a prisoner in the Victor Verster prison at Paarl, to honour him in this way, and I had written to him on 8 December 1989. I sent the letter by hand to the prison, having contacted the head of the prison and received an assurance that it would reach Mr Mandela. When there was no reply from Mr Mandela by the end of that year, I waited until the end of the first week of January 1990 and then phoned James Gregory, the warder responsible for him at the Victor Verster prison. (The telephone number had been obtained when Mr Mandela contacted the university about a member of his family who wanted to study there.) I asked James Gregory whether Mr Mandela had received the letter and he enquired whether that was the letter about the honorary degree. When I confirmed that was the case, his short answer was 'no'. I asked how that could be and he said that the authorities in Pretoria had refused to release the letter to Mr Mandela! I was astounded as there had been much publicity about Mr Mandela's freedom to communicate, and I told Gregory that he would read about it in the newspaper that same afternoon. Gregory asked me to give him quarter of an hour, with my assurance that I would not take action during that time.

Ten minutes later he phoned me back and said that Mr Mandela would be honoured to receive an honorary degree from the University of Cape Town. I asked Gregory where Mr Mandela was and his reply was that he was standing next to him. I told him that I would like him to ask Mr Mandela to be so kind as to confirm what he had told me in writing and that I would send for the letter the next day. Accordingly, on 10 January, I received a letter from Mr Nelson Mandela, on prison notepaper with a stamp on it signifying clearance by the prison censor. When I received the letter, I realised that I had an historic document in my possession. All of this happened three weeks before F W de Klerk's speech in parliament and four weeks before Mr Mandela's release from prison. Given that Nelson Mandela was to be released from prison within two months, it was extraordinary that the authorities had refused to let him receive my original letter, but what was even more surprising was a phone call which I received from Jan Steyn, who was passing on a request from the Minister of Justice, Kobie Coetsee, saying that the Government understood that the university was to confer an honorary degree on Mr Mandela and I was asked to delay the award and not make the matter public. My reply was that the news would be in that afternoon's newspapers. The announcement stated that we hoped that 'he would be free to accept the honorary degree in person'.

My lunch with Mr Mandela at Bishopscourt started with the two of us meeting alone in one of the reception rooms. I was enormously impressed by him, as were countless others. His personality, his positive attitude to life and his commitment to a non-racial democracy simply shine through everything that he does. Above all, he has committed himself to peaceful reconciliation in South Africa and has set an example for all South Africans and indeed for the world. He is a truly remarkable man. I discovered that day that he is also one of the most courteous people I have met.

I chaired a committee at UCT consisting of representatives from all segments of the university, including the students and the trade union plus the ANC, to plan the ceremony at which the honorary degree would be conferred. One point of contention was that the student leaders and the trade union questioned Mr Oppenheimer's role in the ceremony because of their criticisms of the Anglo American Corporation. The registrar, with whom it was first raised, indicated that the matter was non-negotiable and at the next meeting, when I was present, I told them it was inconceivable that the degree could be conferred by anyone else. Few universities were fortunate enough to have a chancellor of his distinction, great dignity, compassion, concern and commitment. UCT's chancellor was elected by convocation, representing the important constituency of nearly 50 000 men and women graduates. At no time did Mr Mandela raise the question. When one of the students said to me that they objected that Mr Mandela would have to kneel in front of Mr Oppenheimer I said, 'Well if that's your problem, then the whole thing falls away because when honorary degrees are conferred, the chancellor stands' and indeed that had usually been the case. Another extraordinary request that the student leadership made was that at the ceremony the choir of the University of the Western Cape should be asked to sing. Given that the University of Cape Town had a choir and that the St George's choir was directed by Barry Smith, a member of the College of Music of the university, I was astounded at the suggestion, but it took quite a lot of discussion before the students dropped their bizarre idea. It wasn't the only bizarre idea I heard from the student sector. A vice-chancellor needed a great deal of patience and self-control to sit through hours of debate with certain students before quite simple and obvious decisions could be made.

Mr Mandela received the honorary degree at a specially arranged ceremony on our main rugby fields in front of the oldest buildings of the university, at 4.30 pm on Friday 30 November 1990, but before that occurred a number of events took place in relation to the ceremony. The first was fixing the date. Originally we decided on 28 June, when the two of us met at the Archbishop's home, but it turned out that this was not possible because he was due to meet President George Bush at that time. Many phone calls and consultations followed and while I was travelling in the United States I tried repeatedly to make contact with Mr Mandela in order to finalise the date, only to discover he was in Algeria. I can confirm that it is not easy to contact anyone in Algeria phoning from the United States! We had to ensure that Mr Oppenheimer's diary could accommodate a mutually acceptable date. Margaret Touborg, president of the UCT Fund, and I were to fly from New York to Chicago, and when we reached La Guardia airport, our flight had been cancelled, so we stood in line for an alternative flight and eventually walked onto an aircraft without reserved seats. It became apparent that only one seat was available on the plane. Margaret insisted that I take it, saying that we would meet at Chicago airport. I sat down and saw her talking to a woman cabin attendant. As we got on, I had asked that cabin attendant whether there was a telephone on the plane (it turned out there was not) because I was still trying to call Mr Mandela. Margaret asked the flight attendant, 'Did you hear my companion ask whether there was a telephone?' and she said 'yes.' 'He's a South African, you can hear it from his accent and he was trying to phone Mr Nelson Mandela.' The flight attendant was suitably impressed. Margaret went on to say the two of us had to be in Chicago on this plane and we had to make contact with Mr Mandela on arrival. The cabin attendant turned round and announced at the top of her voice, 'This lady has to get to Chicago on this flight and she has to contact Mr Mandela. Would anybody give up a seat for her and take the next plane?' Half a dozen people immediately stood up and Margaret got a seat.

At the UCT dinner after Mr Mandela had received the honorary degree, I related this story in my speech and pointed out that one of the features that make him unique is that his name can get one a seat on an aircraft from New York to Chicago!

I also saw Mr Mandela in Shell House, the ANC headquarters in Johannesburg, to discuss the ceremony and other university matters. My appointment was for 8.30 am. When I arrived his personal assistant, Jessie Duarte, told me he was meeting with the executive of the ANC but would not be long. She said the meeting had started at 6.00 am! Promptly at 8.30 Mr Mandela appeared, apologised to me for keeping me waiting and told me he had called a meeting of the executive because the De Klerk Government had sent the army into the Transkei, contrary to a previous agreement with the ANC. He kept the executive waiting while we completed our business, certainly not because I was anyone of importance but because of his innate politeness and good manners. An extraordinary man.

The announcements of February 1990 set in train a chain of events which profoundly changed the lives of all South Africans for the better and had enormous implications for the university. We were immediately aware of the fact that publications, which were formerly banned for political reasons, were now freely available and that we had the opportunity to appoint staff who would otherwise have been prohibited for political reasons from coming to South Africa. We set about planning a strategy to recruit some of the outstanding scholars whose expertise had been denied South Africa for so many years.

The confrontation between protesting staff and students and the police became much less frequent, but didn't disappear during 1990. For example, at the beginning of August a march by students to the local police station, in an attempt to present demands dealing with the remaining parts of the security legislation still in place, was met with a strong police contingent and was broken up with tear gas and water cannon.

Some marches had been without incident. When about 1 000 students marched to the State President's residence protesting against the segregated educational system in South Africa, a senior police officer accepted their petition on behalf of the Government and that was the end of the matter. A previous march involving thousands was planned from Cape Town, starting at St George's Cathedral, which was packed when Anita and I arrived. Archbishop Desmond Tutu met with a number of us in the vestry where we spoke with Cheryl Carolus, the main organiser of the march. Lionel Louw, one of UCT's lecturers in social work and a parson, stood in the pulpit and gave one of the most fiery speeches I have ever heard. Thousands marched peacefully through Cape Town on that day, with no police action. This was largely because Robin Renwick, the British Ambassador, had prevailed on De Klerk to allow the march to take place.

Some student organisations protested about 'academic exclusions'. The university insisted that only students who had adequate grades could pass and that those who did not show adequate progress should leave the university. The readmission and review committee held the line on this despite the student agitation. There was a call in some student quarters to 'pass one, pass all', something the university simply would not contemplate. It was pointed out that the criteria for readmission were not 'middle class' oriented and if this was an elitist policy it was so only in the sense that only students who had succeeded at UCT were promoted. The students had alleged that the criteria for promotion from one academic year to another were 'middle class and elitist.' 'Elite' is by definition the best part of a group and those who succeed in their studies are in that sense 'elite'. Black students constituted some 37 per cent of the first-year intake in 1990 (by 1996 they had risen to more than 50 per cent), and the numbers of African first-year students increased by 30 per cent on the 1989 enrolment in comparison with the previous year. Most of these students wanted a degree worthy of the hard work they had put into their studies and we would not be pushed into diminishing the academic rigour of our programmes.

Bernard Louw, who for many years had been the able secretary to the Committee of University Principals, was a senior official in the Department of National Education in the early '90s and told me that when he was transferred to head African education, he realised for the first time how under-resourced and how poor the standards were in that department. This illustrated how segregation of education departments, resulted in senior officials being ignorant about what was happening to education as a whole, and South Africa had 20 education departments all based on the racial classification of the Government. African education was seriously neglected. It was a disgrace.

Dr Ramphele chaired a committee which brought out a comprehensive report on sexual harassment. We decided to make the report public, even though it was likely to lead to criticism of UCT, because we believed the university had a leadership and educational role to play in these matters as well. Subsequently many organisations looked to Dr Ramphele and her committee for advice. UCT adopted a sexual harassment policy and code of conduct. I presided over two disciplinary cases dealing with allegations of sexual harassment and in both instances the staff member accused was found guilty and disciplined.

It took longer to introduce a comparably comprehensive code on racial harassment, mainly because the committee established to deal with it got bogged down on definitions of what constituted race! This meant that the policy on racial harassment was adopted some time after the one on sexual harassment and led to some students alleging that the university did not take racism seriously. The policy indicated that the university would strive to create a safe working environment for all and was committed to redressing past discrimination and specifically to addressing problems posed by racism, racial discrimination and racial harassment. The policy declared as disciplinary offences racial slurs or harassment and racial discrimination (except in those cases where university policy is formulated specifically to redress past discrimination). Over the years three cases of alleged racism on the part of white staff towards black students were brought to my attention. Thorough investigation failed to support the allegations and those accused were people whose record showed them least likely to have racist attitudes. Naturally the accused were upset by the charges and in one case legal steps dealing with defamation were narrowly averted.

These examples of allegations of racism illustrate the complexity of the problem and, given our history, this is particularly true in South Africa. There have been a number of instances in the democratic South Africa where public figures have been accused of racism, usually to the astonishment of those who know them well. Some argue that the label has been used as a reaction to criticism when the accuser wishes to avoid facing the real issues, but this is too simplistic an answer, although it may be true in some cases. All South Africans, black and white, have to realise that they have been traumatised by their history; that they are all capable of racial prejudice and that only when each one of us faces this squarely will racism begin to diminish. When the accusation is made without apparent foundation it may reflect unrecognised prejudice on *both* sides with *both* honestly denying it. Racial (and other) prejudice occurs in all societies. Human beings are unlikely to free themselves of it entirely, but societies can create structures to minimise its impact. It was important for UCT to give credibility to the claim of the 1980s that it was a non-racial island in a sea of racism. Of course UCT has a lot of progress to make in both racial and sexual harassment and some individual members of the university community may harbour deep prejudices, but the culture and rules of the institution must aim to make them an ineffective, very small minority. Only time will tell to what extent UCT (as well as South Africa) succeeds.

On the whole, the integration of the residences at UCT, which started in 1981, proceeded remarkably smoothly. The black students' life experiences and cultural values were usually distinct from those of the white students. The value of formal house dinners and other 'traditions' in residence were questioned and a great deal of discussion and tolerance was needed by all. The senior students, wardens and sub-wardens all played important roles, and while there were some problems none became major and all were resolved within the 'house'. It has always been my conviction that UCT, and particularly its residences, should be places where students of different backgrounds could live, learn and play together and that this would be a major contribution to the new South Africa.

From the mid-eighties proportionately fewer white students sought residence accommodation, for a combination of at least three reasons. Firstly, fashions change and at times living in private homes close to campus becomes highly desirable. Secondly, the cost of residential accommodation on campus could be higher in any one year than off-campus housing. Thirdly, some parents of new white students (or returning students) and the students themselves may have been unenthusiastic about UCT's policy of integrating the residences. It seemed to me that the last was the least important; no parent or student expressed that view to me. Indeed they usually complained that the black students were getting preference with regard to accommodation. To some extent this was true because their need was so much greater – we could persuade few householders in surrounding suburbs to give them lodgings while white students were easily accepted. We were criticised for this by some out-of-town white parents who refused to allow their children to come to UCT because we could not accommodate them on campus, and were critical of our residence admission policy.

Black staff also had problems with housing. In terms of the Group Areas Act the university held title to houses in white areas which had been 'bought' by black staff members in the late '80s. There was a binding agreement that if that staff member wished to sell the house, all the proceeds reverted to him or her in exactly the same way as if they held title. Fortunately complaints from white neighbours were sent to the Attorney-General for action and not dealt with directly by the police, as had been the case in the past. There were a number of such complaints. Each time I phoned Mr Rossouw, the Attorney-General, and each time he said the file would fall off his table and that no action would be taken! In terms of the Group Areas Act each 'population group' or 'race' had to live in its 'own' area. One of our black members of staff lived on a road which formed the boundary between the coloured and white group areas in Woodstock. His wife was expecting another child and there was an ideal house with additional accommodation for sale on the opposite side of the road. Because it fell within the white group area, they were not allowed to live there. They could not cross the road! I appealed to the Administrator, Gene Louw, but he would not help.

Violent episodes between students on the campus occasionally occurred, but never between black and white students. In some instances there were stabbings, sometimes between students and sometimes the assailant was from off-campus. It was against the university rules for a student to carry an offensive weapon on his or her person on the campus. All firearms had to be deposited at the campus control office. Some students argued that they had to carry a knife because when they went home or visited the African townships some of the areas were potentially very violent and they required a knife for self-defence. This argument was not accepted, but I have no doubt that some of them continued to carry knives. A notice was posted on all boards stating that carrying offensive weapons could result in my recommending expulsion. Alcohol abuse played a role in stabbing incidents on campus which could result in serious injuries. Assailants were dealt with by the courts of the land.

The use of drugs, other than alcohol, did not seem to be a problem on the university campus. Many students probably did experiment with dagga (marijuana) but widespread use of marijuana was not thought to be a reality and more hard-line drugs were seldom known to be used at UCT. The director of the students' health service and a clinical psychologist confirmed this impression. Of course students with drug problems would not often go to the students' health service.

The newspaper *Weekly Mail and Guardian* came into possession of documents which showed that the National Student Federation (NSF) leaders had met with the secret (security) police to discuss strategy and tactics. The Moderate Student Movement (MSM) at UCT was affiliated to the NSF. According to the police document labelled 'Operation Aristotle', local NSF officials at liberal campuses had police code names, for example 'Source N834'. Police and NSF officials planned the NSF shift away from NUSAS-bashing towards promoting the free market, a shift that was echoed faithfully by the MSM at UCT. NSF members and security police held a joint workshop in March in 1990 to plan their activities for 1991. The police admitted that the *Weekly Mail* document was genuine. In a press release announcing the disbanding of the NSF, the president, Danie Kriel, announced that he had informed all affiliates after the exposé that the NSF had been receiving state funding, but he did not refer to the meetings and communication with the security police. Karl Kruger, the then chair of the MSM at UCT, said that they had accepted NSF funding in good faith and believed that it was donated by private enterprise. When pressed to say why they had not queried the source of their funding he acknowledged that their trust might have been misplaced. Political opponents regarded the versions of the events as given by the NSF and the MSM as far from the truth. The MSM had in fact ceased to exist halfway through the last semester of 1990 and Kruger and others were then involved in the formation of Students for the Free Society (SFS) which was to promote the values of 'classical liberalism'! None of these events surprised me in the least.

It was felt that we ought to express our thanks to the university's major donors, but what could we give them? Anita suggested that funds be set aside for the production of portfolios, each limited to an edition of ten, incorporating original works of art as well as reproduction of works in UCT's archives. She had been involved in the production of two other portfolios and these contacts were helpful in identifying the typographer, printer, box maker and fine artists* who were asked to contribute to the first portfolio once Ellalu O'Meara and she had established the theme (botanical studies), format and colour range. The second portfolio contained prints of John Parker's architectural drawings and a large etching by Lynn Smuts featuring a view of Table Mountain. Special functions were arranged for each presentation to a major donor to UCT.

Anita and I spent two months at the beginning of 1991 at Princeton, where I published a booklet on the tension between access and quality in higher education. The late Ernie Boyer, and Heidi Greenberg at the Carnegie Institute, were of enormous help to me. Harold Shapiro and his wife were very helpful to us as was Jeff Herbst, who had been asked to 'look after us'.

---

* A contemporary South African artist.

We journeyed elsewhere, including China, where we were the guests of the Chinese Association for International Friendship and travelled with Tony and Lil van Ryneveld; Tony was a member of the UCT council. This was the most memorable of our overseas journeys. During a short visit to Taiwan, Anita and I went for a walk in Taipei shortly after arrival. We were in a broad boulevard and saw what we thought was a hotel with marble steps and columns. As our experience in China had been that hotels had very good shops we went inside to see if we could buy something. At the ornate desk it became clear to us that we were in a brothel!

While we were in Princeton Robert Kirby, the satirist, wrote and submitted a play entitled 'Panics' to the Standard Bank Grahamstown festival. The programme notes relating to the play which appeared in the booking kit publicising the festival were judged by the university's lawyers to be defamatory. The play, a skit on university procedures, was set in an English-speaking university and the derogatory names given to its vice-chancellor and to a faculty dean were clearly anagrams of my name and of the dean of music. (Mr Kirby and his wife had started legal proceedings against UCT just before this, arising out of her experience in a master of music degree programme. The case was eventually dropped.) In the end the university decided not to take action and the play appeared to amused audiences at the festival and subsequently at the university's Baxter Theatre. In Princeton I was oblivious of these events and was astonished, when I returned to Cape Town, to hear allegations that UCT was trying to censor a play. I was sorry not to see the play myself as I have always found Kirby's satire amusing and I am sure I would have enjoyed seeing it.

Anita and I were privileged to visit Germany and France as the guests of the respective governments.

Three new deputy vice-chancellors were appointed at the end of 1990, anticipating the retirement of Professor John Reid at the end of 1991 and Professor Leatt leaving UCT at the end of May 1991 to take up the position of vice-chancellor of the University of Natal. Both Professors Reid and Leatt had been outstanding deputy vice-chancellors at UCT. John Reid had been with me virtually from my appointment as vice-chancellor and had brought to the post his unique insights, courage and compassion. Both Jim and John had been of enormous help to me during the many problems we had faced and had consistently given me loyal support. The new deputy vice-chancellors were Professor Wieland Gevers, professor of medical biochemistry; Professor Martin West, professor of social anthropology; and Dr Mamphela Ramphele, who would be a part-time deputy. I had to twist Mamphela's arm to become a deputy vice-chancellor. When I convinced her to become a deputy in a part-time capacity I was very much aware it wouldn't be long before she would have to do it full-time. Wieland Gevers was responsible for academic administration amongst other duties, and was an excellent deputy vice-chancellor. An internationally renowned researcher and an outstanding teacher, he brought a wealth of experience, the capacity for sustained hard work and complete commitment with him. Martin West was of great help to me in all the fields he was responsible for: student affairs, industrial relations and later international contacts. He was an excellent deputy vice-chancellor. I was extraordinarily fortunate in having three such outstanding people to join Professor Dave Woods as deputy vice-chancellors.

The biggest crisis of 1991 was the strike called by the transport and general workers' trade union (TGWU) on the campus from 24 to 30 September. Despite the cut in funds from treasury, provision had been made for salary improvements. The non-academic pay-classes at the university were divided into 12 grades. All the non-academic staff in pay-classes 4–12 were now members of a trade union and negotiations with that trade union had resulted in the acceptance of the 16,5 per cent increase in salaries from 1 July. Similar improvements were agreed to after discussions with the academic staff, who were not unionised. Protracted negotiations had taken place over a period of months between the university and the union representing classes 1–3.* At the beginning of July the union had submitted 23 demands, including an approximately 50 per cent increase in salaries. Given that the university's employment packages at this level were unsurpassed throughout the country, some universities paying its workers 50 per cent of the UCT package, the university took the view that the demand was unrealistic. At the end of July the demand was reduced to an increase of some 25 per cent and, in return, the university made a counter offer of 13,5 per cent plus fully funded medical aid instead of the 80 per cent subsidy, thereby effectively offering an increase of 16,5 per cent, one equivalent to the increase accepted by all other members of staff. In August the union declared a deadlock after unsuccessful mediation and a strike ballot resulted in a decision to strike.

For a few days nothing happened. We knew that the strike would be announced to the workers by the raising of a red flag on the campus and some students caused some considerable consternation amongst union members when they raised a red flag on the flagpole above Jameson Hall without the knowledge of the union, which had not yet completed its preparations. On the morning of Tuesday 24 September, I was driving towards the hospital at about 7.40 am when I saw large numbers of UCT workers with red arm bands and red scarves around their heads, carrying red flags, some

---

* Classes 1–3 were the lowest income groups.

of them obstructing the traffic on the public roads. I realised that the strike had begun. Early on 24 September the strikers put up barricades on the entry roads to the upper campus, causing serious traffic disruption. Reluctantly, the university obtained a Supreme Court interdict against the union to stop actions which would interfere with legitimate campus activities. The university gave the union permission for protest meetings on campus as long as they did not disrupt the university's normal functions. On the afternoon of 24 September a large group of striking workers protested at the Bremner Building and gained entrance to it by breaking down the barrier gate. My colleagues and I left the building by a side door and, as we did so, a group of two or three striking workers hung out of an upstairs window and jovially and triumphantly wished us farewell and said we would meet again soon!

We debated having a meeting at Glenara but thought that the house could then become a target, and so we went to the dean's office in the College of Music on the middle campus. I drew heavily on the advice of the deputy vice-chancellors and the registrar and throughout the strike they gave me enormous support, as did Mr Malcom Roach, the deputy registrar (buildings and services), and his assistant, Mr Neville Gaunt, Mr Derek Edwards, who was deputy registrar of personnel, and Ms Joy Fish in industrial relations. Rochelle Kapp, a graduate in English, had succeeded Annamia van den Heever as my personal assistant at the beginning of September, and this was her baptism of fire. She rose to the occasion in a superb manner. She was cool and calm at all times. I was particularly fortunate in my personal assistants, Annamia van den Heever (1986–1991), Rochelle Kapp (1991–1993) and Stephen Langtry (1994–1996). All three are outstanding people, utterly reliable and very able. Maggie Sükel, my personal secretary, took all the tension in her stride and the other secretaries in my office, and indeed the staff in the Bremner Building and the non-striking staff in the university in general handled the situation remarkably well.

We didn't expect the workers to stay in the Bremner Building very long. The majority of them ordinarily stopped working at 4.30 pm and we expected them all to go home at that time, which they did! Early the following day, a group of students approached me and urged me to close the university for the day. They reported that some students had erected barriers at the north and south entrances and exits of the campus, and there could be violence, resulting in injury. They convinced me that the situation could get out of control and I closed the university for the Wednesday. Subsequently I learned that two or three of those students were in fact the ringleaders of the small group of 40–60 students who had become actively involved in the strike and were behind illegal and violent acts.

On the Thursday, the striking union was active on the medical school campus. This was probably linked with the fact that the then State President, Mr F W de Klerk, was opening the new Groote Schuur hospital adjacent to the medical school campus. The strikers put lives at risk by impeding the flow of medical supplies between the medical school and the hospital. They also prevented doctors from travelling to the Red Cross Children's Hospital. It was only after a prolonged negotiation with the dean of medicine that the strikers relented. Some violent episodes occurred. On the upper campus, students again erected barricades at the entrances and exits and disobeyed my directive to remove them. We had decided to be on the campus very early in the morning and asked some senior academic colleagues to join the deputy vice-chancellors and myself, and some senior members of the administration, to try to dissuade students from putting up the barricades and to seek to prevent clashes between students, because we had good information that the great majority of the student body was opposed to the small group of mainly black students who were actively supporting the strikers. The situation became quite serious when some members of staff tried to remove the barricades physically and were resisted by students. All members of staff were asked to avoid any such involvement. The dean of arts kicked at a burning tyre and his trouser legs caught alight before the flames were rapidly extinguished, but a very dramatic photograph appeared in most of the newspapers of the world! On hearing about this, I immediately left for the hospital where I was relieved to find he had superficial burns and was not seriously injured.

We had refused to close the university on the Thursday and small groups of students went to some of the lecture theatres to disrupt the lectures, in some instances by turning fire hoses on in the lecture theatres and flooding them, and in others by shouting, singing and screaming. Later in the morning most of the lectures resumed, and the forbearance and self-control demonstrated by the vast majority of the students and the staff were really remarkable. The vast majority did not react with abuse or physical violence of any kind, but they were very annoyed. There was clear intimidation of staff and students. Fifty floors were flooded and the libraries had to be closed for part of the day. As explained before, I could not call for help from the police.

The strikers were supported by SASCO, which was closely linked to the ANC, and the Azanian Student Congress, AZASCO, which was closely linked to AZAPO. I had a conversation with Mr Nelson Mandela to see whether the ANC could bring any pressure to bear on SASCO, given the violent and anti-social behaviour of some students. Archbishop Desmond Tutu was also contacted and on the Thursday morning he came to the campus.

Together with Dr Mamphela Ramphele and some members of the SRC he negotiated with the leaders of these students who were supporting the strikers, and tried to defuse a very tense situation. Each day the events ended at about 4.30 pm, which was the end of the working day, and that gave us some breathing space. On Friday 27 September the weather came to our aid and it poured with rain. The strikers and the students were again on the campus, as were we, but the activities were few and far between and their attempts to put up barricades and disrupt lectures were not as energetic as they had been on the previous day. Dave Woods and I stood at the north end of the campus in the rain and were soaked. By about 10.30 am it was clear that although the strike was continuing, there was no untoward action on the campus and Dave Woods and I returned to my office with our shoes full of water. We went in to see the registrar and, to our delight, he was able to produce dry socks for us because he was moving house that weekend and he had a case of clothes with him. We padded about our offices while our shoes dried at a safe distance from heaters and our clothes gradually dried out.

A special meeting of the general purposes committee was held on the Saturday morning and a unanimous decision was taken in favour of keeping the university open and of holding a university assembly at lunch time on the Monday to call for peace and to reject violence. The assembly was advertised in the press and the speakers were the Archbishop of Cape Town, the Most Reverend Desmond Tutu, Professor Charles Villa-Vicencio of the department of religious studies, and myself. It was agreed that none of us would refer to the strikers' demands and the university's response to them. The Jameson Hall was packed for the assembly. I said that I was encouraged by the response of the university community to my call to resolve problems through dialogue and discussion and not through violence. The university's priority was to go on with the academic year and make sure students were adequately prepared for their upcoming examinations. Reference was made to the university's right to take disciplinary action against anyone who acted illegally or broke the university's rules and regulations and it was emphasised that there was no vendetta or victimisation, that the university was only interested in justice and in the proper disciplining of people who had acted in an intolerable manner. I was also able to announce that an interim agreement between the university and the union had been reached late that morning, just before the assembly had convened and that the strike was over. Archbishop Desmond Tutu asked the university community to participate in the peace process in South Africa. 'Dialogue and negotiation, not confrontation and violence were needed at UCT as elsewhere in the country, to promote a peaceful future for all South Africans. Differences in religion, skin colour and culture should help unite and not separate people in this country,' said Archbishop Tutu. He said that as a person who believed in peace and justice, he accepted the right of workers to strike and the right of students to support striking workers but condemned those involved in raising barricades, disrupting lectures, and intimidation. 'Don't raise your voices; improve your arguments,' he said. He encouraged the university authorities to do everything possible to evoke a feeling of 'togetherness' among all sectors of the UCT community, so that all staff and students would believe they were part of an organisation which had the interests of the entire community at heart.

Charles Villa-Vicencio also spoke of peace and of negotiation, but in addition he indicated that he thought the striking workers' demands were reasonable. I was very cross indeed.

The assembly approved a statement condemning the violence and calling for peace. Although the student leadership had not associated itself with the assembly on the grounds that insufficient consultation had taken place before it was called, the SRC endorsed the wording of the statement.

There had been considerable intimidation of workers by workers during the strike. On one occasion a middle-aged woman who was on her way to work was forced into the boot of a car, which was then closed on her, and she was driven off. We heard about this shortly afterwards but could not trace where she was. Urgent representations were made to the union officials who denied all knowledge of the incident. Subsequently the woman reappeared, but was too terrified to give any account of what had happened. In a number of incidents members of staff in pay-classes 1–3 who wished to work, were forcibly prevented from doing so and one member of the staff in one of the residence kitchens was forcibly taken to a meeting half a mile away on the upper campus. One kitchen worker had her hands put on the hot plate of a stove. I was surprised and dismayed at the violence which the striking workers indulged in and equally disturbed by the violence on the part of the students. Subsequently I have come to realise that strikes often become violent, and it does seem to me that this is a serious matter which is not being adequately addressed in South Africa. I support, and the university has always supported, the right of workers to strike and of students wishing to do so, but there can be no support for those who prevent others from going about their legitimate business. There certainly can be no condoning of violence.

Ironically, the union finally accepted an offer which in real terms was the same total package which they had been offered originally. What the union finally agreed to was a re-packaging of that offer so that by reducing the pensionable salary and replacing it with an increased non-pensionable allowance, the union was able to accept a 17 per cent increase in pay. This, in budgetary terms, represented the same total amount of money as the original 13,5 per cent pensionable salary increase would have cost. Given the disruption which the strike caused and the violence and bad publicity which the university received, the strike could only be described as disastrous. It was also quite unnecessary.

We were determined to take disciplinary action against those who had acted irresponsibly and had broken the university's rules, or had acted illegally. Due process was followed, both with regard to the students and the staff. Disciplinary procedures were brought against 50 employees for disruption, barricading and intimidation during the strike. Seven were dismissed, 26 were given final written warnings and 17 were acquitted on grounds of insufficient evidence. In each case the worker had submitted that the actions taken had been mandated by the union, but the university industrial relations management committee had examined the issue and concluded that acting under a mandate from a trade union did not absolve an individual from responsibility. The university court found 16 students guilty and acquitted 1. The 16 students pleaded guilty to charges including disobedience to instructions given by an authorised member of the university staff, blocking entry to the campus by means of physical force or threat of violence, and behaving in a threatening, discreditable or offensive or abusive manner. Of the 16 students 10 were expelled and 6 were rusticated. The expulsions and rustications were suspended on two conditions: i) that the students were not found guilty of further offences; ii) that they render community service, which in the case of some of the students was up to a maximum of 360 hours.

It was significant that the students stated, '... in accordance with their organisational position abhorring violence in any form, they regret the unfortunate incidents of 24, 25, 26 and 27 September to which they have pleaded guilty.' The entire process took about one year! This was due to the fact that the staff disciplinary procedures had to be completed first, that it took time to identify the students and to gather the evidence (some witnesses were reluctant to get involved and newspapers would not release photographs as a matter of principle), and the students requested a series of postponements. It was also a reflection of our cumbersome, formal disciplinary procedures involving senior lawyers on both sides. The actions demonstrated the university's commitment to ensure that acts of violence and intimidation were not tolerated. We recognised that the strike had left deep scars in the university and that we had actively to work at healing the wounds.

The vast majority of the students, black and white, thoroughly disapproved of the violence and disruption perpetrated by a small number of students in support of the strike. A significant number of workers who did not belong to the union also disapproved of the union's action and many, including union members, were disturbed by the course of events. Years later, in 1998, one of the students who had built burning barricades and had been involved in other violent acts was interviewed in one of the newspapers. To my surprise he regarded his actions as part of the struggle for democracy! He indicated in the article that he had been quite prepared to throw stones at other students who were trying to remove the barricades, but that it hadn't been necessary. He is now a director in the civil service and a private secretary to a Minister, and he views his present position 'as a product of this struggle'. He does admit that such actions created divisions in the ranks of SASCO. In my view those students who helped the strikers were hardly making a contribution to the struggle for a free and democratic South Africa. The photograph which accompanied the interview showed our intrepid struggler standing at a burning barricade with a large rock in his hand.

Student protests directed at internal university problems, of which there were a number, were usually carried out by a small number of students, e.g. 50 or 100. The strategy used to deal with them was to allow the protest to continue without taking disciplinary action and containing any disruption of the work of the university to a minimum, allowing the protesters increasingly to isolate themselves. When the protest was over, disciplinary action was taken against those where there was evidence which allowed charges to be brought. There were always problems with identification and witnesses. If heavy-handed action is taken during a protest the 50 protesters become 1000 and the issue becomes the action taken against them and not the original cause of the protest. The strategy was effective.

Demise of legalised apartheid 1992-1994

I continued to have people of high quality working closely with me. They included Professor Michael Savage, professor of sociology, who acted as deputy vice-chancellor between August 1992 and June 1993 while Dave Woods was on study leave. Professor Peter Horn, professor of German, acted as deputy vice-chancellor from October 1993 to October 1994 as a leave replacement. Helen Zille* was appointed as director of the university's development and public affairs department in October 1993, a post she filled with great distinction. A journalist of considerable ability who had subsequently formed her own consulting company, Helen Zille brought to the task a professionalism and dedication which were outstanding.

When Professor David Hall was appointed as the director of the Graduate School of Business he immediately started looking for suitable quarters for the school, which was still housed in prefabricated buildings. He fixed his attention on the old breakwater prison at the harbour, when the Victoria and Alfred Waterfront, which has proved to be such a great success, was in its infancy. We were shown around the buildings (including the death cells and treadmill!) and flown over it in a helicopter. We were being subjected to a 'hard sell'. Money was the problem and the figures of future student numbers and other sources of income were significantly inflated. I was against UCT taking this step but yielded to the majority view of council. The renovated prison and the new buildings have provided superb accommodation and the development has been a success: the financial problems have been overcome. In 25 or 50 years' time, if anyone bothers to ask what I achieved at UCT, the Graduate School of Business will be mentioned, but it is something for which I deserve little credit.

I was amused by what happened at a meeting at the headquarters of the Committee of University Principals chaired by John Samuels, who was the head of the ANC education desk. This was part of a series of discussions between the ANC educational group and the vice-chancellors of universities. While trying to set a date for a further meeting it became clear that all

---

* Helen Zille is now Minister of Education in the Western Cape Parliament.

the vice-chancellors of the so-called historically black universities were unable to attend on a particular day. Knowing full well what I was doing, I turned to Sibusiso Bengu,* the vice-chancellor of the University of Fort Hare, who sat next to me, and asked him whether I had misdiarised the other meeting. He replied that was not a meeting which I was expected to attend. He asked me for a lift to the airport and as we drove along the highway he apologised for the fact that I was excluded from the other meeting, explaining that the vice-chancellors and rectors of the 'historically black universities' had decided to meet together to try to address their particular problems, that Jakes Gerwel, rector of the University of the Western Cape, had been asked to convene the meeting but had declined to do so, and so he himself was convening the meeting. I thanked him for telling me and I said to him, 'Do me one favour, Sibusiso, do not start a black Broederbond.'

There was cause for celebration during the year when the Government repealed the quota legislation. As a consequence, on the recommendation of the academic freedom committee, the date MCMXCI (1991) was inserted on a plaque which had been installed in 1960, as a protest against the Extension of University Education Act, which had denied universities the right to decide who to admit, and specifically prevented the university from admitting students of colour without a permit issued by a Cabinet Minister. The inserted date indicated when this denial of academic freedom was repealed. It was decided not to insert a date on the plaque erected in 1968, which acknowledged the loss of academic freedom in general and was erected after council had withdrawn its offer of appointment to Archie Mafeje in the light of threatened Government action. That date would only be inserted when all restrictive legislation was removed. It was also decided to mount a display case in the Jagger Library explaining the context and history of the 1960 and 1968 plaques and to install a third plaque to record important events in the struggle for academic freedom.

Robin Renwick, the British Ambassador, continued working towards the creation of a democratic state in South Africa. Ever since his arrival in the country he had played a very significant role in this regard and, in addition, he understood the university's mission very clearly and was influential in obtaining financial support for black students, including support for the academic development programme. He and his charming wife Annie became very good friends of ours. Two United States Ambassadors, Ed Perkins and William Swing, also left a deep impression on me. I first met Ambassador Perkins at a mayoral reception given in his honour on his arrival in Cape Town by Mayor van Zyl, who was a member of the National

---

* Minister of Education in the first democratic government in South Africa, now retired.

Party. The mayor asked the ambassador if he had visited any other cities in South Africa. Perkins replied in the affirmative and, on the mayor enquiring further, identified them as Soweto, Mamelodi and other black residential areas. Van Zyl was quite taken aback. Given the university's public stance and the location of parliament in Cape Town we regularly met many visiting politicians, fact-finding commissions, business men and other groups as well as diplomats from foreign countries.

Amongst those who received honorary degrees from UCT in 1992 was Max du Preez, the editor of the *Vrye Weekblad*, a newspaper published in the Transvaal. He had courageously exposed the hit squads and assassinations carried out by the South African security forces. The university was honouring him for his courage in these actions and for defending democracy. Interestingly, just after the announcement had been made that Du Preez was to get an honorary degree, I was at a dinner party where the then State President, De Klerk, and his wife Marike were also guests. When he came into the lounge and sat down he looked at me and said, 'Why are you honouring Du Preez?' I asked him why he asked the question and he said, 'Well, he's one of my enemies.' I replied, 'We are honouring him because he has exposed murder and hit squads and has promoted democracy. Why is he one of your enemies?' There was no reply.

Even in 1992, public meetings on the campus could give rise to some difficulty. There was to be a campus debate on violence in South Africa and the panel of invited speakers included a representative of the Inkatha Institute. The rules for inviting such speakers to the campus had not been followed and it was late on the day before the meeting was due to take place that Martin West, the deputy vice-chancellor responsible for these matters, had been informed of student objections, particularly by SASCO, to the proposed participation by a speaker from the Inkatha Institute. Professor West then arranged a meeting for the morning of September 2 and at that meeting the members of SASCO said the debate was likely to be 'peacefully' disrupted, given the students' sensitivity to the question of violence in South Africa. They advised him that SASCO was unlikely to 'go along' with the staging of a protest, provided they could state their point of view from the start and indicate why they opposed the speaker from Inkatha being present. Martin accepted this but when he arrived at the meeting found it to be a fairly boisterous one. The president of SASCO made his statement and then, before the meeting calmed down, two of the invited speakers decided not to participate on the grounds that not much of the allotted time remained. Martin then announced that the debate was being postponed. It was never re-convened. While the circumstances were different from our previous experiences where freedom of speech had been denied, that was again the net result of actions by students.

I was invited to the University of Otago in New Zealand as the William Evans Distinguished Visitor. This gave Anita and me great pleasure because we were able to spend two weeks with Robin and Bunty Irvine, Robin being the vice-chancellor of the university and, as I have already indicated, the Irvines were very dear friends. Later in the year, after attending a meeting of the International Association of Universities in Alexandria, Robin and Bunty, Anita and I had the enormous pleasure of sailing up the Nile together. The re-establishment of our links with other universities in Southern Africa was symbolised by my attending the thirtieth anniversary of the Eduardo Mondlane University in Maputo, Mozambique. President Chissano is the chancellor of the university and the visitors were given the opportunity to meet with him on a number of occasions. I found him very well informed and very keen to promote co-operation in higher education. When I thought back on the way in which the South African Government had vilified Frelimo, of which he was one of the leaders, I realised the extent to which propaganda was used in international affairs and warfare. Chissano is an outstanding man.

During 1993 an African senior lecturer, after a thorough process of review, had not been granted tenure. Originally the recommendation was that his probationary period, under certain conditions, should be prolonged but he declined to respond to this offer. After extensive further negotiations, his contract with the university came to an end and he claimed to students that racial prejudice was involved. As a result I received requests from a number of black student organisations and some of the black members of staff to reinstate him. In each instance I was able to reassure them that every consideration had been given to the lecturer and that the proceedings had been fair and just, that the committee of review did not consist only of white people, and that they should have confidence in the proceedings. I also indicated to them that the lecturer had all the facts and that he was in a position to give them the details, something which he had consistently refused to do. I indicated to them that what had passed between the committee of the university and the staff member was confidential to him and that only he could release that information and if he chose not to do so, there was nothing I could do about it.

Because of these repeated expressions of concern, the council invited an independent panel to review the procedures. The panel consisting of Professor Hugh Corder, professor of law, and Mr W A Mgoqi, a distinguished African attorney and member of the university council, had expressed confidence in the procedure. Following further requests by the students for a review of the position, the council appointed yet another committee to review both the procedure and the substance as it affected the whole matter and asked Professor Kader Asmal* and Professor Walter Kamba[†] to review it in detail and to report to council. A number of the students objected to both Professor Asmal and to Professor Kamba being appointed to undertake this task, claiming that the former was friendly with members of staff in the department and the latter was not a South African.

The terms of reference were wide-ranging. The committee of review had the lecturer's full record, and described the university council's decision to terminate the probationary appointment as procedurally fair and substantively correct. It also dismissed suggestions of racial bias or victimisation. Despite its findings, the report recommended that the lecturer be given a 'further opportunity to demonstrate his ability in the department' and suggested that he be offered 'a further probationary appointment' on condition that he agreed to undergo a professional assessment acceptable to the university council, followed by counselling or treatment if necessary, that he took a course at the teaching methods unit and that he spent the bulk of his time on campus. The report also recommended that the university council pay for the professional assessment and 'any counselling or treatment that may be required'. The council noted the review committee's recommendations and resolved to consider them at its next scheduled meeting. At the same time it resolved to consider any submissions the lecturer or others might make and the lecturer was invited to do so. No such submissions were made. The lecturer's position had consistently been against any suggestion of professional assessment and counselling if needed, and the council confirmed its previous decision to deny tenure. I had chaired the committee of review and the subsequent events underlined for me the difficulties which could arise in a country with such a strong history of racial bias and prejudice. Even when matters were conducted in a fair and proper manner, they were open to the suspicion that racial bias might be involved and it was only after two additional enquiries, one by two eminent jurists from outside the university, that the matter could finally be put to rest.

1994, the year of South Africa's transition to democracy, was also a watershed year for universities. Apart from sharing the nation's relief at having broken the spiral of repression and resistance, the main gain for universities during the year was the Government's stated commitment to formulating a new policy framework for higher education. At the end of the year a National Commission on Higher Education was established, with UCT's academic secretary Mr Jon File one of the thirteen commissioners. The com-

---

* Minister of Water Affairs in the first democratic government in South Africa. Now Minister of Education.
[†] Previous vice-chancellor, University of Zimbabwe.

mission was required to propose goals, policies and institutional requirements for a higher education system that could meet the country's needs in the twenty-first century.

The major event of 1994 was the general election and the subsequent installation of Nelson Mandela as the President of the democratic South Africa. Senate and council took steps to ensure free and fair electioneering on campus. The professor of public law, Hugh Corder, was appointed as an ombudsperson and the university also appointed an eight-person electoral committee, four students and four staff members. The ombudsperson had a range of powers including the right to bar any organisation from electioneering or campaigning on the campus if they violated UCT's rules, which ensured that all parties had equal opportunities. Although the meetings were sometimes noisy and the discussions vigorous, all were able to speak freely. The extent of tolerance for divergent views went a long way towards healing the scars that remained after the events of 1986 when Dr Conor Cruise O'Brien had been prevented from speaking.

After an election which inspired the world, South Africans of all political persuasions celebrated the inauguration of President Nelson Mandela at the Union Buildings on 10 May 1994. Anita and I were privileged to be there and were deeply moved by the proceedings. There was a particularly poignant moment when military helicopters flew directly towards the assembled guests. A hush fell over the crowd, some heads turned nervously, then wild cheering broke out. Up to that time helicopters had been a symbol of oppression: the police had used them extensively in crowd control and in dealing with staff and student protests on and off the campus during the difficult times in the 1980s. The sound of a helicopter had always filled me with dread, but here they were celebrating the inauguration of President Nelson Mandela and suddenly they belonged to all of us in a symbol of the new era. UCT's Choir for Africa sang at the inauguration.

On May 13 we raised the new South African flag above the Jameson Hall in a lunch-time ceremony during which both national anthems were sung. The university had not flown a national flag for more than forty years. On July 20, during the annual T B Davie memorial lecture, the torch of academic freedom was relit, thirty-four years after it was extinguished in protest against the Extension of University Education Act which sought to exclude students from the universities on the basis of race. These were important and moving events.

The demise of apartheid also opened new opportunities to forge and strengthen bonds with academics throughout sub-Saharan Africa. In February a delegation of scientists and engineers from sub-Saharan universities visited UCT to foster research co-operation and promote staff development. The universities, represented by their vice-chancellors or deans of science, were the Universities of Zambia and Zimbabwe, the Eduardo Mondlane University of Mozambique, the Jomo Kenyatta University of Kenya, the Universities of Dar es Salaam, Tanzania, and Kinshasa in Zaire and the University of Botswana. The visit was funded by the Rockefeller Foundation, which had offered a launching grant to explore the feasibility of scientific co-operation between UCT and other sub-Saharan universities, in order to encourage good scientists and engineers to remain in Africa.

A great deal of work was done during 1994 to build on these contacts and to develop joint scientific research projects to address pressing problems across the continent. USHEPIA, the University Science, Humanities and Engineering Partnerships in Africa, resulted from this, managed by a committee chaired by Professor Martin West, and funded by the Rockefeller Foundation, the Carnegie Corporation and the Mellon Foundation. In 1996 32 scholars, most of whom are members of the academic staff of universities in sub-Saharan Africa, outside of South Africa, entered the programme to do their PhD degrees on the UCT campus, and a further 12 in 1998. Six more scholars are expected to enrol in 1999. Efforts are being made to raise funds so that these scholars can continue their research work on their home campuses. It is believed that scholars who do their post-graduate work on this continent are more likely to remain in Africa than would have been the case if they studied in the United States or Europe. This programme is proving to be a great success and I hope that it will expand in the future. Regional co-operation was also promoted between the five tertiary institutions in the Western Cape through the activities of the Western Cape Tertiary Institutions Trust. The greatest achievement was the co-operation between the five institutions' libraries which culminated in the establishment of the Cape Library Co-operative (CALICO). An attempt was made to establish a joint school of public health, but this was not as successful. In my view co-operation and rationalisation between the five institutions is likely to become increasingly important in the future as will be the case in the other regions of South Africa.

We were forced to review the security measures at large student functions when a woman was raped near the Rag 'big bash' party in orientation week. The rape survivor was not a student and could not identify her assailant, partly because she was drunk at the time. We were concerned about the amount of alcohol consumed by the students and introduced stricter measures to control this. Our statistics were almost identical to those published in the USA showing over 60 per cent of damage to property and over 70 per cent of all instances of violence by students were related to alcohol abuse. Both the voluntary students' 'buddy campaign', which helped anyone who had become inebriated, and the members of the gender initiative did excellent work. These problems raised the question of the role of the police on campus. The history of police action on the campus had made them unwelcome, but times had changed. The SRC was opposed to the police being involved but a student referendum showed clear support for a police presence on campus when it was needed. There was very strong support amongst black women. A joint campus security committee was established with the police and the police commenced their patrols. This was a far cry from the 1980s.

UCT experienced a second strike towards the end of the year. The salary negotiations with the union ended in deadlock after the majority of workers in the union bargaining unit of pay classes 1–3 voted to reject our final offer of a 6 per cent increase and a once-off R400 bonus. The union held a two-day strike on October 26 and 27 during our examination period. I felt that the decision to strike was completely unreasonable, given the fact that nobody doing equivalent work in the country was paid more than they were, and I also worried about the possibility of examinations being disrupted. It made me very depressed. Anita and I had arranged to go to an auction on the evening before the strike to bid on some furniture for the house into which we planned to move when I retired. I found that attending a public auction was a good way of taking my mind off the impending strike and certainly helped to lift the depression.

About 140 striking workers took part in demonstrations on the first day. They blocked traffic on one of the public highways and marched to the Jameson Hall. They made considerable noise outside the hall in which examinations were being held. After about three or four minutes the group left when asked to do so. A similar demonstration took place outside the sports centre, where examinations were also being written and again the strikers dispersed in a few minutes. They went to the students' union, overturned rubbish bins and disturbed those writing exams in that building. Then they moved to the chemistry building where they caused damage by turning on fire hoses and letting off fire alarms. They finally returned to the new science lecture theatre and after that to the sports centre where they again made a lot of noise, disrupting the exams.

The examination periods were extended by 40 minutes. There was no student involvement in the strike on this occasion. SASCO and other student organisations made it clear that their sympathy was with the strikers but that they could not support any action which interfered with examinations. A group of black students from the residences told the strikers that they earned much more than their parents, and did not have their support. The academics association also issued a statement distancing itself from the strike. The general mood in the examination halls was good, the noise levels were not high and they weren't sustained for any length of time. The feeling was that the additional forty minutes would make up for any difficulties which the students had experienced. But it was very worrying that these disturbances had happened at all. On the second day the strikers confined their activities to the middle campus, except for a march around the Bremner Building. The settlement in the end put more cash into the strikers' pockets but reduced short-term and long-term pensionable benefits and the total budgeted amount was not increased. It was very questionable whether this was in the interests of the striking workers. I was very impressed with the manner in which the industrial relations committee had handled the strike, particularly Martin West and Joy Fish, and by the co-operation which we received from the deans. At other strikes in South Africa at that time there was a tendency to take hostages so I was very concerned when there was a request for Martin West to address the strikers. We obtained an undertaking that he would not be detained against his will and he was accompanied by Jon File and Malcolm Roach. Astonishingly, the strikers gave him a standing ovation!

The road of transformation
1995-1996

Transformation of the university had already become a major issue in 1993 and has continued to be so. It is often the case that discussion on transformation becomes shallow because many who use the term freely are unable to be precise about what they mean. It is, of course, easier to deliver slogans than to pose reasoned arguments and in-depth analysis. There is still too much sloganeering in contemporary South Africa.

For my colleagues and me transformation was a process which began more than a decade earlier. UCT was no Johnny-come-lately to the debate. It started with the steady enrolment of black students in increasing numbers, in housing them in the residences, in the development of the sophisticated academic development programme, in the equal opportunity policy in hiring academic and administrative staff, in the policies on sexual and racial harassment, the review of symbols and rituals and, more recently, in the review of the constitution of the university council and senate, the revision of degree structures and curricula and of student governance, as well as the creation of a university transformation forum. UCT published a booklet entitled 'The transformation of the University of Cape Town' which recorded, inter alia, the university's drive for equal opportunity and black advancement. There were student protests claiming that UCT was not moving fast enough. The major protest resulted in a presentation of demands to the council which was very well handled by the chairman, Ian Sims.

A weekend workshop of the full transformation forum was held in August 1994. There were representatives from the council, the executive, senate, the various staff groupings and the students. Detailed documentation was provided concerning national higher education policy, the university's admission policy, readmission rules, the way in which academic and residential fees were derived, full details of the general operating budget, the financial aid policy and the readmission of students in debt to the university, as well as the function of the academic development programme. There was full and frank discussion. As vice-chancellor I often had to grit my teeth and listen to what seemed to be endless discussion around issues which, to me at least, seemed to have a clear and simple answer. Students can be very loquacious, at times aggressive and somewhat disorganised in their thoughts and take up a lot of time, but it is important to listen and to be patient. It was not always easy to achieve this. A statement of intent was adopted and a representative executive committee was formed. It was agreed that all decisions would be reached by consensus and that the transformation forum would only be advisory. This was important because there were some who wanted the forum to have executive powers, but that was unacceptable. The governance of a university must remain the ultimate responsibility of the council for all matters except those strictly academic matters which are the responsibility of senate and where council would be unwise to interfere. Any parallel body which usurps those powers can only undermine the university and ultimately destroy it. It is my view that some South African universities' transformation forums have taken powers upon themselves which are to the detriment of the institutions they purport to serve.

The UCT transformation executive was active in 1995 and 1996 and reached consensus on the way in which my successor should be chosen and on a new mission statement, and made a lot of progress regarding the constitution of the council. There was some distrust at first but this was soon overcome by the determination of all members to make it work. The recommendations on the mode of election of the new vice-chancellor and the mission statement were accepted by senate and council. In the election of my successor the selection committee recommended the candidate, senate endorsed the recommendation and council made the appointment, while the university transformation forum exco approved the legitimacy of the process. The search and selection committee was responsible for advertising the post, inviting applications and nominations, for undertaking a search process, compiling a short list of candidates and making this known to the university community, and arranging for each short-listed candidate to address the different sectors of the university community and to make a major public address in the Jameson Hall. Following that, the search and selection committee decided upon its recommendation to the senate and after the approval of senate the recommendation was approved by council. Three people were short-listed: Professor Njabulo Ndebele, who was the vice-chancellor of the University of the North, Professor Dave Woods, and Dr Mamphela Ramphele, who were both deputy vice-chancellors of the University of Cape Town. Professor Ndebele withdrew from the process and the council formally appointed Dr Ramphele on 19 October. Professor Dave Woods was appointed vice-chancellor of Rhodes University, so that in the end both universities were extremely fortunate to have an outstanding person appointed as the new vice-chancellor. I was delighted with the appointment of Dr Ramphele, a person of great ability who I knew would lead the university very successfully in the years that lay ahead. I was equally delighted that Dave Woods's exceptional talents would be able to flourish as he gave equally strong leadership to Rhodes University.

It must be said that the procedure was quite unique for the University of Cape Town. Similar procedures were used at other universities in South Africa at the time and were shaped by the dominant contemporary requirement that the chosen candidate should be able to claim demonstrable support and legitimacy throughout the diverse university community. The process was clearly crucial to a successful outcome and so it proved to be. From the outset I decided not to become involved in any way in the process of selecting my successor. This has always been the tradition at UCT. Great credit must go to Martin West, who worked tirelessly to ensure that the transformation forum and its executive functioned well.

The political changes resulted in new international contact in 1995 and 1996. In January 1995 I attended the meeting of the African Association of Universities in Maseru. It was useful meeting colleagues from the rest of Africa and we were able to hold further discussions about our co-operative USHEPIA programme. I was struck by the fact that with two courageous exceptions the Nigerian vice-chancellors all toed the Government line and would not criticise the unacceptable events in higher education in their country, to say nothing of what was happening to Nigeria as a whole. This reminded me of the Afrikaans university heads during apartheid. Later in the year I was elected to the Administrative Board of the International Association of Universities at the New Delhi meeting. The following year the Association of Commonwealth Universities held its meeting in Malta. The meeting ended with a morning 'business' session chaired by the Maltese vice-chancellor, assisted by the secretary-general of the association, Dr A Christodoulou. As the session came to an end someone from the floor asked if any action was to be taken concerning the Nigerian vice-chancellors who had been forbidden by their Government to attend. The answer from the platform was inconclusive. A colleague from South Africa repeated the question and the chairman and secretary-general both said that they were handling the matter. The meeting then started to break up but this was too much for me. I spoke as loudly as I could, saying, 'Any organisation which does not act on a matter such as this does not deserve to exist!' People who were walking out turned round and sat down again. The chairman agreed to reconvene after lunch and to present a statement for approval, and an appropriate statement was approved. I felt a bit awkward and embarrassed, but it had to be done. I had had experience of organisations failing to act in the face of injustice to its members, and that is exactly what would have happened without that intervention.

In 1995 we had a crisis in student government because only 19,4 per cent of the students voted for the new SRC and the constitution demanded a vote of at least 25 per cent. We were forced to ask the student parliament, formed in 1996, to approve an interim structure, which had great difficulty in giving leadership to the student body during the ensuing twelve months. Fortunately the required number of votes saw an SRC elected the following year. This apathy may well have been related to the political changes in the country as opposition to apartheid no longer formed the basis of student politics. The outgoing SRC president, Maxwell Vusani, suggested that other factors might include disillusionment with the SRC, alienation of white students because most of the candidates were black, and the bad weather on election day!

It was quite clear that a submission had to be made to the National Commission on Higher Education and that the university transformation forum was already fully committed to the matters which it had in hand, so I decided to send a submission to the commission in my own name based upon the deliberations of a working group which I had set up. The views of members of the university were sought from faculty boards and senate and the UTF exco was informed of the procedures and asked to submit ideas for inclusion in the submission to the national commission. The university transformation forum exco was concerned that it had not been consulted earlier, but understood the practicalities involved. Jim Leatt, by now a consultant in Cape Town, was of great help in preparing our submission. UCT recommended a systematic approach to higher education based on quality, equity and autonomy and responsive to the demands of development in South Africa and of a globally competitive economy. It pointed out that the higher education system should be built on the integrated planning and funding of the range of academic programmes and that South Africa required a more flexible approach to the allocation of these programmes in tertiary institutions across the country. The successful implementation of the approach we suggested would require sound planning to determine the appropriate academic programme mix required for national development and economic growth and the appropriate distribution and funding of programmes in various institutions.

During the year the commission recommended urgent interim measures to deal with the national student financial aid crisis which was an annual event and loomed again for 1996. It was my view that this was a matter of urgency and that the commission should make recommendations for the establishment of a national bursary and loan scheme, in order to find a long-term structural solution to the problem. I was appointed by the Minister of

Education and the Minister of Finance to a committee charged with helping to raise funds for the interim scheme for student financial aid, which would be operating during 1996. At the first meeting I expressed the reservation that the Government was not committed to solving the problem and had to allocate R300m to show its commitment. To its credit it did so, but the committee was not a success. In 1997 a group of us developed a policy document on student financial aid and presented it to Government, and I hope a bill will be presented to parliament soon.

In accordance with our submission to the commission, the academic planning committee, under the leadership of Wieland Gevers, was developing a programmatic approach to the university's academic offerings to students. This was in keeping with the content of the new mission statement.

The commission failed to deal with some of the crucial issues in higher education. I have already pointed out its lack of action in student financial aid but it also did not address the diversity in higher education and neglected research. The commission avoided major areas which were politically sensitive, and this was unfortunate.

The issue of student fee indebtedness is one which receives a lot of attention in South Africa. A number of institutions apparently have very large student fee debts. In 1992 student fee debt at UCT was R1,5 million, in 1993 R4 million and in 1994 R4,8 million. The university has a clear policy not to release a student's results if more than R400 is outstanding and not to allow students indebted to a greater amount to graduate. This may seem harsh, but without such a rule there would be no inducement to pay fees, even by those who can afford to do so. In the weeks running up to graduation and once the examination results have been posted, I was always amazed at the amount of money streaming in from students who had allegedly been unable to pay their fees. UCT went to extraordinary lengths to provide financial aid for needy students, putting millions of rands of its own money to this purpose, underwriting loans from a commercial bank and putting student financial aid as the top priority of its national and international fund-raising. This played a big role in restricting the size of the student debt. We were grateful to many including the Overseas Development Agency and the British Council which, largely on the advice of Ambassador Renwick, recognised the quality of UCT's education. Baroness Chalker, the Minister of Overseas Development, was also a strong supporter. Many other donors gave essential, generous support. Institutions which did not have repayment rules similar to those of UCT, and did not place such an emphasis on student financial aid in budgetary allocations and in their fund-raising programmes, inevitably accumulated larger amounts of student debt.

The establishment of a multi-media centre at UCT was made possible through the support of generous donors in South Africa and the United Kingdom. Mary Roberts, Professor George Ellis's wife, made a major initial donation which started the ball rolling in a spectacular way. The centre has proved to be a great success and in particular gives opportunities for the learning of Xhosa and English. UCT's ideal is to ensure that all students are fluent in both languages It will not be easy to achieve, but a start has been made. The centre is also developing novel methods of presenting educational material to students.

It was in 1995 that the implications for the quality of patient care and the opportunities for teaching and research at the major teaching hospitals in the Western Cape started to become clear. The old Cape Province had been divided into Western, Northern and Eastern Cape and the Western Cape was the site of two major teaching hospitals. The funding for the Western Cape health services was inadequate for the proper running of the teaching hospitals of the two medical schools, especially in view of the new emphasis on primary health care and the development of clinics in peri-urban and rural areas. The university medical school had strongly supported the thrust towards primary health care but had warned against shifting funds too rapidly and failing to protect centres of excellence in teaching hospitals. I was particularly pleased that Glaxo plc, United Kingdom, agreed to fund a chair of primary health care at the University of Cape Town, which brought into focus and placed special emphasis on that discipline in the medical faculty.

The health department of the Western Cape Province came forward with a proposal which they hoped would help them meet the large budgetary deficit. The plan called for Groote Schuur and Red Cross Hospitals (the two hospitals linked to the University of Cape Town) to become referral hospitals or 'super-specialist tertiary hospitals' while it envisaged Tygerberg Hospital (the teaching hospital of the Stellenbosch medical school) becoming a general specialist hospital for the greater Cape Town area. This proposal did not find favour with the University of Stellenbosch. The proposal implied that all hospitals would no longer be linked to medical schools and that both medical schools would have equal access to Groote Schuur and Red Cross Hospitals as tertiary hospitals. Tygerberg Hospital would become a general specialist hospital serving both medical schools.

In response to the health department's proposals many meetings took place. I formed a committee at the medical school and I chaired the meetings. One evening a small group of us met as a sub-committee and after many hours of discussion it became clear to us all that the best way forward in a situation of seriously shrinking resources was to establish a single medical school. We accordingly suggested that the two medical schools should fuse. We believed that this would secure quality patient care, teaching and research There has always been some tension between the medical schools. As a result a *'bosberaad'* (brainstorming session) was held, attended by members of both medical schools and the provincial health department. In the end there was a better understanding by all and a general realisation that we all had to work together. Unfortunately Stellenbosch rejected the concept of fusing the medical schools. The crisis continued, the goal posts kept shifting and the budgetary deficit steadily increased, but by the time I retired in August 1996 no solution to the overall problem had been found. Many beds have been closed at all three hospitals, essential equipment has not been bought, the pharmacopoeia has contracted and, very foolishly, the Government has allowed staff to take voluntary retrenchment; many outstanding nursing and technical staff in particular availed themselves of this offer, greatly increasing staff shortages in all three hospitals. If the teaching hospitals in South Africa are not preserved the future for health care is bleak, especially but not only for the poor.

Towards the end of 1995 a dispute between Professor William Makgoba, a deputy vice-chancellor of the University of the Witwatersrand, and some of the professors of that university entered the public arena. There were allegations that his curriculum vitae was not accurate and in January Professor Makgoba alleged that his detractors had obtained a copy of his curriculum vitae from the University of Cape Town appointments office. He revealed that he had been a candidate for a post of deputy vice-chancellor at the University of Cape Town, but had not been short-listed and that his CV had therefore been in the possession of the appointments office. He further alleged that questions about his academic credentials arising out of the conflict with the University of the Witwatersrand had influenced the search/selection committee's decision not to short-list him for the post of vice-chancellor of the University of Cape Town.

These were very serious allegations because, if true, they would reflect on the confidentiality of our appointment procedures and on the integrity of the search/selection committee. I personally made a detailed study of the appointments office, interviewing all members of staff. I also spoke to every member of the search/selection committee. I found that the security procedures in the appointments office made it extremely unlikely that the CV could have been obtained from our confidential files. The weight of the evidence therefore suggested that the person at UCT (and it had been confirmed that it had come from somebody at UCT) had obtained the CV from another source before faxing it from a Rondebosch shop. There was no truth in the allegations that the selection/search committee had in any way been influenced by allegations of irregularity in Professor Makgoba's CV. Each member of the committee confirmed that view and stated that they had had no knowledge of the matter when the committee had met. I was later pleased to receive Professor Makgoba's assurance that he had confidence in the integrity of the selection process, and did not believe that the committee had been influenced in that way.

A university assembly was held at which the new mission statement, which resulted from the work of the transformation forum and had been approved by senate and council, was adopted. The mission defined UCT as being an outstanding teaching and research university, educating for life and addressing the challenges facing our society. Each of these was dealt with in detail and the statement ended with a commitment to academic freedom, critical scholarship, creative thought and free enquiry.

The chancellor, Mr H F Oppenheimer, retired at the end of June 1996 and spoke movingly at the graduation ceremony. He referred to the university's commitment to academic freedom and spoke of his own opposition to apartheid. Harry Oppenheimer was UCT's fourth chancellor and held office for 29 years. I have the greatest respect for him. A thoughtful and courteous man, his wide knowledge of international and national contemporary affairs and his wisdom have made his advice and opinions invaluable. I kept him informed of major events as they occurred and always greatly valued his interest and support. The chancellorship is ceremonial but we were blessed to have a great South African as our chancellor at a critical point in our history, a chancellor who symbolised our belief in academic freedom, justice and non-racialism. It was a great privilege for Anita and me to get to know Bridget and Harry Oppenheimer. They are both remarkable people. On two occasions he hosted memorable dinners for us in London. He has been generous in his support of the university.

In July 1996 Professor John Martin, a very distinguished engineer from UCT's Department of Civil Engineering, was appointed a deputy vice-chancellor when Dave Woods left UCT. John Martin died in office in October 1999.

In August we had our second transformation forum, which was held over a weekend, and which was attended by representatives of all sectors of the university and proved to be a great success. There was a commitment to the transformation process.

I retired officially at the end of August 1996. During my years as vice-chancellor I had generously been awarded four honorary degrees, from the universities of Aberdeen, Toronto, Sheffield and Cape Town. In 1997 the University of Princeton awarded me an honorary doctorate in law. Anita and I were received with great warmth and friendship at all four overseas universities and we look back on these occasions with great pleasure. I was given the honorary fellowship of the College of Medicine of South Africa, which was also very gratifying.

At the last vice-chancellor's concert while I was still in office, the UCT choir (predominantly white) and the UCT Choir for Africa (predominantly black) sang together for the first time. They announced that they planned to do so regularly in the future and that they knew I would want them to do so.

It is legitimate to ask what UCT, as a university, achieved during these tumultuous years. The university was successful in progressively enrolling more black students over these fifteen and three-quarter years. (See Appendix for Tables I–IX.) Table I documents student enrolments by 'population group' and gender over time. African student enrolments rose from 316 in 1984 to 3489 in 1995, coloured enrolment from 1168 to 2007 and Indian from 276 to 823 while white enrolment dropped from 10140 to 8558. The average annual increase in African enrolment was 24,4 per cent. Under apartheid, universities were obliged by law to record the racial classification of the students. When that legislation was repealed, I proposed at the Committee of University Principals that universities ask students to give the information voluntarily so that progress in black enrolment could be monitored. The rector of the Rand Afrikaans University stated that his university had resolved not to do this as it was 'immoral' – this from a university which had supported apartheid! Of course the net result was that it would be difficult to monitor black enrolment. Some Afrikaans universities have tried to avoid changing their 'character' by enrolling black students predominantly for night courses or for distance education. The deception cannot last. Table II shows the proportion of South Africa's university students studying at UCT. FTEs refer to full-time equivalent students. SAPSE is the South African post-secondary educational system used to gather educational statistics. Table III gives the proportion of UCT students in 1984 and in 1995. The striking increase in African students and in postgraduate enrolments is noteworthy, as is the number of students enrolled in commerce, engineering, science and medicine.

It is clear from the tables that the policy to increase enrolment of black, particularly of African, students succeeded. In 1996 more than 50 per cent of the entering class was black. This was the result of our growth, access, admissions and readmissions policies, of the success of the academic development programme, of our emphasis on financial aid and student housing. Table IV records the number of students in UCT housing over an eleven-year period. The success of our adding to our stock of student housing and the accommodation provided for black students is apparent. The successful mixing of students in the residences had an important role to play in increasing understanding and trust between people with widely divergent life experiences.

Our policy of equal opportunity, affirmative action and employment was not as successful in correcting the imbalance in the staff, as can be seen in Table V. This is because of a number of factors, among them the slow turnover of academic staff and the lack of funds to create new (and needed) posts (the support of the Mellon Foundation and other donors for contract lectureships has been of real help in this regard), the movement of many talented blacks and women into Government, the civil service and commerce and industry (the university simply cannot compete with the employment packages offered at senior levels), and the fact that UCT's budget was stretched to the limit over all these years due to falling Government allocations and the funds needed to ensure the steady increase in black student enrolment. UCT is tackling this problem with vigour and will be helped by the stabilisation of the civil service and the redistribution of more funds to the staffing area. UCT made and is making a contribution to strengthening civil society in a country populated by many diverse people, by ensuring that the future graduates understand each other better after sharing common experiences on the campus. Those universities which failed to do this in the 80s and in the first half of the '90s did a disservice to our nation.

People who are going to work in and contribute to South Africa are far better prepared on a campus like UCT where students from all sections of the community work and play together, than they are from those institutions which may wish to be less diverse in the make-up of their student body. I always told parents and alumni that if they wanted their children to be part of the future they should send them to UCT.

Secondly, there was a strengthening of scholarship and research over these years due to the talent and hard work of many able academic staff members, supported by conscientious administrative and technical staff. I placed emphasis on scholarship and research in my inaugural address and later in the mission statement which I issued, and was surprised by how positively people responded. We scrutinised teaching and research ability in making appointments, in *ad hominem* promotions, in granting sabbatical leave, in giving tenure, and we emphasised the importance of scholarship and research in our weekly meetings with members of academic departments. We began to ask for curricula vitae updates before we made our visits and stressed vigour in scholarship. We emphasised the value of the Fellowship awarded for exceptional contributions to knowledge and the Distinguished Teacher Award for outstanding teaching. UCT consistently received more funds from statutory research councils in open competition and has had and has more A-rated scientists than any other South African university (Table VI). The figures refer to 1999 but reflect the position over the past ten years. A-rated scientists work at the highest international level as judged by international peer review. B & C scholars are judged as outstanding and worthy of financial support. P refers to outstanding young investigators who get financial support for five years, while Y refers to bright young investigators. The figures reflect the strength of UCT's scholarship. The university sustained a good publication record in peer-reviewed journals and books. The institution of merit awards for outstanding scholarship in the professoriate was a pointer to the importance placed on excellence in research, scholarship and teaching. UCT's academic staff travelled widely to foreign universities and they, the university's publications and the overall quality of postgraduate students studying at foreign universities, all enhanced the reputation of the university.

In the late '80s and early '90s some white South Africans became concerned about declining standards in South African universities. This concern continues to be expressed quite frequently. It stems partly from the decreasing financial resource base universities are experiencing but more importantly from the increasing enrolment of black students, many from poor educational backgrounds. Some of the concern is rooted in racism – in the belief that blacks cannot succeed at the same level as whites. It may also arise from the potential difficulties which can occur if students in the same class have widely divergent levels of achievement because of different school systems. The academic development programme helps to overcome this, as does a rigorous selection process, plus much more care being given to teaching techniques and the learning process. UCT has learned a great deal and our critics should remember that it is much more difficult for anyone to get a degree at UCT now than it was when the parents of the current students were undergraduates themselves. The problem is not that standards are falling but rather that the reverse is happening, although those whose main source of information is the cocktail and dinner circuit often seem to be reluctant to acknowledge that it is so.

The facts mentioned above speak for themselves, plus the fact that students not making the grade are not promoted and may well be required to leave the university, something which was not nearly as vigorously applied when I was an undergraduate student. What is true is that, like many universities in the world, there tends to be a greater percentage of students who get third-class degrees, but bear in mind that the classes are bigger and that this represents a raising of standards. UCT's current achievements also speak for themselves. Table VII shows the academic success rates by 'population groups' and Table VIII, academic progress. Table IX shows the degrees awarded.

Of course apartheid damaged all of South Africa's universities and all other aspects of South African life. We were less able to recruit scholars from overseas because of apartheid, especially in the '80s and early '90s and the censorship and denial of freedom of expression imposed from without (and from within as we have seen) were damaging, as were the banning, harassment by the police and the enforced exile of some of apartheid's opponents. UCT weathered the storm well and is positioned to make important contributions to South and Southern Africa. It deserves and must get the support of Government and of South African society as a whole and of donors at home and abroad, so that it can fulfil its historic task of helping to ensure the development of South Africa and the consolidation of its democracy. I am grateful to all who worked over the years to make UCT a better place of learning and scholarship. They include members of the executive, the administration, the academic staff, students and generous donors both in South Africa and abroad.

Dr Mamphela Ramphele is an outstanding vice-chancellor who is leading UCT into the future with ability and determination. I greatly admire what she is doing at and for the University of Cape Town. She leaves the University in the second part of 2000 to take up an important post at the World Bank, and her successor deserves the wholehearted support of all who believe in the university's mission and its role in ensuring a prosperous and democratic future for South Africa.

On 28 August 1996 the council gave Anita and myself a memorable farewell dinner at the Mount Nelson Hotel in Cape Town, where we saw my portrait by Hayden Proud, a distinguished painter, for the first time. Confronting my likeness as interpreted by him was a strange experience.

The following month a large number of students gave a farewell party for me and a welcoming party for Dr Ramphele in Jameson Hall. There were bands, speeches by students, and generally it was a very happy occasion. Mr Tokyo Sexwale, who was then the Premier of Gauteng Province and a prominent member of the ANC, made a speech of tribute to me and Dr Ramphele. In it he said that I had formed deep footprints in education in South Africa and that as I moved off into the sunset I could be happy with what I had achieved. I told Anita that it reminded me of going to the movies on a Saturday morning as a little boy. I usually saw the Lone Ranger or Hopalong Cassidy. At the end of the movie they always rode off into the sunset on their horses, silhouetted against the sun on a hill, but what impressed me was that they always rode back into the movie house the next Saturday morning. It wasn't my intention to do that, but I certainly did not intend to disappear.

Tables

Table I: Student enrolments by 'population group' and gender

Year	African M	African F	African T	Coloured M	Coloured F	Coloured T
1984	231	85	316	708	460	1168
1985	253	86	339	687	468	1155
1990	944	471	1415	682	955	1937
1991	1135	564	1699	982	969	1951
1992	1329	641	1970	943	927	1870
1993	1627	790	2417	918	918	1836
1994	1964	983	2947	941	971	1912
1995	2290	1199	3489	964	1043	2007

Average annual growth 1984–1995 (in percentages)

| | 23,00 | 27,50 | 24,40 | 2,80 | 7,50 | 5,10 |

(Source: Table 2.7, annual SAPSE returns 1994; 1995 from UCT records.)

Table II: The proportions of South Africa's university students studying at UCT	
	1995
White residential university students	10,0%
African residential university students	3,9%
	1993*
'Natural science' students[1]	9,3%
Black 'natural science' students[1]	6,9%
Masters and Doctoral students (FTEs)	11,8%
'Natural science' Masters and Doctoral students (FTEs)	14,2%
Black 'natural science' Masters and Doctoral students (FTEs)	8,5%
	1991
Engineering students	15,6%
Black engineering students	18,2%
African engineering students[2]	36,0%

* 1993 figures exclude former TBVC universities
1 'Natural sciences' as defined by the SAPSE system
2 A more important indicator is graduation stastistics. Over the six-year period 1986 to 1991, UCT produced 57 (or 28%) of the 292 African engineers who graduated from South African universities

	Indian			White			Total		
M	F	T	M	F	T	M	F	T	
186	90	276	6190	3950	10140	7315	4586	11900
186	96	282	6092	3976	10068	7218	4626	11844
308	184	492	6033	4224	10257	8267	5834	14101
343	213	556	5986	4219	10205	8446	5965	14411
367	227	594	5738	4105	9843	8377	5900	14277
405	269	674	5412	3855	9267	8362	5832	14194
429	293	722	5015	3675	8690	8349	5922	14271
473	350	823	4834	3724	8558	8561	6316	*14877
,90	13,2	10,50	-2,30	-0,80	-1,70	1,50	3,00	2,10

* This total does not include elective students and those registered for certificate courses.

Table III: Proportions of UCT students

	1984	1995
Women students	38,5%	42,5%
African students[1]	2,7%	23,6%
Postgraduates	22,4%	29,2%
Students in the Faculties of Commerce, Engineering, Science and Medicine	57,4%	60,6%

Proportions of first-year UCT students

	1984	1995
Women students	47,3%	46,6%
African students	3,0%	31,06%
Students from the Western Cape	59,9%	47,8%
A, B and C aggregates[2]	68,3%	71,8%

1 Approximately 75% of UCT's African students come from schools administered by the former Department of Education and Training and the Transkei Education Department
2 Calculations are based on the formula used by the education departments and not the stricter SAPSE formula. The figures do not imply that 25% of UCT's students have D and E aggregates, as aggregates cannot be calculated for foreign school-leavers and mature-age entrants

Table IV: Students in UCT student housing

	1984	(%)	1995	(%)	Change
White	2 089	(94%)	910	(23%)	-56.5%
Coloured	37	(2%)	190	(5%)	514%
Indian	14	(1%)	170	(4%)	1 214%
African	73	(3%)	2 610	(68%)	3 575%
Total	2 214	(100%)	3 877	(100%)	175%

Table V: Permanent staff by personnel category*

	1984	1995	change
Teaching and research staff	630	749	18%
% Professors and Associate Professors	30%	42%	
% white	97%	92%	
% African	1%	4%	
% women	21%	24%	
Executive/Professional/Specialist	153	184	20%
% white	97%	85%	
% African	1%	4%	
% women	41%	54%	
Technical/Administrative/Trades	840	1026	22%
% white	82%	62%	
% African	1%	2%	
% women	65%	69%	
Service staff	1065	831	-22%
% white	2%	4%	
% African	11%	11%	
% women	18%	34%	
Total	2688	2790	

* Personal Categories as defined in the SAPSE system. These do not correspond entirely to UCT definitions; e.g. a Professor acting as Dean who spends <50% of her time on research and teaching would be classified in the Executive/Professional category. The figures do not include more than 2000 temporary staff employed each year as tutors, student receptionists, temporary lecturers and administrators, etc. Neither do they include contract research staff (more than 300 in 1993).

Table VI: Rated researchers in the natural sciences

	A	B	C	P	Y	Total
University of Cape Town	22	48	79	5	14	168
University of Witwatersrand	8	38	61	4	18	129
University of Pretoria	3	25	69	2	21	120
University of Natal	5	32	47	4	16	104
University of Stellenbosch	2	22	44	2	10	80
University of Orange Free State	2	8	43		14	67
Potchefstroom University		9	24		5	38
Rand Afrikaans University	4	8	20	1	6	39
Rhodes University		11	20		3	34
University of the Western Cape		3	12	2	9	26
University of Durban-Westville		4	19		1	24
University of Port Elizabeth		3	16		5	24
Unisa	1	3	6		3	13
University of the North			7		2	9
University of the Transkei			6			6
University of Fort Hare			5		1	6
University of Zululand			4			4
University of the North-West	1		1			2
Medical University of S/Africa			2			2
Vista University			2			2
University of Venda						
Total	48	214	487	20	128	897

Table VII: Undergraduate success rates by 'population group'

(Success rate = % of courses taken that are passed)

	1989	1990	1991	1992	1993	1994	1995
African							
First-time entering	64	67	71	69	65	70	72
Other	70	72	74	73	73	72	72
Coloured							
First-time entering	67	65	66	66	71	67	67
Other	79	78	81	79	83	82	80
Indian							
First-time entering	62	69	70	66	65	70	72
Other	78	80	81	83	84	81	81
White							
First-time entering	83	85	84	86	85	84	86
Other	88	88	90	91	91	90	90
Total							
First-time entering	78	79	79	79	78	76	78
Other	85	84	86	86	86	84	83

(Source: Table 2.9 and 2.11, annual SAPSE returns.)

Table VIII: Undergraduate academic progress: 1995

Undergraduates	Students registered in 1995	% qualified	% continuing in 1996	% 'excluded on academic grounds'	% discontinuing studies in 'good academic standing'
African					
First-time entering	857	—	88,00	6,60	5,40
Other	1989	18,00	70,00	5,90	6,10
Coloured					
First-time entering	423	—	79,70	14,40	5,90
Other	1105	28,60	60,30	5,40	5,70
Indian					
First-time entering	185	—	81,70	12,40	5,90
Other	429	22,30	70,90	2,70	4,10
White					
First-time entering	1272	—	90,10	3,30	6,60
Other	4121	32,60	59,40	1,60	6,40
Total					
First-time entering	2737	—	87,40	6,50	6,10
Other	7644	27,70	62,90	3,30	6,10

Table IX: Degrees and diplomas awarded: 1995

	African	Coloured	Indian	White	Total
Undergraduate	359	316	95	1 345	2 115
Postgraduate	274	169	53	1 089	1 585
Total	633	485	148	2 434	3 700
Percentage	17,10	13,10	4,00	65,80	100,00

(Source: Table 2.13, 1995 SAPSE returns.)

Index

AECI 129
Abrahamse, LG 72 73 74 75 83 93 97 105 106 107 112 115 118 119 130 141 143 162 165 188 198 199 202 211 215
Abrahamse, Nel 73
academic boycott 36 109 180 182 204
academic exclusions 224
academic freedom committee 41 143 181
academic freedom plaques 238
academic support programmes 76 77 176 246 256
Ackerman, Raymond and Wendy 185
African Association of Universities 248
African Scholars Fund 20 141
African National Congress (ANC) 30 31 51 175 176 177 178 180 182 207 210 216 218 220 222 223 232 237
Afrikaans Studentebond (ASB) 120
Aggett, Neil 126 127
Albert Einstein Medical School 35
Alberts, René 192
Alexander, Ray 101 175 219
Allwood, Cliff 29
Ames, Prof. Frances 41 90
Amoore, Hugh 42 73 74 169 187 188 200
Anglo American Corporation 107 129 132 215 222
Annan, Lord 133
Appenteng, Kofi 132
Arias, Win 35
Ash, Sir Eric 133
Asmal, Prof. Kader 241
Association of Commonwealth Universities (ACU) 170 171 248
Athenaeum, the 170
Auer, Bernard 131
Axelson, Prof. Eric 72
Azanian Peoples Organisation (AZAPO) 232
Azanian Students Congress (AZASCO) 232
Azanian Students Movement (AZASIM) 152 153 166
Azanian Students Organisation (AZASO) 175 180

Barben, Tanya (née Simons) 101
Barlow, Malcolm 132

Barlow-Rand 215
Barnard, Dr Chris 33 47 48
Barnard, Dr Marius 101 211
Baxter Theatre 99 230
Baxter, William Duncan 99
Beattie, Sir Carruthers ('Jock') 84 95 153
Benatar, Prof. Solly 67 111
Bengu, Sibusiso 238
Benino, José Miquez 182
Bieber, EPH 134 188
Biko, Steve 46 85 86 89 90 91 120 127
Black Sash 72 173
black students' society 210
Bloch, Graeme 101 139 147 208
Bloch, Manfred 3
Boesak, Rev. Allan 195 208 209
Booysen, Prof. P 167
Borain, Nic 145 149 153
Boraine, Dr Alex 120 153
Boraine, Andrew 120
Bosenberg, Dr 1
Boshoff, Prof. Carel 125
Botha, Minister JC ('Stoffel') 157
Botha, Minister Roelof ('Pik') 144 145 168
Botha, State President P W 57 157 159 160 163 164 168 188 211 212
Bowen, Bill 130 199 202 207
Boyer, Ernie 228
Bozzoli, Prof. G 111
Bradburne, John 63 64 65 66
Bradlow, Drs Frank and Edna 116
Brink, Prof. Andries 34 35
British Council 75 170 250
Brock, Prof. Jack 17 26 27 39 40 41 48 49 50
Broederbond 97 125
Bromilow-Downing, Prof. B 60 61 68
Brown, Dr Helen 15
Budlender, Debbie 101
Budlender, Geoff 55
Burger, Christine 156 165
Burger, Dr JG 34 66 67
Burns, Dr Derek 32
Buthelezi, Chief Mangosuthu 29 30 31
Buthelezi, Princess Irene 29 30

Campbell, Colin 132 186
Cape Library Co-operative (CALICO) 243

Index

Cape Provincial Administration 111 211
Cape Supreme Court 195
Cape Technikon 106 168
Carnegie Corporation 86 121 127 128 131 132 244
Carolus, Cheryl 101 225
Carr, Prof. AD 92 93 152 173 204
Carter, Sir Charles 75
Cartwright, Jean, and family 4 5
Cecilia Makewane Hospital 96
Centlivres, Hon. Albert van de Sandt 22
Central Middlesex Hospital 25
Centre for African Studies *see* Oppenheimer Centre for African Studies
Centre for Conflict Resolution 120 121
Centre for Jewish Studies *see* Kaplan Centre for Jewish Studies
Chalker, Baroness 250
Chapman, TN 134 218
Chaskalson, Adv. A 183
Chinese Association for International Friendship 229
Chissano, President 240
Christian Brothers College 6
Christian National Education 125
Christodoulou, Dr A 248
Ciba Foundation 51
Civil Rights League 41 80
Clarke, Dr Elaine 58
Clase, Minister P J 168 188 201
Cleymans, Prof. 140
Coetzee, Minister Kobus 188 221
College House 79
College of Medicine of SA 89 253
College of Physicians and Surgeons 19 45
Committee of University Principals (CUP) 96 97 117 143 166
Committee of University Rectors (CUR) 166
Congress of South African Trade Unions (COSATU) 184 189 217
Consolata House 154
Consultative Business Movement (CBM) 218
Corder, Clive 40
Corder, Prof. Hugh 240 242
Cormack, Allan 120
Criminology, Institute of 129
Crossroads 58 59 150 174
Crouse, Prof. Cas 168
Crowson, Prof. Lamar 147 148
Crowson, Estelle 147 148
Cullinan, Sarah 93 94
Curtis, Neville 120
Customs and Excise 56

Dall, Prof. George 175 188 211
Davie, Dr TB ('Tom') 22 84
Dartmouth College 199
De Beers Corporation 107 215
Defence and Aid Fund 39
de Klerk, Minister FW 147 148 163 166 167 168 178 188 198 199 202
    State President 220 221 223 232 239
de Klerk, Prof. JN 87 88 89 90
de Lange, Prof. JP 122
de Lange Report 122 123 124 125
de Villiers, Prof. JC 167
de Villiers, Wim 96
de Vries, Prof. Mike 168 186
de Wet, Prof. Jack 53 82 140
de Wet, Madge 55
Democratic Party 30
Dempers, Leon 131
Diemont, Judge Marius 152 153 167 188 195
District Six 15 102
Dittmer, Beryl and Eric 131
Dominguez, Prof. 140
Donald, John 210
Dove, John 64
Dowd, Captain Raymond 172 191
Dowdle, Dr Eugene 20 35 41
Driekoppen Residence 21 28 29 31 36 42 44
Dugmore, Cameron 180 205
Duminy, Dr JP 29 40 42
du Plessis, Prof. DJ ('Sonny') 17 18 23 111 118 183
du Preez, Max 239
Durand, Prof. 176
Durbach, Andy 156
Durr, Leslie 215
du Toit, Stephanus 53
Dyer, David 131

Eales, Prof. Len 20 35
Ebert Stiftung 171
Ebrahim, Minister Carter 163 164
Eduardo Mondlane University 240 243
Edinburgh University *see* University of
Edwards, Derek 231
Elleston Junior School 6
Elliott, Prof. Guy 45
Elliott, Julian 107
Ellis, Prof. George 251
Elsworth, Margaret 20
End Conscription Campaign 81 82
Erasmus, Prof. J F P 17
Erwin, Alec 217
Esack, Farid 205
Eskom 129
Essau, Rev. Matt 208
Evans, Akosua 132
Extension of University Education Act 22 108 113 139 238 242

Index

Falconer, Prof. AW 84 95
Farlam, Adv. 156
Farr, AZ 134
Feinstein, Andrew 174
Fick, Johan 120
Fielden, John 73
File, Jon 175 177 241 246
Financial Mail 193
Finberg, Barbara 132
Fish, Joy 231 245
Flowers, Lord 133
Folb, Prof. Peter 58 59 91 106 127
Ford Foundation 132
Forman, Prof. Frank 14 17 18 19 25 26
Forum 74
Fort Hare University *see* University of Fort Hare
Foster, Don 129
Fourie, Danie 94
France-Libertés Foundation 216
Fredericks, Wayne 132
Freemasons 7
Friends of Nusas (FONS) *see* National Union of SA Students
Fuggle, Prof. Richard 104
Fuller Hall 81

Garfield Western Foundation 133
Gaunt, Neville 231
Gauntlett, Adv. Jeremy 200
Gay and Lesbian Association (GALA) 116
Geeling, KLG 134
Gelfand, Prof. Michael 63
general election 1994 242
Georgetown University 186 200
Gerard, Whitney 130 131 132
Gerwel, Prof. Jakes 165 168 175 176 208 209 238
Gevers, Prof. Wieland 229 230 250
Glaxo, PLG 251
Glaxo, Welcome 133
Glenara 95 97 99 105 121 143 146 154 155 158 199 205 231
Glendower Hotel 137 149
Goosen, Glen 175
Gordon, Dr H 41
Graaff, Sir De Villiers 41
Graduate School of Business (GSB) 29 237
Gray, Allan 133
Grayce, Dr Isaac 15
Greenberg, Heidi 228
Gregory, James 221
Groote Schuur Hospital (GSH) 16 28 34 35 54 66 67 68 77 78 211 231 251
Groote Schuur Residential Hotel 154
Group Areas Act 75 97 122 126

Hales, MH 134

Hall, Prof. David 237
Hamburg, Dr David 127 128
Hamilton, Charles 131
Hammersmith Hospital 24
Hani, Chris 176
Hanson, Sir John 170
harassment, racial 225 226
  sexual 225
Harrison, Prof. Gaisford 33
Hartzenberg, Dr 140
Harvard Medical School 31
Harvard University 199
Haskins, Caryl and Edna 132
Hathorn, Peter 148
Haysom, Cheetah 131
Haysom, Nick ('Fink') 127
Healy, Father 186 200
Heese, Prof. H de V 79
Herbst, Jeff 228
Hendrickse, Rev. Alan 57 163
Heunis, Minister Chris 174
Hirschberg, Dormee 71
Hoffenberg, Dr Raymond ('Bill') 20 39 40 41 42 48 50 57 100 133
Hoffenberg, Margaret 39
Hoffman, Sir Leonard 132
Hofmeyr, Willie 101
Horn, Prof. Peter 237
Horwitz, Dr Marshall ('Mark') 14 17 26 27 48
Horwood, Senator Owen 55 118 119
Howie, Judge C T 201
Human Sciences Research Council (HSRC) 122 125 126
Hunter, Donald 16 25

Ilchman, Alice 132
Immelman, Prof. Edward 54
Imperial College 133
Independent Development Trust (IDT) 73 136
Inkatha Freedom Party 31 153
Inkatha Institute 239
Internal Security Act 101 167 205
International Association of the Liver 50
International Association of Universities (IAU) 240 248
International Atomic Energy Agency 40
International Committee of Scientific Unions 182
Intervarsity 110 166 218
Irma Stern Museum 93
Irwin, Robert 132
Irvine, Robin and Bunty 24 82 240
ISCOR 129
Isenberg, Dr JJ 87
Isselbacher, Dr Kurt 35

Jacomb, Sir Martin 170
Jackson, Prof. Peter 20 57
James, Prof. RW 22
Jewish Studies *see* Kaplan Centre for Jewish Studies
Jomo Kenyatta University 243
Jones, Dr Avery 25
Joseph, Helen 147
Jowell, Prof. Geoffrey 133

Kamba, Prof. Walters 24
Kane-Berman, Dr Jocelyn 211
Kannemeyer, Colonel 207 208
Kaplan (Isaac and Jessie) Centre for Jewish Studies 106 180
Kaplan-Kushlick Foundation 106
Kaplan, Mark 139
Kaplan, Prof. Maurice 70 117
Kaplan, Mendel 106 107
Kapp, Rochelle 231
Karl Bremer Hospital 33
Karl Popper Fellowships 112
Keeton, Dr Roy 68 69
Kellogg Foundation 132
Kgosana, Philip 27
Khanyile, Nombelela 189
Khanyile, Vusi 179 189 202 203 206 207
Khayelitsha 142
Kies, Dr Bryan 66
King David Country Club 19
King Edward VIII Hospital 68
Kings College Hospital 25
Kinnear, Dr Andrew 104 215
Kipps, Prof. Arthur 61 62 68
Kirby, Robert 229
Kirsch, Prof. Ralph 32 39 57 58 59 214
Klatzow, Peter 185
Klug, Sir Aaron 132
Koornhof, Minister Piet 144 145
Kottler, Prof. R 36
Kotze, Brigadier 156
Kresge Foundation 132 215
Kriel, Danie 228
Kritzinger, Prof. Leon 52
Krone, GN 134
Kruger, Deputy Minister Jimmy 55
Kruger, Karl 228
Kruger, Miss ME 14
KTC squatter camp 159 173 174
Kurtz, Daniel 130 131

Lamprecht, Prof. JH 138 139 167
Landau, Dr Arthur 115
Lang, Dr 90
Langa High School 208
Langtry, Stephen 231
Leatt, Prof. James ('Jim') 165 175 178 188 190 204 229 249

Leevy, Carrol 35 131
le Grange, Minister Louis 157 158 163 188
Leo Marquard Hall 194
Levetan, Laura 101
Levy, Dr Norman 90
Liberal Party 39 41
Liesbeeck Gardens 132 215
Linbury Trust 133
Linda, Tomasinqa 194 198
Livesey, Derek 105 174
Livingstone Hospital 68
Lloyd, Sheilah 78 100 111 148 186
Louw, Anita, *see also* Saunders, Anita 147 148 149
Louw, Dr Appie 155
Louw, Bernard 224 225
Louw, Administrator Gene 227
Louw, Prof. JH ('Jannie') 17 36 46 60 61 68 83
Louw, Lionel 224
Louw, Dr Nicholas 212
Louw, Stephanie 155
Louw, Stephen 155
Lusaka – visit to ANC *see* African National Congress
Luyt, Lady ('Betty') 79 80
Luyt, Sir Richard 64 70 71 78 79 80 81 82 83 84 85 86 92 95 96 104 111 117 169 171

Macara, Tom, Rew and John 25
Mafeje, Archie 238
Mahomed, Adv. I 183
Mai, Vincent 132
Makatini, Johnny 178
Makgoba, Dr William 252 253
Malan, Dr Nico 33 34
Malan, Wynand 153
Mandela, Nelson 159 161 165 178 192 205 211 220 221 222 223 232 242
Mandela, Winnie 178
Mandela, Zinzi 169
Mangope, Chief 30
Marks, Prof. Solly 26
Marshall, Jerome 114 115
Martin, Prof. John 253
Marzullo, Sol 131
Masekela, Barbara 176 217
Massachusetts General Hospital 31
Massachusetts Institute of Technology (MIT) 199
Mass Democratic Movement (MDM) 213 216
Matanzima, Chief 30 98
Mathew, Arnold 104 105
Mauerberger Foundation 116 117
Mauerberger, Morris 116 117
Mayer, Prof. Jean 165 216

Index

Mbeki, Thabo 218
McEvoy, Brother 17
McGregor, Alistair 8
McGregor, Charles 132
McKenzie, Prof. David 70
McMurray, TB 45
Meachin, David 131 132
Medical Association of South Africa (MASA) 41 46 86 87 88 89 90 127
Medical University of South Africa (Medunsa) 144 187
Mellon Foundation 130 132 136 243 255
Menell, Irene 134
Meyer, Deputy Minister Roelf 202
Meyers, Dr Mendel 18
Mgogi, WA 240
Middelmann, Hans 99 130 215
Milne, Dr Malcolm 24 32 57
Minister of
   Co-operation and Development 144
   Education and Culture 163 188
   Education and Training 123 163
   Finance 118 119 250
   Foreign Affairs 144 168
   Health 211
   Home Affairs 31
   Internal Affairs 123
   Justice 27 40 189
   Labour 33
   Law and Order 146 157 163 188 202 214
   National Education 101 118 122 123 143 144 163 166 167 168 188 198 199 200 201 249
Mission statements 162 253
Mitterrand, Mme Danielle 216
Moderate Students Movement (MSM) 154 195 197 228
Modise, Billy 177
Moharroe, Prof. P 175
Mompati, Ruth 177
Moolman, Dominee 167
Moore, Charles 64 65 66
Moosa, Essa 213
Moosa, Mahommed 207
Moran, Anne 131
Morope, Murphy 207
Mostert, Judge 57
Motlana, Dr Ntato 153
Mott Foundation 130
Mouat, Pax 71
Moulder, Dr James 98 99 185
Mouton, Prof. 144
Mpetha, Oscar 127
Mulder, Minister 'Connie' 57
Mullins, Mrs Dorothy 137
Multi-media Centre 250 251
Munnik, Dr LAPA 34 68 69

Murray, Prof. Andrew 55
Mutemwa 63 64 65
Mwanza, Dr JM 177
Mzamane, Chris 175

Nash, Margaret 173
Nathan, Laurie 121
National Commission of Higher Education 241 249 250
National Education Crisis Committee 179
National Party 15 53 218
National Students Federation 153 154 197 227 228
National Union of South African Students (NUSAS) 41 54 80 110 115 120 127 154 157 169 190 197
Naudé, Dr CF Beyers 146 169
Ncayiyana, Prof. Daniel 88 104
Ndebele, Prof. 247
Nel, Deputy Minister Louis 163 164
New Somerset Hospital 27 66 68 70
Ngcoba, Clifford 207
Niemoller, Pastor Martin 126
Nobel Prize 120 132
Norman, Rev. Michael 141
Ntsantwisi, Chief Hudson 30
NUSAS see National Union of SA Students
Nyandimus, Denford 65
Nzo, Alfred 175

O'Brien, Dr Conor Cruise 179 180 181 182 183 189 191 194 204 242
Odendaal, Major 158 173 191
Ogilvie Thompson, Julian 107
Olivier, Prof. Nic 29
Olivier, Administrator P J 23
O'Malley, Brendan 96
Omar, Dullah 195 196 206 219
Omar, Farieda 196
O'Meara, Ellalu 228
Open Society Fund 112 132
Oppenheimer Centre for African Studies 107
Oppenheimer, HFO 40 76 107 154 215
Oppenheimer, Nicky 133
Opperman, Dirk 34 35
Overseas Development Agency 250
Oxford University 133 139

Paap, Prof. Anton 53
Page, Stanley 10 11
Pan African Congress (PAC) 27 30
Parker, Gordon 131
Parker, John 228
Patel, Ebrahim 184
Peat, Marwick and Mitchell 72 73
Peers, JR 194 195
Peninsula Maternity Hospital 15

Index

Peninsula Technikon 117 163 167 204 208
Perkins, Ambassador Edward 238 239
Pheiffer, Steven 132
Philip, Kate 102 156
Phimister, Prof. Ian 160
Pifer, Alan 85 121 130 131 132 179
Pimstone, Dr Bernard 62
police – involvement with students 54 55 101 105 114 115 156 157 158 159 160 161 162 167 171 172 173 174 190 191 192 196 197 204 205 206 213 214
Popper, Karl 112
Pretorius, Daniel 196 197
Pretorius, Mr (Secretary to State President) 46
Price, Prof. Tom 29
Princeton University 130 199 207 229 254
Progressive Federal Party 183 208
Progressive Party 29 41 101 120
Proud, Hayden 257

Quirk, Lord 133
quota system for universities 126 143 144 238

Rabie, Chief Justice 126
Radcliffe, Geordie 212 213
Rademeyer, Prof. 167
Radloff, Godfrey 19
Rafelski, Prof. Jan 140 141
Rag 104 141 142 213 243
Ramphele, Dr Mamphela 91 128 134 175 176 225 229 233 247 257
Rand Afrikaans University (RAU) 21 122 144
Read, Amy 120
Read, Leonard 94 97 120 131 187
READ organisation 141
Red Cross Hospital 233 251
Reddy, Prof. 176
Reid, Prof. John 78 93 126 131 144 151 153 179 189 199 203 217 229
Reid, Ron 106
Relly, Gavin 107
Renwick, Ambassador Robin 133 224 238 250
Republic Festival 117 118 119
residences, integration of 137 149 226
Reuter Foundation 133
Rhodes, Cecil John 1 107 168
Rhodes Trust 133
Rhodes University 132 143 165 170 173 193 199 216 248 249
Rhodesia Leprosy Association 64
Roach, Malcolm 215 231 245
Robb, Frank 72 73
Robb, Noël 72
Roberts, Gareth 133

Roberts, Mary 251
Robertson, Prof. HM 41
Rockefeller Foundation 132 243
Rockefeller Brothers Fund 132
Ross, Prof. Alec 75
Rossouw, Attorney-General 227
Rotberg, Robert 1
Royal College of Physicians 24
Royal Postgraduate Medical School 24

Sainsbury, Lord 133
Saint, Prof. Charles 5
St Francis Xavier Seminary 7
St George's Cathedral 54 81 178 209 213 224
Samuels, John 175 237
Sanders, Dr Hannah-Reeve 67 147 212
Sandler, Diane 129
SASOL 129
Saunders, Albert 2 3 4 5 6 7 10 11 19
Saunders, Anita *see also* Louw, Anita 3 24 100 133 154 155 158 162 170 171 185 186 200 201 202 213 216 224 228 229 240 242 244 253 257
Saunders, Jane 36 95 96 205 213
Saunders, John 31 32 36 95 96 142 159 187
Saunders, Lilian 1 2 4 5 7 8 11 155
Saunders, Nanette 2 4 9 11
Saunders, Noreen 19 20 24 25 26 28 36 44 46 47 60 77 79 83 95 130 141
Savage, Prof. Michael 237
Sax Appeal 104
Schaffer, Prof. Walter 28
Schmid, Dr Rudi 35
Schrire, Prof. Robert 144 145
Schrire, Prof. 'Val' 15 57
Scott, Associate Prof. Ian 76
Sea Point Boys Junior School 6
Sebe, Chief Lennox 30 138
Seligman, Adv. S C 200
Selikowitz, Judge 195 196
Selzer, Dr Golda 18 19
Sexwale, Tokyo 257
Shapiro, Harold 228
Shapiro, Dr S 41
Sharpeville 27 190
SHAWCO *see* Students Health and Welfare Organisation
Shell South Africa 73 122 128 132 137 215
Shippey, Dr TC 106 168
Simons, Prof. Jack 100 175 176 182 220
Simons, Mary 100
Simons, Ray *see* Alexander
Simons, Tanya *see* Barben
Sims, IJ 106 134 246
Sisulu, Albertina 185

Skea, Ella 45 46
Skewes, Prof. Sammy 28 32
Slabbert, Dr F van Zyl 82
Slemon, John 99 215
Smith, Barry 222
Smith, Joan 77 78
Smit, Prof. Dirk van Zyl 129
Smuts Hall 81
Smuts, Lyn 228
Sobukwe, Robert 30
solitary confinement 129
Somerset Hospital see New Somerset Hospital
Sonn, Franklin 163 168 208
Sons for Young Azania (SOYA) 166
Sonnenberg, Richard 129 146
Soros, George 111 112 113
South African Broadcasting Corporation (SABC) 57 143 212
South African Bureau of Racial Affairs (SABRA) 29
South African College 185
South African Communist Party 175 209
South African Council of Education 123 124 125 126
South African Council of Higher Education (SACHED) 175
South African Institute of Race Relations (SAIRR) 169
South African Medical and Dental Council (SAMDC) 87 89 90 127
South African Medical Journal 87 88 89
South African National Students Congress (SANSCO) 190 197
South African Students Congress (SASCO) 232 236 244
South African Students Organisation (SASO) 54 120
South African Tertiary Institutes Sports Council (SATISCO) 210
Southern Life Insurance Co. 218
Soweto 68 70 122 177 191
Spencer, Prof. Ian 58 59
Spencer, John 132
Spong, Mrs 13
Springer, Sir Hugh 170 171
Standard Bank of South Africa 136
Standard Charter Bank NY. 130
Stanford University 199
State President see Swart, CR, Botha, PW, and de Klerk, FW
States of Emergency 27 86 158 162 165 171 173 188 198 205 214
Stern, John and Bella 9
Stein, Edgar 9
Stellenbosch University see University of Stellenbosch
Stewart, James 177

Steyn, Judge JH 126 137 221
Steyn, Victor 152 153
strikes on campus 230 231 232 233 234 235 236
Stubbs, Gladys 78
student fees and debts 250
Student Parliament 249
Students for the Free Society (SFS) 228
Students Health and Welfare Organisation (SHAWCO) 39 58 59 104 105 142 174 213 214 215
Students Jewish Association 203 204
Students Muslim Association 203 204
Students Representative Council (SRC) 54 110 115 116 117 127 139 149 153 157 165 166 174 175 180 190 192 194 196 197 209 210 212 213 232 244 249
Stutterheim, Dr Niko 118 143
Sükel, Maggie 187 231
Suppression of Communism Act 39 101
Supreme Court 118 195 201 202 205 216 231
Susman, DR 134
Sutherland, Carla 175 180 194
Suzman, Helen 30 147 189
Swing, Ambassador William ('Bill') 238
Swart, State President CR 46

Tebbutt, Judge PH ('Pat') 134 200 215
Tempelsman, Maurice 132
Terblanche, Prof. John 32 36 37 50 51 57 141
Terrorism Act 127 129
Terry, LA 194
Tertiary Education Fund of SA (TEFSA) 136
Themeli, Zeko 180 196
Tindale, Sibylla 133
Thomas, Albert 149 150
Tokyo Declaration 129
Tomin, Dr Julius 139
Toms, Dr Ivan 105 214
Touberg, Margaret 132 133 223
transformation (of UCT) 246 247 249 253
Transport and General Workers Union (TGWU) 230 231
Treurnicht, Dr A 140
Trey, Dr Charles 32 33
Trollip, Senator 119
Troskie, Prof. 52
Trunan, Glen 105
Truth and Reconciliation Commission 88 91
Tshwete, Steve 217
Tucker, Dr 90
Tufts University 165 216
Turfloop see University College of the North

Index

Turner, Dr 87
Tutu, Archbishop Desmond 178 179 208 218 224 233 234
Tygerberg Hospital 34 251

UCT Choir 253
UCT Choir for Africa 242 253
UCT Foundation 131 134
UCT Fund Inc., New York 130 131 132 165
UCT Trust, United Kingdom 132 133
UCT Regiment 85
Uluntu 122
Umkhonto we Sizwe 176
Unibell squatter camp 57 58 59
UNISA see University of South Africa
United Christian Conciliation Party 194
United Democratic Front (UDF) 197 208 213
United Party 41
Universities Act 118
University Amendment Bill 143 144
University Assemblies 143 173 233 234 253
University Court 195 235
University House 29 31 42
University of
  Aberdeen 202 253
  Bristol 133
  Bologna 212
  Bophuthatswana 21
  California 75
  Chicago 75
  Botswana 243
  Dar-es-Salaam 243
  Durban-Westville 21
  Edinburgh 171
  Fort Hare 22 138 139 144 167 238
  Kinshasa 243
  Lancaster 75 200
  London 75
  Natal 55 99 119 132 143 167 173 193 199 216
  New Jersey 199
  North, (College of the) 21 54 175 247
  Orange Free State 21 143
  Otago 82 240
  Port Elizabeth 21 167
  Potchefstroom 21
  Pretoria 21
  Rhodes see Rhodes University
  Sheffield 133 253
  South Africa (UNISA) 73
  Stellenbosch 21 34 40 41 45 67 107 166 168 186 201 215 216 218 251 252
  Tanzania 243
  Toronto 253
  Virginia 154

Vista see Vista University
Warwick 75
Western Cape 21 58 117 133 143 163 165 167 173 175 176 187 193 199 200 204 208 216 222 238
Witwatersrand 21 22 23 111 118 132 143 166 173 187 193 199 216 252
Zambia 177 243
Zimbabwe 243
Zululand 21 31 153
University Science, Humanities and Engineering Partnerships in Africa (USHEPIA) 243 248
University Teachers' Association of SA (UTASA) 40
Urban Foundation 73
Uys, Prof. Dirk 70
University Transformation Forum (UTF) see Transformation

van Aswegen, Dr Jerry 66
van der Heever, Annamia 231
van der Merwe, General Johan 202
van der Merwe, Prof. HW 120
van der Merwe, Dr Schalk 58
van der Poel, Dr Louis 68 69
van der Ross, BJ 134
van der Ross, Prof. Richard 163 164 167
van der Walt, Prof. JL 125
van der Westhuizen, Prof. John 113
van der Westhuizen, Brigadier 59
van Dyk, Captain 42
van Eck, Jan 208
van Huysteen, H 187
van Niekerk, Prof. JP 214
van Niekerk, Dr Raymund 148
van Niekerk, Minister W 211
van Ryneveld, Tony and Lil 229
van Zyl, ex-Chief Justice 129
van Zyl, Prof. Fransie 34 41 42 45
van Zyl, Mayor 238 239
Varsity 55 145
Viljoen, Dominee D J 125
Viljoen, Minister Gerrit 97 98 118 119 143 144 168
Viljoen, Dr Marais 46 88
Viljoen, Minister Marais 55
Villa-Vicencio, Associate Prof. Charles 175 233 234
Viollier, Prof. 140
Vista University 140 167
Vlok, Minister Adriaan 197 202 214
Vogelpoel, Dr Louis 15
Volkskongres 125
Vorster, Prime Minister B J 43 57 168
Vusani, Maxwell 249

Walker, Louis 132

Walker, Unity 19
Walt, Alec 132
Watermeyer, Judge 55
Waters, Dr Anthony 74
Welsh, Prof. David 181 183
Wesleyan University 132 186
West, Prof. Martin 229 230 239 243 245 248
Western Cape Tertiary Institutions Trust 243
Whisson, Dr Mike 74
Williams, Cynthia 188
Williamson, Judge DM 205
Wilson, Prof. Francis 83 128
Wilson, John 128
Wingate, Orde 64 79
Witdoeke 173 174
Wolfson Foundation 133
women students, centenary of 185
Woods, Prof. Dave 204 230 233 237 247 248
Woolsack, The 154
Woolworths 146
World Bank, Washington 134
Worrall, Dr Dennis 194 195 196

Yach, Solly and Estelle 117
Yale University 145
Yeld, Nan 76
Yzerfontein 36 37 171

Zille, Helen 237